P9-DTW-219

Teaching Innovations in Economics

TEACHING INNOVATIONS IN ECONOMICS

Strategies and Applications for Interactive Instruction

Edited by

Michael K. Salemi
University of North Carolina at Chapel Hill

William B. Walstad
University of Nebraska–Lincoln

Edward Elgar
Cheltenham, UK • Northampton, MA, USA

Published by
Edward Elgar Publishing Limited
The Lypiatts
15 Lansdown Road
Cheltenham
Glos GL50 2JA
UK

Edward Elgar Publishing, Inc.
William Pratt House
9 Dewey Court
Northampton
Massachusetts 01060
USA

A catalogue record for this book
is available from the British Library

Library of Congress Control Number: 2010934039

ISBN 978 1 84844 825 4 (cased)

Printed and bound by MPG Books Group, UK

CONTENTS

TABLES AND FIGURES

TABLES

FIGURES

CONTRIBUTORS

Joann Bangs, Associate Professor of Economics, Department of Economics, St. Catherine University (St. Paul, Minnesota)

Niels-Hugo Blunch, Assistant Professor of Economics, Department of Economics, Washington and Lee University (Lexington, Virginia)

Patrick Conway, Professor of Economics, Department of Economics, University of North Carolina at Chapel Hill (Chapel Hill, North Carolina)

Michael Curme, Associate Professor of Economics, Farmer School of Business, Miami University (Oxford, Ohio)

Ann E. Davis, Assistant Professor of Economics, School of Management, Marist College (Poughkeepsie, New York)

Tisha L.N. Emerson, Associate Professor of Economics, Hankamer School of Business, Baylor University (Waco, Texas)

Indradeep Ghosh, Assistant Professor of Economics, Department of Economics, Haverford College (Haverford, Pennsylvania)

Monica Hartmann, Associate Professor of Economics, Department of Economics, University of St. Thomas (St. Paul, Minnesota)

Denise Hazlett, Professor of Economics, Department of Economics, Whitman College (Walla Walla, Washington)

Gail Hoyt, Professor of Economics, Department of Economics, University of Kentucky (Lexington, Kentucky)

Jennifer Imazeki, Professor of Economics, Department of Economics, San Diego State University (San Diego, California)

Prathibha Joshi, Associate Professor of Economics, Division of Business & Social Science, Gordon College (Barnesville, Georgia)

Mary Kassis, Associate Professor of Economics, Department of Economics, University of West Georgia (Carrollton, Georgia)

Kirsten Madden, Associate Professor of Economics, Department of Economics, Millersville University (Millersville, Pennsylvania)

Mark Maier, Professor of Economics, Department of Economics, Glendale Community College (Glendale, California)

KimMarie McGoldrick, Professor of Economics, Robins School of Business, University of Richmond (Richmond, Virginia)

Roisin O'Sullivan, Associate Professor of Economics, Department of Economics, Smith College (Northampton, Massachusetts)

Kathy A. Paulson Gjerde, Associate Professor of Economics, College of Business, Butler University (Indianapolis, Indiana)

Brian Peterson, Associate Professor of Economics, Department of Economics, Accounting and Management, Central College (Pella, Iowa)

Robert Rebelein, Associate Professor of Economics, Department of Economics, Vassar College (Poughkeepsie, New York)

Jennifer K. Rhoads, Graduate student, Department of Economics, University of Illinois at Chicago (Chicago, Illinois)

Michael K. Salemi, Professor of Economics, Department of Economics, University of North Carolina at Chapel Hill (Chapel Hill, North Carolina)

John J. Siegfried, Secretary-Treasurer, American Economic Association, and Professor of Economics, Emeritus, Department of Economics, Vanderbilt University (Nashville, Tennessee)

Katherine Silz Carson, Professor of Economics, Department of Economics and Geosciences, United States Air Force Academy (Colorado Springs, Colorado)

Judith A. Smrha, Associate Professor of Economics, Business and Economics Department, Baker University (Baldwin City, Kansas)

Derek Stimel, Assistant Professor of Economics, Menlo College (Atherton, California)

Sue Stockly, Associate Professor of Economics, College of Business, Eastern New Mexico University (Portales, New Mexico)

José J. Vazquez-Cognet, Lecturer, Department of Economics, University of Illinois at Urbana-Champaign (Urbana, Illinois)

David Vera, Assistant Professor of Economics, Department of Economics, Kent State University (Kent, Ohio)

William B. Walstad, Professor of Economics, Department of Economics, University of Nebraska–Lincoln (Lincoln, Nebraska)

FOREWORD

The purpose of the Teaching Innovations Program (TIP) is to improve the quality of economics instruction in America's colleges and universities, thereby enhancing the understanding of economics by the nation's college students and graduates. Financial support for TIP was kindly provided by the National Science Foundation from 2004 through 2010.

The Teaching Innovations Program is one of the more recent efforts in a half century of American Economic Association Committee on Economic Education sponsored projects aimed at improving the teaching and learning of economics. TIP was enthusiastically supported by the officers and Executive Committee of the Association in 2000, when the Executive Committee appropriated a modest $25,000 grant to provide seed money for five economics education projects. Four of those projects were eventually funded: TIP by the National Science Foundation; a project studying the production of Ph.D. economists by the Ford and Spencer Foundations; a project studying the use of new technologies in economic education by the Andrew W. Mellon Foundation; and a project studying the long-term effects of learning economics by the Calvin K. Kazanjian Economics Foundation, Inc. Together the four projects attracted over $1.3 million dollars of support.

TIP comprises three main components: workshops, online instruction, and opportunities for scholarship in the area of economics education. This volume represents some of the scholarship produced by the Program.

From 2005 through 2009, TIP conducted ten workshops that provided more than 335 college and university economics instructors with knowledge about interactive teaching strategies. The interactive teaching strategies were demonstrated to the participants, and they were helped to decide which of the strategies would fit best with their unique teaching circumstances. The workshops also provided an opportunity for the participants to share their knowledge of teaching with new colleagues, and to develop a community of teaching scholars that will last into the future. Almost all of the participants reported that the workshops were at least as good a use of their time as their next best alternative.

A set of seven online instructional modules were created to provide interactive instruction to the participants at the point in time when the participants planned to implement a particular strategy. The modules include: assessment, case analysis, cooperative learning, context-rich problem solving, interpretive questioning and discussion, classroom experiments, and interactive methods for large-enrollment courses. The experts who developed the modules mentored participants at the time they chose to adapt the interactive teaching strategies. The close proximity of training and implementation enhanced participant understanding and increased the likelihood of success.

The Teaching Innovations Program provided participants opportunities to engage in the scholarship of teaching by presenting interactive teaching strategies to instructors who did not participate in the Program. One way of accomplishing this was by organizing sessions at annual meetings of economics associations, at which participants presented papers describing their teaching innovations. Participants also developed original teaching materials, wrote papers on teaching, served as discussants of papers on teaching, and participated in other teacher education programs.

TIP concluded with a January 2010 academic conference. A group of 21 TIP participants was selected and grouped into seven teams based on the TIP online teaching modules they completed. Teams were joined by their respective module expert from the TIP staff. Each team then wrote a paper describing the teaching strategy and its innovative classroom use. The papers were presented at the conference, along with four others describing the purpose of TIP and overall outcomes of the project. The papers were subsequently revised in light of comments received at the conference, and now appear as the chapters in this volume, which is published in hope of sharing the benefits of the TIP workshops with a broader population of college and university economics instructors.

This volume and the six years of hard work constructing its foundation represent one among several ongoing projects of the American Economic Association's Committee on Economic Education, all aimed at improving the knowledge and understanding of economics by the nation's residents. For more information about the Committee's programs see its website at http://www.vanderbilt.edu/AEA/AEACEE/index.htm.

John J. Siegfried
Secretary-Treasurer,
American Economic Association, and
Professor of Economics, Emeritus,
Vanderbilt University

PREFACE

The Teaching Innovations Program (TIP) introduced undergraduate economic instructors to interactive teaching strategies and mentored them as they began to adopt those strategies. TIP participants first attended a residential workshop to learn about different interactive teaching strategies. They next enrolled in online modules that provided further instruction and mentoring as they adapted selected interactive strategies to their own classes. Finally, participants wrote about their TIP-based teaching experiences, made presentations at professional meetings, and discussed their program experiences with interested colleagues.

TIP was sponsored by the Committee on Economic Education (CEE) of the American Economic Association which has a long tradition of supporting teacher education programs for economists (Salemi, Saunders, and Walstad 1996). TIP grew out of a conference sponsored by the CEE, funded by the AEA, and held in San Antonio in the spring of 2000 (Salemi et al. 2001). The conference was held to identify research and action priorities for the CEE, to organize teams to work on each priority, and to discuss funding options. One of the five priorities identified at the conference was a new teacher-education program that would focus on interactive teaching and learning.

Conceptualizing TIP was one thing; finding funding for it was another. We submitted our first and second applications for National Science Foundation (NSF) funding in 2000 and 2001 and were unsuccessful. Our third application in 2003 was successful and TIP was funded by a five-year grant from the National Science Foundation (DUE #03-38482).

We received funding from NSF in February 2004. There was too little time that year for us to plan and conduct spring workshops so we worked on other components of the project. One advantage of our one-year delay in offering workshops the first year was that it created cost savings that we used to fund a sixth year of activity. We devoted 2004 to designing the prototype for our workshops and follow-on instructional modules. We also did extensive work on advertising and publicizing the project and on recruiting and selecting workshop participants. Each spring from 2005 through 2009, we offered two TIP workshops for economics faculty members. The project also developed seven follow-on instructional modules that were used by many TIP participants. Although the NSF grant officially ended at the end of January 2010, the TIP module instructors gave the last cohort of TIP workshop participants until June 2010 to complete the module work and conduct their classroom innovations.

The division of labor for administering and conducting the grant activity worked smoothly throughout the project. Walstad served as the Principal Investigator (PI). He was responsible for administering the grant, budgeting funds, contracting for expert services, managing the website, handling project evaluation, and providing general oversight for all phases of grant activity. Co-principal investigator Salemi served as workshop director throughout the project and worked on workshop site arrangements, workshop design and program, applicant selection, staff mentoring, and workshop reporting.

Both PIs developed the prototype for the follow-on instructional modules and recruited the module experts. Both served on the instructional staff of several workshops. Walstad was the expert for the assessment module; Salemi for the discussion module. The PIs also organized sessions at professional meetings that at first served as introductions to TIP and later showcased the TIP-related accomplishments of program alumni.

Other economists played key roles in TIP and made valuable contributions. KimMarie McGoldrick (University of Richmond) served on the instructional staff of many workshops, was instructional staff leader at several, was program expert for the cooperative learning module, and headed up the scholarship of teaching phase of TIP. Mark Maier (Glendale Community College) served on the workshop instructional staff, was program expert for the context-rich problems module, and coordinated the online instruction phase of TIP. Patrick Conway (University of North Carolina at Chapel Hill) served on the instructional staff and was the program expert for the teaching with cases module. Denise Hazlett (Whitman College) was a workshop instructor and program expert for the classroom experiments module. Gail Hoyt (University of Kentucky) served on the workshop instructional staff and was program expert for the module that taught instructors how to use interactive strategies in large enrollment courses. Tisha Emerson (Baylor), Kirsten Madden (Millersville University), and Robert Rebelein (Vassar College) are TIP alumni who joined the workshop instructional staff.

In addition to our colleagues above who served as skilled instructors and module experts for TIP, we also must acknowledge the valuable help and support we received from other quarters. We are grateful to the American Economic Association (AEA) for its support of TIP, and in particular to John Siegfried, Secretary-Treasurer of the AEA, and Michael Watts, current chair of the AEA-CEE, for their help and guidance throughout the project. We also want to thank the staff of the AEA, and Marlene Hight in particular, for helping us publicize TIP in various AEA publications, obtain venues for TIP workshops, and arrange the logistics for the TIP final conference in 2010. We are grateful to Susan Houston at the AEA for her work on the TIP webpage at the AEA-CEE website. In addition, we greatly appreciated the advice we received from Myles Boylan at the National Science Foundation on how we could make the best possible case to the Foundation. Sharon Nemeth (University of Nebraska–Lincoln) too deserves thanks for her many and tireless efforts in support of the administration of TIP grant. Finally, we thank Alan Sturmer (Edward Elgar Publishers) for encouraging us to prepare this book and guiding us through its completion.

Teaching Innovations in Economics describes in detail the components of TIP and reports on the accomplishments of economics instructors who participated in TIP between 2005 and 2010. Chapters 1 through 3 describe the three phases of TIP – the workshops at which participants were introduced to interactive teaching and learning strategies, the follow-on modules which assisted participants in implementing those strategies in their own courses, and opportunities created by TIP for its participants to contribute to the scholarship of teaching and learning. Chapters 4 through 10 showcase the contributions of TIP alumni to the development of each interactive teaching and learning strategy supported by TIP: cooperative learning, experiments, discussion, formative assessment, context-rich problems, teaching with cases, and interactive teaching strategies for large-enrollment courses. Chapter 11 reports the findings from a retrospective evaluation of TIP undertaken by participants as the program ended.

We are proud of all that has been accomplished through TIP. The chapters in this book provide readers with a rich sample of program work and outcomes. TIP informed and influenced many economists who teach undergraduate economics to students in colleges and universities throughout the nation. TIP gave these economics instructors the education and support they needed to adapt and apply new interactive teaching strategies. We believe that the greatest and longest-lasting benefits of TIP will accrue to the thousands of students who TIP participants now instruct with their new or expanded set of interactive teaching strategies for economics.

Michael K. Salemi
William B. Walstad
July 1, 2010

REFERENCES

Salemi, M.K., P. Saunders, and W. Walstad (1996), "Teacher training programs in economics: Past, present and future," *American Economic Review*, Papers and Proceedings, **86** (2), 460–64.

Salemi, M.K., J.J. Siegfried, K. Sosin, W.B. Walstad, and M. Watts (2001), "Research in economic education: Five new initiatives," *American Economic Review*, **91** (2), 440–45.

CHAPTER 1

Developing Teacher Expertise for Economists through a Workshop Experience

Michael K. Salemi

Between 2004 and 2010, the Committee on Economic Education (CEE) of the American Economic Association (AEA) sponsored the Teaching Innovations Program (TIP). The primary goal of TIP was to guide instructors of college-level economics courses in the use of interactive teaching strategies which, despite their proven efficacy, are underused (Becker and Watts 1996; 2001). A secondary goal was to promote the scholarship of teaching and learning.

TIP provided a three-phase instructional experience to its participants. In the first phase, participants attended a three-day workshop at which they were introduced to a variety of interactive strategies and completed exercises designed to help them determine which strategies would work best for them. Between 2005 and 2009, TIP offered two workshops per year for a total of ten at a variety of U.S. locations. In phase two, participants completed follow-on instructional modules designed to help them implement their chosen interactive strategies in their own courses. In phase three, participants designed interactive strategies of their own and wrote about their experiences in teaching with them.

In this chapter, I describe the workshop component of TIP and explain how it helped staff and participants meet the program goals.[1] The first section of the chapter places the TIP workshops in their appropriate historical context. The second describes the workshops and the workshop venues. The third section explains how participants were recruited and describes the participants and the instructional staff. The fourth and fifth sections of the chapter describe the workshop curriculum and document how participants evaluated their workshop experience. The sixth section provides information about the cost of the TIP workshops and the final section concludes.

I. HISTORY

The TIP program's workshops were the latest installment in a long history of efforts by the AEA to provide its members with effective teacher education. The first efforts began in 1973 using funds from the Sloan Foundation. The original Teacher Training Program (TTP) started with a pilot program in 1973 and led to publication of a resource manual. The success of the pilot led to a five-year grant from the Lilly Foundation and a series of five workshops held between 1979 and 1983 which based instruction around the resource manual. Hansen, Saunders and Welsh (1980) provide a detailed report on these first efforts to establish a national teacher education program.

In 1990, Phillip Saunders and William B. Walstad published *The Principles of Economics Course: A Handbook for Instructors,* subsequently replacing the original resource manual. The publication of the handbook served as a springboard for the next wave of six TTP workshops which were held between 1992 and 1994 and again funded by the Lilly Foundation. The 1992–94 workshops served 236 participants. The workshop curriculum, participant evaluations, and the longer-run impact of the workshops on participants are described in Salemi, Saunders and Walstad (1996). Walstad and Saunders (1998) updated the original *Handbook* and expanded its scope to the undergraduate major's curriculum in economics.

The first two series of teaching workshops provided participants with training about traditional teaching skills including lecturing, preparing for and leading discussion, creation and evaluation of fixed and constructed response examinations, and course management skills. The next series of workshops were a change in direction.

In two important articles, Becker and Watts (1996; 2001) documented that instructors of college-level economics taught primarily using "chalk and talk" despite widespread evidence in the educational literature that more hands-on approaches to learning resulted in better outcomes. The next series of workshops, sponsored by the AEA Committee on Economic Education, focused on promoting the use of active and interactive teaching strategies.

Three new workshop formats were developed. First, the CEE and the then National Council on Economic Education (now Council for Economic Education) used funds provided by the Calvin K. Kazanjian Economics Foundation, Incorporated, to develop a prototype "Active Learning Workshop" which was held at UNC-Chapel Hill in 1996 and 1997. Second, the CEE began in 1997 to sponsor one-day active learning workshops as part of the annual meetings of the Allied Social Science Association (ASSA). The ASSA workshops are held on the second day of the meetings, comprise three two-hour sessions, and continue to be offered.

Third, between 2001 and 2003, the Kazanjian Foundation provided funding to 24 regional workshops that served over 750 participants and focused not only on helping participants adopt active learning strategies but also on building regional teaching communities. Goodman, Maier and Moore (2003) describe the regional workshop program in detail.

The workshops held as part of the Teaching Innovations Program are, thus, the most recent installments in a history of efforts by the Committee on Economic Education and its partners to help instructors teach college-level economics using state-of-the-art teaching and learning strategies.

II. VENUES

Table 1.1 provides an overview of the ten workshops that were conducted under the aegis of TIP. The workshops served a total of 335 participants and were held at a variety of venue types and in a variety of locations. All of the venues provided residential facilities and on-site dining.

We chose the Rizzo and Georgetown Centers and the MIT Endicott House because they are affiliated with universities and are designed to meet the requirements of an academic conference. We chose the Chicago Marriott Suites because its location near O'Hare airport provided participants with an opportunity to minimize the travel time associated with the workshop. We chose Hotel Santa Fe, Hotel Mar Monte and the St. Anthony Hotel because they are located in places that we believed would attract participants. While all of our venues were attractive in one way or another, our choice of venue did not appear to matter – every one of the workshops was oversubscribed.

III. RECRUITMENT

We recruited participants in a variety of ways. First, between 2005 and 2009 we published an annual conference brochure[2] that described the workshops, explained to prospective participants what they could expect, introduced the staff and workshop agenda, and set out the application procedure. We mailed copies of the annual brochure to every economics department in the United States and distributed copies at the meetings of regional economic associations and conferences where the program included economic education sessions. Second, we constructed and maintained a TIP web page that we linked to the web page of the AEA CEE. On the TIP web page, we

Table 1.1: Teaching Innovation Program Workshops

Date	Venue	Number of Applicants	Number of Participants
May 20–22, 2005	Paul J. Rizzo Conference Center, UNC-Chapel Hill, NC	100 (13*)	34
June 3–5, 2005	Georgetown University Conference Center, DC		35
May 19–21, 2006	Chicago Marriott Suites O'Hare, Rosemont, IL	76 (8)	35
June 2–4, 2006	Hotel Santa Fe, Santa Fe, NM		32
May 18–20, 2007	Hotel Mar Monte, Santa Barbara, CA	80 (9)	32
June 8–10, 2007	MIT Endicott House, Dedham, MA		34
May 30–June 1, 2008	St. Anthony Hotel, San Antonio, TX	83 (3)	35
June 6–8, 2008	Paul J. Rizzo Conference Center, UNC-Chapel Hill, NC		31
June 5–7, 2009	Hotel Santa Fe, Santa Fe, NM		34
June 12–14, 2009	Chicago Marriott Suites O'Hare, Rosemont, IL	81	33
Total		**420**	**335**

Note: *The number in parentheses is the number of applicants in a given year who were judged to merit participation in a workshop but whom we were unable to accommodate because of space constraints. Each of these applicants was given a right of first refusal for the workshops offered in the following year. Some applicants to whom we offered a right of first refusal did not enroll in a workshop.

provided a detailed explanation of TIP, posted a copy of our most recent brochure and provided a link to an online application form. We accepted applications between early September and mid-January.

Third, we published annual advertisements for TIP and its workshops in the *American Economic Review*, the *Journal of Economic Perspectives*, and the *Program of the Allied Social Science Association Meetings*. The ads[3] provided a brief overview of TIP, identified the dates and locations of the next workshops, and explained how to apply. Fourth, we added workshop announcements to the email "blasts" that the American Economic Association sends several times each year to every member for whom they have an email address.

The application procedure required prospective participants to complete an online application form in which they provided their contact information, a description of the institution at which they taught economics, their position at that institution, and their preferred workshop. Prospective participants also submitted a description of the economics course into which they intended to introduce interactive teaching strategies. They were also required to submit a letter in which their department chair indicated that the candidate was suitable for TIP and that the department would support the candidate's efforts to use interactive teaching strategies. A $100 participation fee which we used to defray the workshop venue costs was required of each prospective candidate.

We designed our application process to filter out applicants who would be willing to attend a workshop but unlikely to adopt interactive teaching strategies and develop their skills as interactive teachers through participation in phase two of TIP. Our filter was effective. Over the five years during which we accepted applications, we judged 41 applications to be incomplete and 16 applications to be unacceptable. In all those cases, we did not approve the application.

Our recruiting efforts were successful in the sense that each year we received more applications from suitable candidates than we could accommodate. Table 1.1 reports the number of applications we received in each of the years we recruited. When we received more suitable applications than we could accommodate, we assigned participation rights to earlier applicants and offered later applicants rights of first refusal for workshops to be held the following year.[4] Table 1.1 reports in parentheses the number of applicants offered rights of first refusal each year.

Finally, as we promised NSF, we offered travel support to TIP participants who were employed by minority-serving post-secondary educational institutions. We announced the availability of this support in our brochure and allowed participants to apply for this travel support when they completed their online application. For the ten workshops together, we provided $8238 of travel support to 13 different applicants.

IV. WORKSHOP CURRICULUM

The heart of the workshop is its curriculum[5] and I will describe the TIP workshop curriculum in some detail. We designed the workshop so that two features would characterize each of the workshop sessions. First, we included a substantial hands-on component in every workshop session whereby participants could gain first-hand experience of the target interactive teaching and learning strategy. Participants completed cooperative learning exercises, wrote discussion questions, played the role of subjects in an experiment and answered prompts with clickers. We believe that the hands-on opportunities we provided were crucial to the success of the workshops.

Second, all workshop staff made a point of modeling the behaviors that characterize successful interactive teachers. Presenters called participants by name, probed answers when appropriate, displayed enthusiasm for their technique and its benefits, listened carefully to participant responses, and promoted interaction among participants. We believe that it was essential for presenters to show participants how interactive teachers behave both to gain credibility and to provide participants with working models of interactive teachers.

The workshops began at 1:00 pm on a Friday and concluded with an optional lunch at noon on the following Sunday. The first session provided participants with an overview of the workshop and a review of the case for interactive learning. In the first four workshops, we devoted 1.5 hours to these two topics but later combined and shortened these sessions to 45 minutes to allow participants more free time on Saturday afternoon. As a substitute, we asked participants to read Salemi (2002) before the start of the workshop.

In the second session, participants worked on a team assignment in which they formed teams, interviewed teammates, discussed what instructors can do to promote student learning, and prepared a presentation of their conclusions. The team assignment served as an icebreaker that introduced participants to one another and helped them become comfortable working together. It also helped participants focus on the idea that teacher development begins with a consideration of student learning.[6] Participant teams gave presentations based on their assignments on Saturday morning immediately after breakfast.

During the third and fourth sessions on Friday and during four sessions on Saturday, workshop instructors introduced participants to a variety of interactive teaching strategies. We attempted to offer a slightly different program at each of the two workshops held in a given year. At one workshop, we covered strategies that we believed would be most interesting to instructors who taught small enrollment courses. At the other, we included two sessions targeted to instructors of large enrollment courses. In the course of the workshop, we designed and presented sessions on nine different interactive strategies.

A session on *cooperative learning* was included in every workshop. The session helped participants to identify the elements of successful cooperative learning exercises, to understand how to match cooperative learning exercises with a variety of student learning objectives including problem-solving, and to learn how to develop and implement a cooperative learning exercise. The session was hands-on. During it, participants completed three cooperative learning exercises all designed to promote deeper understanding of the benefits of interactive learning.

A session on *classroom experiments* was also included in every workshop. The session had three parts. In the first, participants played the roles of students and completed a classroom experiment. At some workshops, participants completed a double-oral-auction experiment that investigates what happens when markets are opened to international trade. At some workshops, participants completed an asset trading experiment that investigates how asset-price bubbles inflate and pop. At the conclusion of the experiment, the workshop instructor explained to participants the importance of carefully debriefing experiments and outlined a number of debriefing strategies. Finally, the instructor explained logistical issues that teachers face when they use experiments.

A session on *interpretive questions and discussion* was part of every workshop and was typically held on Saturday so that participants would have ample opportunity to read an article provided by the instructor.[7] The discussion session introduced participants to inquiry-based discussion and began by explaining the differences between inquiry-based discussion and common definitions of discussion. The instructor began the session by explaining why discussion helps students attain higher-cognitive mastery of economic concepts. Because the key to successful inquiry-based discussion is preparation of well-crafted discussion questions, the instructor then explained how to categorize questions by their types and their roles in a discussion. Participants then wrote and revised discussion questions for the article they had read. At the end of the session, participants compared their questions and explained how the questions they wrote were motivated by the learning objectives they had chosen.

The session on *assessment*[8] was also part of every workshop. Most instructors routinely use summative assessment strategies to judge and grade student work and to measure student achievement. Few instructors use formative assessment – assessment designed to provide feedback to students in a way that shapes their learning and directs instruction. In the session, participants identified differences between formative and summative assessment and learned how instructors can use each type of assessment to enhance learning. Participants shared examples of different assessment techniques they have used and the instructor introduced them to a variety of new assessment techniques. Participants discussed the advantages and disadvantages of different assessment strategies and participated in an activity designed to help them prepare assessment activities for their own courses.

As mentioned earlier, some workshops included two sessions of interest to instructors of *large enrollment courses*. The first such session provided instructors with a variety of strategies that promote an active learning posture on the part of students in courses where lecture is the norm. In the session, participants identified the impediments to interactive learning in large enrollment courses and learned how master teachers of large enrollment courses overcame those impediments. The instructor provided participants with advice on how to create fertile ground for interactive learning by constructing a proper blend of course objectives, ground rules, classroom atmosphere, incentives, instructional style and pedagogical technique. The instructor also demonstrated various techniques, including short writing assignments, think–pair–share activities, and participatory exercises that promote student engagement. The instructor finally provided examples of nonstandard lecture materials that promote student interest such as the use of audio and video clips and animated PowerPoint graphs.

The second session targeted to instructors of large enrollment courses concerned the use of *"clickers"* to promote interactive learning. Clickers are radio senders that students use to respond to prompts given by the instructor. The instructor collects student responses with a radio receiver hooked to a computer through a USB port. The instructor can ask for anonymous responses as would be appropriate in a survey of student opinion or can enter student responses in an electronic record book as would be appropriate for a small stakes quiz. In the session, participants used clickers to record their responses to a variety of prompts. The instructor explained how each type of prompt could be used to promote student engagement and illustrated how the clicker system could be used in non-standard ways, for example, to auction off an item or to record votes in a "town hall meeting." The instructor closed the session by explaining the logistics of clicker use and by presenting evidence that clickers do enhance student engagement.[9]

In one workshop each year, we offered a program that substituted away from large enrollment course instruction and toward additional interactive strategies most appropriate in small enrollment courses.

In the *writing as interactive learning* session, participants reviewed types of writing assignments used in economics courses and learned why writing is a form of interactive learning. They reviewed ten in-class writing activities that promote interactive learning and discussed how to match those assignments to different learning objectives. Participants completed a writing activity designed to show how writing activities can be interactive. Finally, participants were guided in drawing conclusions about the kinds of writing activities that are best suited for their own classroom settings.

In the *cases* session, participants discussed the similarities and differences between teaching with cases and other active learning strategies. They identified ways in which the case method helps students meet a variety of learning objectives. They learned that the best cases pose problems with no obvious answers, identify actors who must solve a problem, require students to use the information in the case, include enough information for a substantial analysis of the target issues, and require students to work at the level of analysis and beyond. During the session, participants worked on the case of George, a fictional student who washed cars for spending money and was offered a baseball card in lieu of a cash payment. The participants decided what George should do.

Context-rich problems are problems that are more like the problems that decision makers encounter in the real world and less like the problems that economics instructors typically ask their students to solve. Context-rich problems are short scenarios in which the student is the major character with a plausible motivation and a particular problem to solve. Context-rich problems do not specify what rules or tools students are to use in solving the problem. Frequently, context-rich problems provide more information than required to solve the problem, including some that is irrelevant, so that students must differentiate between information that is germane and information that is not. A traditional problem might ask students to compute the present value of a sum of money to be paid in the future. A context-rich problem that targets the same skills might suggest that two brothers share an inheritance and that one brother wants his "fair" share of the inheritance immediately.

In the session on context-rich problems, participants learned the defining characteristics of a context-rich problem and then practiced writing and refining a context-rich problem appropriate to one of their own courses. The session concluded with suggestions of how context-rich problems might be incorporated within a variety of teaching formats.

The TIP workshop included three Sunday morning sessions. In one session, participants exchanged teaching ideas. The workshop staff asked participants to tell them by early Sunday morning whether they would like to make a brief presentation on their own interactive teaching innovations. The *participant teaching ideas* session was typically very lively and underscored the idea that TIP was at its core a collaborative effort to improve instruction.

In a second Sunday session, a TIP instructor explained to participants what they could expect by participating in *phase two of TIP*. The instructor explained how participants could preview phase two instructional modules, how they could enroll, and what sort of activities they would undertake as they completed their chosen module. Finally, the instructor logged on to the Blackboard site at the University of Nebraska–Lincoln where the modules are housed and navigated through one of the modules.

In the third Sunday session, participants completed a final and very important *team assignment* in which they made and discussed their preliminary choices to participate in phase two of TIP. They chose a course in which they would integrate interactive strategies, set out reasons for choosing that course, chose an interactive strategy that they wished to introduce, received feedback on their choices from their peers, and identified both potential barriers to success and strategies for overcoming those barriers. In our view, it was very important to close the TIP workshop with a session in which participants made specific plans about continued work to implement interactive teaching strategies.

The workshop ended with a 15-minute quiet period in which participants evaluated the workshop, and an optional lunch. We provided box lunches for all participants so that those with early flights could leave as soon as they completed their evaluations.

Opportunities for socialization and networking have always been an important part of our teaching workshops. With that in mind, we scheduled a cash-bar reception before dinner on the first evening of each workshop. The reception allowed participants to relax and continue conversations that they had begun during the Friday afternoon sessions. We always followed the reception with a dinner. On Saturday evening, we provided dinner to participants when the workshop was held at a university conference center or at a hotel not close to restaurants. When the workshop was held within walking distance of a commercial area, we freed participants to have dinner on their own. We also provided participants with breakfast on Saturday and Sunday mornings and with lunch on Saturday and Sunday.

The opportunities to socialize and continue conversations begun during the formal sessions were a very important part of the workshop. Staff regularly observed participants discussing workshop business during breaks and meals and evening free time. It was clear that participants valued the opportunity to talk shop with like-minded colleagues.

V. WORKSHOP STAFF

The staff for the TIP workshops comprised three instructors. However, for the first two workshops, held in 2005, we increased the staff to five: Denise Hazlett of Whitman College, Mark Maier of Glendale Community College, KimMarie McGoldrick of the University of Richmond, William Walstad of the University of Nebraska–Lincoln, and me. Having a larger staff allowed us to obtain a wider set of opinions on the workshop curriculum, the success of initial presentations and the suitability of our hands-on activities. It also allowed us to discuss what combinations of presenters would make the best workshop teams. In 2006, we recruited Gail Hoyt of the University of Kentucky to join our instructional staff and taught the workshop with two separate teams: Hoyt, McGoldrick and Salemi taught at Santa Fe while Hazlett, Maier and Walstad taught at Chicago.

One of the goals of TIP was recruitment of new entrepreneurs to the endeavor of teacher education in college-level economics. Starting in 2007, we began the process of recruiting new instructors for the TIP workshops by selecting Patrick Conway of the UNC–Chapel Hill. Conway is a recognized expert on teaching with cases and we added a session on teaching with cases to the workshops where Pat taught. In 2007, Maier, McGoldrick and I taught the Santa Barbara workshop and Conway, Hazlett, and McGoldrick taught the MIT Endicott House workshop.[10]

In 2008, we asked the first two TIP alumni to join the instructional staff. Tisha Emerson of Baylor University and Robert Rebelein of Vassar became TIP specialists in classroom games and experiments. Conway,[11] Hoyt, Rebelein and I taught the Rizzo workshop while Conway, Emerson and McGoldrick taught in San Antonio. In 2009, we recruited another TIP alumna to our instructional staff – Kirsten Madden of Millersville University. Emerson, Hoyt and I taught the Santa Fe workshop while McGoldrick, Madden and Rebelein taught in Chicago.

Between 2005 and 2009, in sum, we recruited five new resource persons to the TIP program – Conway, Emerson, Hoyt, Madden, and Rebelein. William Walstad and I also recruited and trained Mark Maier and KimMarie McGoldrick to perform several organizational functions that we had done ourselves in previous workshop programs. Mark Maier served as a TIP instructor on teaching with context-rich problems. He also oversaw our follow-on instruction program. KimMarie McGoldrick served as a TIP instructor in cooperative learning activities. She also became the leader of one of our two teaching teams, overseer of our program to create opportunities for TIP participants to contribute to the scholarship of teaching and learning, and took over from me the task of vetting TIP applications.

In sum, the TIP workshop program created both new opportunities for instructors of college economics to learn about interactive teaching strategies and new opportunities for economic educators to take on responsibilities in the creation and administration of programs like TIP.

VI. EVALUATION OF WORKSHOPS

On Sunday, participants evaluated the workshop. The evaluation form appears in Appendix 1D. Briefly, the evaluation asked participants to identify the type of institution where they taught and the number of years they had been teaching. It asked participants to rate each workshop session. It provided four questions to obtain an overall assessment, describe the workshop's greatest strengths and weaknesses, suggest new topics and ways to improve the workshop.

As has been our custom for many years, we ask workshop participants to use benefit–cost language to provide an overall evaluation of the workshop. When asked "What is your overall evaluation of the workshop compared to the opportunity cost of your time," 258 (78%) of respondents said the workshop was "a better use of my time than my next best alternative;" 64 (19%) said the workshop was "as good a use of time as my next best alternative;" 7 (2%) said the workshop was "of some value, but I could have put my time to better use;" and none responded that the workshop was "almost a complete waste of time."[12]

We also asked participants to judge the quality of materials we provided them: 265 (81%) judged the materials to be of high quality that should be used again; 62 (19%) judged them to be of good quality but needing some improvements and none judged them to be of poor quality. When asked about the workshop load, 31 (9%) of the participants said that the load was too heavy and they should have had more time off; 293 (89%) judged that the load was about right; and 5 (2%) said that the load was too light and that more sessions should have been scheduled.

Finally, we asked participants how likely they were to continue with phase two of the program and undertake follow-on instruction to help them implement their chosen interactive strategies: 297 (90%) said that it was "highly likely" that they would participate in follow-on instruction; 29 (9%) said "fairly likely" and 3 (1%) said "unlikely."

Participants were asked to evaluate workshop sessions using the scale "exceptional value" (5), "high value" (4), "solid value" (3), "some value" (2), "little value" (1), and "no value" (0). The results appear in Table 1.2.

Table 1.2: Evaluation of Workshop Sessions

Session	Number	EV	HV	SV	V	LV	NV	Average
Introduction	324	31	34	24	8	2	0	3.8
Team Exercise One	323	30	38	20	9	2	1	3.8
Experiments	328	49	32	15	3	1	0	4.2
Cooperative Learning	329	53	34	10	2	1	0	4.3
Writing	101	42	40	11	5	3	0	4.1
Cases	131	45	34	17	4	0	0	4.2
Large Enrollment Courses	127	43	24	22	9	2	0	4.0
Clickers	65	31	35	29	5	0	0	3.9
Discussion	328	51	29	15	5	1	0	4.2
Context Rich Problems	196	46	34	16	3	2	0	4.2
Assessment	294	32	40	18	8	2	0	3.9
Team Exercise Two	267	34	36	22	7	1	0	3.9
Participant Ideas	189	35	39	16	8	1	1	4.0
Intro to Phase Two	317	28	34	25	9	2	2	3.7

Note: The Number cell reports the number of respondents. The EV, HV, SV, V, LV, and NV cells report the fraction of respondents who indicated that the session had exceptional value (EV), high value (HV), solid value (SV), some value (V), little value (LV), or no value (NV). The average column reports the average score with scores ranging from 5 for EV to 0 for NV.

The number of responses varies because not every session was offered at every workshop and because not every participant evaluated every session. The results indicate that participants strongly approved of all the sessions offered. Averages scores for sessions (computed across all workshops) vary between 3.7 and 4.3 and the distribution of scores is strongly skewed to the "exceptional value" side of the distribution.

Overall, the evaluation data suggest strongly that participants judged the TIP workshops to be very valuable learning experiences and motivated them to participate in additional efforts to improve their teaching through implementation of interactive teaching strategies.

The conclusions reached on the basis of the fixed response evaluations are confirmed by the open-ended comments made by participants. For example, a participant at the 2009 Santa Fe workshop elaborated on his overall evaluation by saying: "I frankly was not sure in advance this would be as good or better than my next best alternative. Ex post, I am definitely convinced it was." In response to the prompt about the greatest strength of the workshop, another 2009 Santa Fe participant said: "I think that the amount of material covered was done in a way that didn't make us lose our attention span. It was not a sequence of boring presentations. I actually felt as though I was learning as we went along. This is probably due in large part to the skill and professionalism of those running the workshop. Overall, it was a fantastic experience and one I would definitely participate in the future." When asked to elaborate on the greatest weakness of the workshop, one 2009 Chicago workshop participant offered: "A weakness might be the limited time to 'digest' information. However, the second phase of the program allows for greater focus on key areas."

Of course, participants are different and some liked some aspects of the workshops better than others. However, in reading through the open-ended comments one quickly realizes that the great majority of participants left the workshop energized and believing that they the workshop had added substantial value to their understanding of teaching and interactive teaching and learning strategies.

VII. WORKSHOP EXPENSES

Table 1.3 reports TIP workshop expenses covered by the grant from the National Science Foundation and administered by the program. It does not include amounts paid by participants for their transportation to and from the workshop venue or extra lodging and meal expenses that participants might have paid in order to arrive at the workshop venue on time.

Overall, the average cost of each workshop was $31,922.42, which amounts to an average cost of $952.90 per participant. Each participant was charged a workshop registration fee of $100. On average, participation fees reduced the per-participant cost of the workshop by slightly more than $100 because a few participants cancelled their participation after the deadline for fee reimbursement.[13] About 69 percent of per participant cost is accounted for by lodging and food and about 27 percent by payments for and travel of instructional staff.

Table 1.3: Workshop Expenses

Expense Category	Average Per Workshop	Average Per Participant
Hotel and Food	$21,879.02	$653.11
Instructional Staff	6,909.81	206.26
Staff Travel	1,697.66	50.68
Minority Travel Support	895.41	26.72
Miscellaneous	540.22	16.13
Sub Total	31,922.42	952.90
Participation Fee	−3,410.00	−101.79
Total of Categories	$28,512.42	$851.11

Note: There were 10 TIP workshops attended by 335 participants. TIP provided travel support for instructors who taught at minority serving post-secondary institutions. The miscellaneous category includes primarily the costs of preparing and shipping participant material binders.

There was variation in expenses across workshops. The least expensive of the ten workshops cost $24,042.35 while the most expensive cost $34,280.23. Some of the variation was due to enrollment, some due to the fact that Saturday night dinner was provided at some workshops and not at others, and the rest due to variation in prices charged by venues.

VIII. CONCLUSIONS

The ten workshops offered by the Teaching Innovations Program are the most recent installments in a long tradition of providing college level instructors of economics with opportunities to improve their teaching. TIP provided a workshop experience to 335 clients, many of whom, as another chapter will document, went on to complete phase two of the TIP program in which they implemented chosen interactive teaching and learning strategies in their own courses. Some TIP participants did more. A third chapter will provide an overview of contributions by TIP participants to the scholarship of teaching and learning. Most of the remaining chapters document participant innovations to the interactive teaching strategies that were the focus of TIP.

Finally, participants gave high ratings to TIP workshops and to all individual workshop sessions. A final chapter will report on participants' retrospective assessment of their workshop experience.

NOTES

1. This paper was prepared for the Teaching Innovations Program Session at the 2010 Allied Social Science Association Meetings. I thank (and indemnify) Kirsten Madden, the paper's discussant, for very helpful comments which I used to revise this paper after presenting it.
2. Content of the 2009 brochure is included as Appendix 1A.
3. See Appendix 1B for the ad copy for the first TIP workshop.
4. Each year, we followed a rolling admission process between September and the end of November so that early applicants could know of their acceptance in time to apply for travel funds at their home institutions. We stopped the rolling admissions process at the beginning of December so that those who applied as the result of hearing about TIP at the ASSA meetings could be considered for admission. We assigned the remaining workshop slots to applicants on or about January 15.
5. See Appendix 1C for the 2009 Hotel Santa Fe workshop program.
6. The importance to teaching of a focus on student learning was a recurrent theme throughout the workshop and throughout phase two of TIP.
7. We faced an important tradeoff in the design of the discussion session. Inquiry-based discussion works best when the target reading is very rich. However, we feared that workshop participants might not find the time to read a long reading prior to their arrival. We thus provided participants with a short but interesting news article on Friday and asked them to read the article carefully before the discussion session on Saturday. At several workshops, the reading was "More Kidneys for Transplants May Go to Young" by Laura Meckler published in the *Wall Street Journal* on March 10, 2007.
8. The assessment session of the TIP workshop was based in part on Walstad (2006), a copy of which was provided to participants as background reading.
9. For more about clickers, please see Salemi (2009) which was provided to workshop participants as a background reading.
10. Gail Hoyt was scheduled to teach but was ill. KimMarie McGoldrick kindly agreed to replace her.
11. Because Pat Conway is at UNC, holding the workshop at the Rizzo Center provided a low cost opportunity to add a session on teaching with cases to the curriculum.
12. These overall responses are quite similar to those reported by Salemi, Saunders and Walstad (1996) for a previous CEE-sponsored workshop series.
13. A workshop application was not considered complete until we received a check for the participation fee. We refunded the fee if we could not accommodate the participant or if the participant cancelled by a date that varied by year but was always early in March.

REFERENCES

Becker, W.E., and M. Watts (1996), "Chalk and talk: A national survey on teaching undergraduate economics," *American Economic Review*, Papers and Proceedings, **86** (2), 448–53.

Becker, W.E., and M. Watts (2001), "Teaching economics at the start of the 21st century: Still chalk and talk," *American Economic Review*, Papers and Proceedings, **91** (2), 446–51.

Goodman, R.J.B., M. Maier, and R.L. Moore (2003), "Regional workshops to improve the teaching skills of economics faculty," *American Economic Review*, Papers and Proceedings, **93** (2), 460–62.

Hansen, W.L., P. Saunders, and A.L. Welsh (1980), "Teacher training programs in college economics: Their development, current status, and future prospects," *Journal of Economic Education*, **11** (2), 1–9.

Salemi, M. (2002), "An illustrated case for active learning," *Southern Economic Journal*, **68**, (3), 721–31.

Salemi, M. (2009), "Clickenomics: Using a classroom response system to increase student engagement in the principles of economics course," *Journal of Economic Education*, **40** (4), 385–404.

Salemi, M.K., P. Saunders, and W. Walstad (1996), "Teacher training programs in economics: Past, present and future," *American Economic Review*, Papers and Proceedings, **86** (2), 460–64.

Saunders, P., and W.B. Walstad (1990), *The Principles of Economics Course: A Handbook for Instructors*, New York: McGraw-Hill.

Walstad, W.B. (2006), "Assessment of student learning," in W.E. Becker, M. Watts, and S.R. Becker (eds), *Teaching Economics: More Alternatives to Chalk and Talk*, Cheltenham, UK and Northampton, MA, USA: Edward Elgar, 193–212.

Walstad, W.B., and P. Saunders (1998), *Teaching Undergraduate Economics: A Handbook for Instructors*, New York: McGraw-Hill.

APPENDIX 1A
TIP Brochure Content for 2009

Teaching Innovations Program
Fifth and Final Year–2009
Workshops for Economics Faculty on
Interactive Teaching in Undergraduate Economics
Bridging the Gap between Current and Best Practice

2009 Workshop Locations
Hotel Santa Fe, Santa Fe, New Mexico
June 5–7, 2009
Chicago Marriott Suites O'Hare, Rosemont, Illinois
June 12–14, 2009

Sponsored By
The Committee on Economic Education
of the American Economic Association
Funded By
The National Science Foundation
TIP Web Site
www.vanderbilt.edu/AEA/AEACEE/TIP.htm

ASSA Meetings

Program staff will report on TIP at the 2009 ASSA Meetings in San Francisco. Please consult the conference schedule to confirm the time and place.

For More Information and to Complete an Application
Email tipecon@unlnotes.unl.edu or visit the TIP Web Site.

OVERVIEW

The AEA Committee on Economic Education (CEE) is sponsoring a Teaching Innovations Program (TIP) for college and university economics instructors. TIP seeks to improve undergraduate education in economics by offering instructors an opportunity to expand their teaching skills and participate in the scholarship of teaching and learning. TIP is funded by a five-year grant from the National Science Foundation.

TIP builds on a long history of work by CEE to promote effective teaching of economics including national workshop programs, teaching sessions at the ASSA meetings, support for regional workshops, and publication of *Teaching Undergraduate Economics: A Handbook for Instructors* by Walstad and Saunders.

TIP will benefit participants and their home institutions. It will help instructors improve their teaching skills and document their commitment to teaching. It will help colleges and universities raise the quality of economics instruction.

Program Objectives

By participating in TIP, instructors should expect to:

- Understand why and how interactive teaching and learning benefit students.
- Translate knowledge about student learning into effective teaching strategies.
- Develop a plan for using interactive learning in their classrooms.
- Adapt teaching strategies presented in the program for use in their own courses.
- Assess student outcomes that result from using interactive learning.
- Prepare effective interactive exercises for student learning.
- Work in teams to enhance the benefits of the program.
- Engage in an on-going dialogue on teaching and learning with participants and program personnel.
- Participate in the scholarship of teaching and learning by preparing and presenting papers related to pedagogy and practice developed during the program.

TEACHING INNOVATIONS PROGRAM PARTICULARS

Phase One is participation in a three-day workshop. At the workshop, participants are introduced to interactive teaching strategies and plan to implement them. Each workshop participant is invited to participate in phases two and three of the project. Although participation in phases two and three is not required, we give preference to applicants who indicate that they intend to participate in phases two and three.

Phase Two is participation in web-based instruction that occurs in the following academic year. Participants complete two modules that help them introduce interactive teaching strategies in a course they are teaching. They review instructional materials, prepare learning exercises for their courses, use their newly created materials in teaching, and complete an assessment designed to help them improve the new materials and their use. During phase two, participants communicate with teammates and program experts. Participants who attend the workshop and complete two follow-on modules receive from the Committee on Economic Education a Certificate of Achievement that serves as tangible evidence of their dedication to teaching.

Phase Three is participation in the scholarship of teaching and learning. TIP organizes sessions at ASSA and regional association meetings devoted to papers on teaching prepared by program participants. TIP also creates opportunities for participants to share ideas and receive feedback about their papers and teaching strategies.

TYPICAL WORKSHOP SCHEDULE

Friday			
1:00–1:45	Workshop Overview	4:15–5:30	Experiments
1:45–2:30	Team Assignment	5:30–6:30	Social Hour
2:30–3:00	Break	6:30	Dinner
3:00–4:15	Outcome Assessment		
Saturday			
8:00–8:30	Breakfast	1:00–2:15	Context Rich Problems* or Interactive Learning in Large Classes†
8:30– 9:00	Team Reports		
9:00–10:15	Interpretive Questions and Discussion	2:15–2:45	Break
10:15–10:45	Break	2:45–4:00	Case Studies* or Teaching with Clickers†
10:45–12:00	Cooperative Learning		
12:00–1:00	Lunch		
Sunday			
8:00–8:30	Breakfast	10:45–11:45	Team Assignment
8:30–9:30	Phase Two and Blackboard	11:45– 2:00	Workshop Evaluation
9:30–10:15	Participant Teaching	12:00–1:00	Optional Lunch
10:15–10:45	Break		

Note: *Chicago; †Santa Fe

Acclaim for TIP

Participants at eight earlier workshops rated them highly.

- Seventy-nine percent of participants rated the workshop a better use of their time than their next best alternative (and 19 percent said it was at least as good a use of their time).
- One participant said that the workshop "was one of the TOP experiences that I have had in a conference in my professional career…a super learning environment."
- Another said "I believe my time spent in these last two days was the best time invested in my teaching career."
- Ninety-three percent of participants indicated that as a result of the TIP workshop, they were highly likely to participate in phase two of the program.

Support from Economics Department Chairs
Department chairs believe that TIP and its Certificate of Achievement have high value.

- Sixty-eight percent said that receipt of the certificate would strengthen a candidate's case for promotion and tenure.
- Eighty percent said they would recommend that young faculty participate in the workshop and follow through to earn a certificate of achievement.

WHO SHOULD APPLY

The program will help novice and experienced instructors introduce interactive teaching and learning into their courses. Preference will be given to applicants who:

- Describe a course in which they intend to implement interactive learning in the term following the workshop.
- Include a letter of support from their department chair indicating that their Department supports the efforts of the applicant and that the applicant is scheduled to teach the course they describe.
- Have not previously participated in a residential teaching workshop sponsored by CEE.
- Express an interest in participating in phases two and three of the program.

Minority Recruitment: TIP will actively recruit women and minority economists. Our budget includes funds to provide partial travel support for participants from U.S. DOE Accredited Post-Secondary Minority Institutions.

Workshop Costs: Program funds will pay for lodging on Friday and Saturday, meals except Saturday dinner, and for program materials. Participants pay a $100.00 program fee and provide their own transportation.

Application Process: To apply, applicants must:

1. Complete and submit the application form available at www.vanderbilt.edu/AEA/AEACEE/TIP.htm.
2. Send an electronic copy of the department chair support letter described above (separately or with application).
3. Pay a $100 program fee. (Send a check payable to *the University of Nebraska–Lincoln* to William Walstad, Department of Economics, University of Nebraska, Lincoln, NE 68588-0402.) We treat applications as incomplete until we receive the check. We will refund the fee if we do not accept you or if you withdraw before March 3, 2009. If you withdraw after March 3, you forfeit the fee.

Acceptance: Applications for the Program will be accepted between September 2, 2008 and January 16, 2009. A rolling admissions procedure will be used. Some slots will be held open until after the 2009 ASSA Meetings.

PROGRAM INSTRUCTORS

Patrick Conway is Bowman and Gordon Gray Professor of Economics and Director of the Center for Faculty Excellence at UNC-Chapel Hill. He is the TIP expert on case use.

Tisha Emerson is Associate Professor of Economics at Baylor University. She is a TIP expert on classroom games and participated in the 2007 TIP workshop in Santa Barbara.

Denise Hazlett is Professor of Economics at Whitman College. She is a TIP expert on classroom games and has received NSF funding to design classroom experiments.

Gail Hoyt is Professor of Economics at the University of Kentucky. She is a specialist in using interactive learning techniques in large lecture settings.

Kirsten Madden is Associate Professor of Economics at Millersville University. She is a TIP expert on discussion and participated in the 2006 TIP Workshop in Santa Fe.

Mark Maier is Professor of Economics at Glendale Community College. He is a TIP expert on context rich problems and author of *The Data Game.*

KimMarie McGoldrick is Professor of Economics at the University of Richmond, TIP expert on cooperative learning and recipient of the Virginia Outstanding Faculty Award.

Robert Rebelein is Assistant Professor of Economics at Vassar. He is a TIP expert on classroom games and participated in the 2005 TIP Workshop at Georgetown.

Michael Salemi, TIP Co-PI, is Bowman and Gordon Gray Professor of Economics at UNC-Chapel Hill and co-author of *Discussing Economics: A Classroom Guide*.

William Walstad, TIP PI, is Hay Professor of Economics at the University of Nebraska–Lincoln and co-editor, *Teaching Undergraduate Economics: A Handbook for Instructors.*

Workshop Experience

All workshop staff have organized and presented at a wide variety of educational programs and conferences. Since 1990, Salemi and Walstad have directed Programs funded by the Lilly Foundation and the Calvin K. Kazanjian Economics Foundation, Inc.

APPENDIX 1B
Advertisement for the 2005 TIP Workshops

Announcing
Interactive Teaching in Undergraduate Economics Course: Bridging the Gap between Current and Best Practices

Sponsored By
The Committee on Economic Education of the American Economic Association
And Funded By the National Science Foundation

The Program

The program is an opportunity for college economics instructors to improve their teaching skills and participate in the scholarship of teaching economics. The program has three parts. The first is a series of three-day workshops that introduce participants to interactive teaching and learning. Workshops will be held each year starting in 2005 and concluding in 2009. The second is a program of web-based, follow-on instruction that will help participants introduce interactive teaching into their courses. The third is a set of opportunities to present papers on new teaching ideas that result from participation in the program.

Application to Participate in the Project

On behalf of the AEA Committee on Economic Education and the National Science Foundation, we invite prospective participants to learn more about the Program and to apply to participate in the workshops that will be held in 2005. To learn more about the program, workshops and the application process, please visit the program web site.

2005 Workshops

May 20–22, 2005: Rizzo Conference Center,
University of North Carolina at Chapel Hill
June 3–5, 2005: Georgetown Conference Center, Georgetown University

Program Web Site

www.vanderbilt.edu/AEA/AEACEE

ASSA Meetings

The Committee on Economic Education is sponsoring a session at the 2005 ASSA meetings in Philadelphia to introduce the Program. Please consult the conference schedule for the specific time and place of this session.

APPENDIX 1C
TIP Workshop Program, Hotel Santa Fe, June 5–7, 2009

Friday, June 5

13:00–13:45	Workshop Overview & Case for Interactive Learning	Mike Salemi
13:45–14:30	Team Assignment One	Gail Hoyt
14:30–15:00	Break	
15:00–16:15	Cooperative Learning	Gail Hoyt
16:15–17:30	Experiments	Tisha Emerson
18:00	Cash Bar Reception followed by Dinner	

Saturday, June 6

07:30–08:30	Breakfast	
08:30–09:00	Team Reports	Gail Hoyt
09:00–10:15	Interpretive Questions and Discussion	Mike Salemi
10:15–10:45	Break	
10:45–12:00	Assessment	Tisha Emerson
12:00–13:00	Lunch	
13:00–14:15	Interactive Learning in Large Enrollment Courses	Gail Hoyt
14:15–14:45	Break	
14:45–16:00	Using Clickers to Promote Active Learning	Mike Salemi
	Participants are on their own for dinner	

Sunday, June 7

07:30–08:30	Breakfast	
08:30–9:30	Phase Two and Bb Technology	Tisha Emerson
09:30–10:15	Participant Teaching Ideas	Mike Salemi
10:15–10:45	Break	
10:45–11:45	Team Assignment	Gail Hoyt
11:45–12:00	Workshop Evaluation	All
12:00	Optional Lunch	

APPENDIX 1D
AEA-NSF Teaching Innovations Program Workshop Evaluation

Please assist us in making revisions to the TIP Workshops by completing this survey. We respect your opinion and would be especially grateful for your suggestions and constructive criticism.

1. Please check one. My institution is a:
   _____ Research University; _____ University; _____ Four-year College;
   _____ Two-year College; _____ Other
   Specify ____
2. The number of years I have been teaching undergraduate economics is: __________
3. Please rate the workshop sessions using the scale: 5=Exceptional Value, 4=High Value, 3=Solid Value, 2=Some Value, 1=Little Value, 0=No Value. *A list of sessions then follows.*
4. As a result of my participation in the TIP Workshop, it is _______ likely that I will participate in the follow-on instruction portion of the TIP program.
   _____Highly _____Fairly _____Not
5. What is your overall evaluation of the Workshop compared to the opportunity costs of your time? The TIP Workshop was:
   ______ a better use of my time than my next best alternative.
   ______ as good a use of my time as my best alternative.
   ______ of some value, but I could have put my time to better use.
   ______ almost a complete waste of my time.
6. What is your reaction to the quality of materials we provided?
   ______ High Quality. The same materials should be used for future workshops.
   ______ Good Quality, but some improvements should be made.
   ______ Poor Quality.
7. What is your reaction to the workload during the workshop itself?
   ______ Too Heavy. We should have had more time off.
   ______ About Right. I was still alert for the afternoon sessions.
   ______ Too Light. We should have scheduled more sessions and covered additional topics.
8. What was the greatest strength of the workshop?
9. What was the greatest weakness of the workshop?
10. What suggestions do you have for including new topics in future workshops? How should we make time for them?
11. What other suggestions would you make for improving the workshop?
12. Were you satisfied with the facilities? Were you able to get the help you needed to make your stay comfortable and enjoyable?

All of the questions that asked participants to choose a response from a list also invited them to make additional comments and allowed space for those comments.

CHAPTER 2

Online Faculty Instruction to Improve Interactive Teaching of Economics

Mark Maier
Tisha L.N. Emerson

Researchers document numerous constraints and barriers to pedagogical change (Henderson and Dancy 2007; Dancy and Henderson 2010; Henderson, Finkelstein, and Beach 2010). Most notably, barriers include teachers' sense of self-efficacy, quality and quantity of pedagogical training, time constraints (i.e., instructor's time, content coverage requirements), assessment difficulties (i.e., external accountability, measuring student performance), and insufficient support and rewards for teaching effectiveness (see Walczyk, Ramsey, and Zha 2007; Sunal et al. 2001; Michael 2007; Henderson and Dancy 2007; Findlow 2008; Abrami, Poulsen, and Chambers 2004). As a result, despite the significant literature on effective pedagogical practices across many disciplines, a recurring theme of failure to innovate emerges. In practice, pedagogical change occurs at a slow pace – if at all. The failure to produce change then is not always a result of faculty who are unaware of best practices, but instead of faculty choosing less effective practices over proven superior practices (Henderson and Dancy 2007). One of the challenges, then, of professional development programs involves overcoming the numerous barriers to innovation.

Research suggests that professional development activities will have a significant, positive effect on teachers' classroom practice if they have certain characteristics. Key features of effective faculty development programs include sustained involvement over a number of hours, opportunities for active learning, follow-up training for skill refinement, and opportunities for faculty to be involved in the development of new pedagogy through collaborative experiences and opportunities to exchange ideas (Garet et al. 2001; Abrami, Poulsen, and Chambers 2004; Hiebert, Gallimore, and Stigler 2002; Major and Palmer 2006; Owston 2007; Postareff, Lindblom-Ylanne, and Nevgi 2007; Henderson, Finkelstein, and Beach 2010). Further, to the extent that professional development programs can address any of the other, external identified impediments to innovation such as assessment difficulties and insufficient support or reward systems, they will be more effective in promoting pedagogical innovation.

Workshops are a common element in traditional faculty development programs. Unfortunately, research demonstrates that even the best organized and delivered traditional faculty development efforts such as short seminars and workshops are relatively ineffective in promoting significant and lasting changes in instructor classroom behavior (Garet et al. 2001; Hiebert, Gallimore, and Stigler 2002; Sunal et al. 2001; Owston 2007; Roy 1998).[1] Single- or multi-day workshops often fail to induce changes in instructor pedagogical practices for two main reasons. First, instructors' workshop exposure to new pedagogies is generally too brief. Second, instructors are rarely afforded post-workshop follow-up (Michael 2007).[2] Thus, while workshops are meant to afford participants with pedagogical training, research suggests that they are not particularly effective nor do they address the many other barriers identified in the literature.

The Teaching Innovations Program (TIP) provided a significant improvement over traditional professional development projects as it addressed many of the barriers to innovation identified in the literature. While the first phase of TIP consisted of a relatively traditional workshop experience, it built the foundation for the next two TIP phases. It is the TIP experience in its entirety that served as the program's major advance over previous pedagogical innovation initiatives.

The purpose of the current chapter is to describe Phase Two of the TIP experience. The remainder of the chapter is organized as follows. Section I presents a detailed description of Phase Two of the TIP experience, including a description of the pedagogical innovation modules. Section II discusses participation levels and participant evaluations of their experiences. Section III describes the logistics involved in Phase Two – from the point of view of both participants and the Phase Two coordinator. Section IV offers recommendations for improvements in future professional development initiatives of the type employed in Phase Two. Appendix 2A provides an example of a participant plan including module instructor comments.

I. PHASE TWO OF TIP

The Teaching Innovations Program (TIP), sponsored by the American Economic Association Committee on Economic Education (CEE) and funded by the National Science Foundation (DUE #03-38482), ran for five years, serving 335 faculty teaching in a wide variety of U.S. colleges and universities.[3] Two workshops were held each year (Phase One) where participants were introduced to seven interactive strategies for teaching college level economics. Upon completion of Phase One, participants were invited to enroll in online instruction in a module of their choice (Phase Two) where they would receive supplemental instruction in applying the innovation in one of their courses.

Phase Two was administered through the use of the Blackboard course management software located at the University of Nebraska–Lincoln. Modules offered instruction in the following pedagogical approaches: Assessment, Cases, Context-Rich Problems, Cooperative Learning, Discussion, Experiments, and Large Enrollment Courses. The TIP Blackboard site included a TIP preview page that provided a summary of each module as well as the modules themselves. With successful completion of two modules a participant earned a certificate of achievement from the CEE.

Finally, TIP offered support for participants to develop scholarly papers and presentations based on their work in one or more modules (Phase Three). Chapter 1 of this volume reports on the TIP workshops in detail, Chapter 3 reports on TIP Phase Three activities, and Chapter 11 reports on participants' retrospective assessment of TIP.

For ease of use and quality assurance, a common format was employed for all seven modules. Each module contained all materials presented at the TIP workshops, required readings for completion of the module, a set of required tasks (including a self-test and development of an implementation plan), additional recommended readings, and examples of participant work.

Each module contained a set of assignments that led participants through six steps for successful implementation of their chosen pedagogical innovation.

1. Participants were provided with a set of required readings with information about the pedagogical innovation and its successful implementation.
2. Participants completed a short self-graded, multiple choice format, assessment to focus attention on the central concepts in the required reading and to initiate discussion with the module instructor if the arguments were unclear or unconvincing.[4]

3. Participants identified the learning goals for the innovation and submitted a work plan for implementation of the innovation. Module instructors reviewed the work plan and provided feedback. Appendix 2A provides an example of a participant plan for a cooperative learning exercise and the detailed comments provided by the module instructor to help the participant refine and implement the plan.
4. After receiving feedback from the module instructor, usually in a week or two, and often involving a back-and-forth discussion about the plan, the participant used the innovation in the classroom.
5. Participants completed a reflective exercise, evaluating the innovation and providing evidence of its outcomes.
6. Participants completed an anonymous survey evaluating the module as a whole.

While each module utilized the same general structure, implementation of the innovation varied from module to module. In the assessment module, participants read about formative and summative assessment and then evaluated methods currently used in their course and added a new classroom assessment technique. A case is a group of source materials on a single subject, drawn from real experience that places the participants in a decision-making analytical role. In the case module, participants learned how to write and teach a case, and then used a case in one of their courses. A context-rich problem is a short scenario using a non-standard application of a important course concept. Participants innovating through use of context-rich problems read about the principles of context-rich problems, wrote three context-rich problems and then used and evaluated a context-rich problem in a course.

Cooperative learning is a structured, systematic instructional strategy in which small groups work together toward a common goal. In the cooperative learning module, participants read about cooperative learning and designed and implemented a cooperative learning exercise.

In an inquiry-based discussion, students investigate the meaning of a text by responding to question clusters created by the instructor. In the discussion module, participants wrote question clusters for a reading and then led a discussion in their classroom. In a classroom experiment, students make economic decisions in a controlled environment that become the data the class later analyzes. In the experiments module, participants chose a classroom experiment, adapted it for their course, and then employed it. Finally, in the large enrollment module, participants implemented activities and format changes that allowed them to add interactive learning to their large enrollment courses.

II. PARTICIPATION AND EVALUATION

A total of 335 economics instructors participated in Phase One of the TIP program. All workshop graduates were invited to enroll in a module in Phase Two. At the end of the project in June 2010, 70 percent of TIP workshop participants had enrolled in a module, 39 percent completed a module, and 27 percent completed two modules and earned a certificate from the CEE. The most frequently selected modules were Discussion, Experiments, and Cooperative Learning, each completed by more than forty participants.

Participants completed an evaluation of the module and their experience. Anonymous evaluation of the modules was overwhelmingly positive, indicating that they were efficiently organized and effective in improving instruction: 96.9 percent of participants indicated that follow-on instruction was "a better use" (61.7%) or "as good a use" (35.2%) "of my time as the next best alternative," 97.4 percent strongly agreed or agreed that they received helpful feedback from the module instructor, and 100 percent strongly agreed or agreed that the module helped them learn how to use the innovation. Table 2.1 provides the responses to seven survey questions.

Table 2.1: Participant Evaluations of Phase Two

	Percent of Responses (n = 193)				
	SA	A	N	D	SD
The module was easy to use.	56.5	38.9	2.6	1.6	0.5
The selection of readings included in this module was useful for learning about the innovation.	62.7	32.6	4.7	0	0
Completing the "check your understanding" assignment helped me learn about the innovation.	44.9	42.2	11.6	1.4	0
The preparatory plan assignment provided a valuable guide as I planned my use of the innovation.	68.4	28.5	3.1	0	0
I received helpful feedback from the TIP module instructor.	88.6	8.8	2.1	0.5	0
Completing the assessment of my innovation was a worthwhile activity.	62.2	31.6	5.7	0.5	0
Overall, this module helped me to learn how to use the innovation.	76.2	23.8	0	0	0

Note: SA = Strongly Agree; A = Agree; N = Neutral; D = Disagree; SD = Strongly Disagree

The module evaluation included two open ended questions: "What I liked best about this module is…" and "What suggestions do you have for improving or changing the module?" Responses to these questions offer additional evidence that participants valued their Phase Two experiences. A typical overall comment called TIP "the best professional development opportunity in my ten year teaching career." Respondents pointed out three reasons for the TIP modules' effectiveness: they followed directly on workshop content; they allowed participants to experiment with an innovation in a course they were currently teaching; and, they allowed for repeated and supportive interaction with experts.

A sample of participant comments to the open-ended questions follows:

General Comments

There is plenty of information in the module to get you started, but the instructor's review of materials really makes all the difference. The feedback, at all stages, is great! What I found most useful was the opportunity to practice the suggestions in the readings by planning for a class, engaging my students in a class discussion, and evaluating the outcome – all with your very prompt, supportive feedback.

The quality of the feedback I received from the moderator was excellent. I think this is what helped me to learn the most.

The instructor was committed to the goals of the project, and was willing to engage in extensive discussion with me. This interchange helped me improve my understanding, and to apply this discussion innovation to my own objectives in my own classes.

I think the feedback from the module leader is a very extraordinary and beneficial part of this program. This is true with this module as well as the others. Fabulous!

Comments on Learning Goals

Participating in this module forced me to sit down and think about the topics that students find particularly difficult in the second principles course and to come up with a strategy to help them.

What I liked best about this module is that this kind of assignment needs a significant amount of thinking-time for the instructor to figure out the goals of the course, and how this assignment can achieve them.

As I said in the earlier assessment, it made me think about what and how I choose to teach. I think that it's very easy to teach on autopilot, and this made me examine my choices.

The suggestions obtained from the module instructor forced me to think through the objectives of this exercise.

While participants overwhelmingly felt that Phase Two was a beneficial experience and helpful in their implementation of active learning strategies in their courses, there were some aspects of the modules that were less successful. Participants felt somewhat constrained by the Blackboard website noting "the web site is not very user friendly" and "It would be helpful to have a website that is designed specifically for this program – not one run through the University of Nebraska web site." In fact, most module instructors chose to communicate directly with participants via email.

The lowest rated section of the module was "check your understanding," usually a multiple choice self-graded test – although the level of dissatisfaction was only 13 percent neutral or disagreeing with the statement that it helped them. Participants wrote, "I wanted the first quiz to be more substantial. Doing well on it did not convince me that I'd really developed more than a superficial understanding of the material" and "I don't like the online quizzes, but I do understand why they need be in the module."

Participants wanted the modules to offer more collaboration with others in the program, commenting: "In the future, I would suggest providing information as it becomes available from current participants on their experiences with this module. What did they learn? What problems did they encounter, if any, and how did they overcome them? What did they find worked especially well?" One suggestion was that "a peer review feature should be added, where one participant would, perhaps informally (or less formally) review another's innovations. This way, all participants would get a chance to see what at least one other person is doing. The enthusiasm for sharing ideas and keeping in touch expectedly died down after we left the conference, and this would be a small way to keep the fires burning."

Participants would have liked more references to the research literature on each pedagogy, especially related to learning goals and assessment, an addition that might have helped with the transition to Phase Three. As one participant explained, "While Phase II seems to easily flow from Phase I, Phase III is quite a stretch. Maybe this is by design. If not, I would suggest a question that asks faculty to think of an extension of the innovation in a way that they are not familiar. This might give TIP participants something to build on for Phase III."

III. LOGISTICS

After completing Phase One, participants were enrolled in TIP Preview, a course on the UNL Blackboard system. Here participants could download all materials used in the Phase One workshop and preview the readings and assignments used in each of the modules. The seven TIP modules also were created as courses within Blackboard and participants were invited to enroll in one of the seven modules in Phase Two. Enrollment involved simply sending an email to the module coordinator indicating the module of their choice and the time frame for their intended implementation. Generally within twenty-four hours of indicating their enrollment intention, the participant was provided full access to the materials for the module of their choice through the Blackboard course management software. The participant was responsible for completing the required reading, self-assessment, and development of learning objectives and implementation plan. The participant would then communicate their learning objectives and plan to the module instructor for feedback. After exchange with the module coordinator, participants implemented the pedagogical change in their course and assessed the outcome.

Participants enrolled in one module at a time and were limited to completing two modules after which they earned a certificate from the CEE. The two-module cap was a direct result of scarce resources and an attempt to limit the workload on any one of the module instructors. As noted above, enrollment was uneven among the modules with greater participation in the Cooperative Learning, Discussion and Experiments modules, but none was completed by more than fifty participants during the project's five years.

The module coordinator's responsibilities focused on TIP's Blackboard site at the University of Nebraska–Lincoln. Although Blackboard courses are designed for traditional instruction, their format was adjusted readily for TIP modules allowing for the posting of readings, submission of participant work and an anonymous survey after module completion. As a well-established university program, technical support was available to the module coordinator when enrollment or course management issues arose. The module coordinator made certain that each module appeared the same to each participant and that all elements were working as planned.

The module coordinator used information stored on Blackboard to keep track of module enrollment and module completion for annual reports prepared for the project principal investigators. In addition, the Blackboard survey tool was used to compile assessment data submitted by participants after they completed each module as well as answers to open-ended questions about the module's effectiveness.

IV. RECOMMENDATIONS FOR THE FUTURE

TIP Phase Two offers a model for future projects in economic education and indeed for other disciplines seeking to foster innovative instruction. Credit for the project's well-designed format goes to co-principal investigators Michael Salemi and William Walstad who envisioned the three-part structure of TIP, and outlined the module format for each instructor. The result was an effective set of modules that benefited over one hundred and fifty instructors who completed at least one module.

As evidenced by the findings in the literature, all too often faculty development workshops stimulate interest in new teaching techniques that are then never employed in the classroom (Roy 1998). In contrast, TIP involved far more than a simple workshop experience. By engaging participants in a continued interaction with module experts (and other innovators in Phase Three), the TIP experience extended the contact hours and provided the workshop follow-up suggested as being necessary in the literature to overcome pedagogical innovation implementation barriers (Abrami, Poulsen, and Chambers 2004; Findlow 2008; Garet et al. 2001; Hiebert, Gallimore, and Stigler 2002; Major and Palmer 2006).

In particular, work in Phase Two was designed to encourage participants to move beyond their usual pedagogical practice. Recognizing that participants would often chose an unfamiliar instructional strategy, Phase Two provided them with support to implement it.

The TIP modules were built on a series of steps from identification of learning goals, to implementation of the innovation, to final assessment. By requiring that participants complete all steps, the module took participants through a cycle of course preparation that is often recommended but not always followed (Wiggins and McTighe 2005, 16; Fink 2003, 73–81). With the support and feedback of module experts, participants likely experienced increased confidence in their ability to effectively implement the new pedagogies in a manner tailored to their particular classroom environment. In addition, the certificate granted for completion of two modules increased the professional rewards and acknowledgement associated with their efforts to innovate. Thus, while it is impossible to know what the innovation level would have been absent the second and third phases of TIP, it is likely that participants realized significantly higher levels of classroom innovation than would have occurred with the workshop experience alone.

The many successes of TIP Phase Two are useful in directing future professional development programs. By addressing many of the barriers to classroom innovation identified in the literature (insufficient workshop follow-up, quality of training, tailoring of innovations to specific situations, and perceived lack of reward/recognition for innovation), Phase Two serves as a model for future professional development efforts, both within economics and in other disciplines. Moreover, the TIP Phase Two modules themselves comprise a rich resource for pedagogical innovation. As a result, we believe that the content should be preserved and extended. Further, given the effectiveness of both the content of the modules and the overall structure, we believe that the content should be made more widely available to economics instructors (including graduate students who currently are teaching or will be shortly) in a manner akin to that in Phase Two.

While there is much to emulate in Phase Two, future professional development efforts also can learn from the small problems experienced in Phase Two as they provide such programs with teachable moments. Areas for improvement include use of alternatives to the Blackboard course management system, greater support for instructors in developing learning goals and assessment, and more intentional linking of complementary pedagogical techniques.

One limitation of Phase Two was its reliance on a university course management system (Blackboard). Since Blackboard was designed for traditional college courses, some of its functionality was less geared toward the needs of a professional development program. For example, the self-assessment function looked like a test and likely reminded participants of graded summative assessment that was not intended. Also, while Blackboard supports communication tools, it is less direct than traditional email. Thus, some module instructors bypassed Blackboard, preferring to use traditional email instead of using the Blackboard communication tools. As a result, module instructors maintained records of participant work, but there was no central repository as could have been possible had all work been sent through Blackboard. In retrospect, while there were advantages of using an existing system that offered ready technical support, a more ideal approach would employ a more flexible course management system that could be formatted specifically for TIP and would encourage archiving of all communications and participant work.

Economic educators and education researchers agree that learning goals need to be identified before pedagogical techniques are selected (Hansen, Salemi, and Siegfried 2002; Fink 2003; Weimer 2002). As a result, all TIP modules first ask participants to specify what students would learn – a step that TIP participants often found to be challenging. Even though participants recognized the importance of writing learning goals, it had not been part of their usual curriculum planning. Future initiatives should provide additional assistance, perhaps in the form of a tutorial, based on *Understanding by Design* (Wiggins and McTighe 2005, Chapter 3) or *Creating Significant Learning Experiences* (Fink 2003).

TIP participants also had difficulty in developing assessment tools. The final step in each module asked participants to assess the innovation's impact on student learning. Because TIP modules were exploratory, often the first time that the participant had used the innovation, the assessment was relatively informal, sharing with the module instructor what went well and what did not. In many cases, the assessment was posted for other TIP participants on the Blackboard web site, and later was the basis for more scholarly work, appropriate for conferences or publication in Phase Three (McGoldrick 2010).

Additional assistance could have been provided, perhaps in a "What is evidence?" tutorial recommending first of all that more data be collected, even if it was not all used in the final report. For example, it is a relatively simple matter to save copies of student work, survey students before an innovation is begun, videotape students in the classroom, or keep a record of the instructor's work and thoughts as the innovation was planned. The tutorial would then offer advice on forming hypotheses from these data, developing empirical measures of student learning, and obtaining necessary approval from institutional human subjects committees.

At the TIP Phase One workshops, innovative pedagogy was interwoven into the sessions so that when, for example, participants investigated classroom experiments, they did so using principles of cooperative learning that had been presented in a prior session. For participants' first classroom use of an instructional technique, it is helpful to focus on one innovation at a time. However, research in physics education suggests that the combined use of innovations has a synergetic effect, improving learning more than the sum of individual innovations (Pollock 2005). Future design of Phase Two modules could include more cross-referencing among modules to encourage follow-on projects that combine more than one active learning technique.

Finally, Phase Two also could be extended to include more links to research both in economics education and in other disciplines in which the module's innovation has been adopted. These resources would build participants' knowledge as they consider Phase Three scholarly projects. In addition, TIP participants could collaborate with other economic educators, beginning to create a "teaching commons," bridging the gap between classroom instruction and education research (Huber and Hutchings 2005). Such a community would be even more informed if it crossed disciplines, sharing the comparative advances of each discipline's work on teaching and learning. See Starting Point: Teaching and Learning Economics[5] for one effort in this direction.

Overall, TIP was a success, reaching more economic instructors than any previous effort in economic education at the college and university level. Phase Two was an important component in this success as it built on the more commonly used workshop model so that participants applied what they had learned in the workshops in an intentional manner, guided by experts in seven different pedagogical modules. Available through a course management system at the University of Nebraska–Lincoln, these modules offered a self-contained introduction to each pedagogy. Interactive coaching with the module instructors then provided TIP participants an opportunity to develop, use, and assess an innovation in a course they were teaching. Participant evaluations of both the modules and instructor assistance were extremely positive on closed- and open-ended questions. Recommendations for improvement focus primarily on ways in which TIP can further assist instructors in developing learning outcomes and assessing student learning. Every effort should be made to preserve the TIP resources already created and to extend their availability to a wider community.

NOTES

1. The ineffectiveness applies to most transmission-oriented workshops, not just those aimed a faculty development (Fixxen et al. 2005).
2. Research demonstrates that individuals learn more (by two standard deviations) through one-to-one tutoring than from traditional instruction (Meltzoff et al. 2009). One-to-one follow-up post-workshop instruction should result in more significant improvements in instructor skills and self-efficacy than from the workshop alone.
3. Maier's role in the project was as staff at two workshop sessions, the instructor for one module, and coordinator of the Phase Two web site instructional modules, enrolling participants, and summarizing the evaluations. Emerson participated in a 2007 workshop and was subsequently invited to join the TIP workshop staff for one workshop each in 2008 and 2009. Emerson also participated in the cooperative learning module in Phase Two.
4. The Experiments module did not include this step.
5. http://serc.carleton.edu/econ/index.html

REFERENCES

Abrami, P.C., C. Poulsen, and B. Chambers (2004), "Teacher motivation to implement an educational innovation: Factors differentiating users and non-users of cooperative learning," *Educational Psychology*, **24** (2), 201–16.

Dancy, M., and C. Henderson (2010), *Barriers and Promises in STEM Reform*, Board on Science Education, The National Academies, Commissioned Papers. Available at: http://www7.nationalacademies.org/bose/Dancy_Henderson_CommissionedPaper.pdf (accessed February 9, 2010).

Findlow, S. (2008), "Accountability and innovation in higher education: A disabling tension?," *Studies in Higher Education*, **33** (3), 313–29.

Fink, D. (2003), *Creating Significant Learning Experiences: An Integrated Approach to Designing College Courses*, San Francisco: Jossey-Bass.

Fixxen, D.L., S.F. Naoom, K.A. Blasé, R.M. Friedman, and F. Wallace (2005), *Implementation Research: A Synthesis of the Literature*.

Available at: http://www.fpg.unc.edu/~nirn/resources/publications/Monograph/ (downloaded February 9, 2010).

Garet, M.S., A.C. Porter, L. Desimone, B. Birman, and K.S. Yoon (2001), "What makes professional development effective? Results from a national sample of teachers," *American Educational Research Journal*, **38** (4), 915–45.

Hansen, W.L., M. Salemi, and J.J. Siegfried (2002), "Use it or lose it: Teaching literacy in the economics principles course," *American Economic Review*, **92** (2), 463–72.

Henderson, C., and M. Dancy (2007), "Barriers to the use of research-based instructional strategies: The influence of both individual and situational characteristics," *Physical Review Special Topics – Physics Education Research*, **3**, 020102-1–020102-14.

Henderson, C., N. Finkelstein, and A. Beach (2010), "Beyond dissemination in college science teaching: An introduction to four core change strategies," *Journal of College Science Teaching*, forthcoming. Available at: http://homepages.wmich.edu/~chenders/Publications/HendersonJCST2009ChangeStrategies.pdf (accessed February 9, 2010).

Hiebert, J., R. Gallimore, and J.W. Stigler (2002), "A knowledge base for the teaching profession: What would it look like and how can we get one?," *Educational Researcher*, **31** (5), 3–15.

Huber, M.T., and P. Hutchings (2005), *The Advancement of Learning: Building the Teaching Commons*, Stanford, CT: Jossey-Bass.

Major, C., and B. Palmer (2006), "Reshaping teaching and learning: The transformation of faculty pedagogical content knowledge," *Higher Education*, **51**, 619–47.

McGoldrick, K. (2010), *Advancing the Scholarship of Teaching and Learning in Economics*. Paper presented at the Allied Social Science Association meetings, January.

Meltzoff, A.N., P.K. Kuhl, J. Movellan, and T.J. Sejnowski (2009), "Foundations for a new science of learning," *Science*, **325**, 284–88.

Michael, J. (2007), "Faculty perceptions about barriers to active learning," *College Teaching*, **55** (2), 42–47.

Owston, R. (2007), "Contextual factors that sustain innovative pedagogical practice using technology: An international study," *Journal of Educational Change*, **8**, 61–77.

Pollock, S.J. (2005), "No single cause: Learning gains, student attitudes, and the impacts of multiple effective reforms," *AIP Conference Proceedings*, **790**, 137–40.

Postareff, L., S. Lindblom-Ylanne, and A. Nevgi (2007), "The effect of pedagogical training on teaching in higher education," *Teaching and Teacher Education*, **23**, 557–71.

Roy, P. (1998), "Staff development that makes a difference," in C. Brody and N. Davidson (eds), *Professional Development for Cooperative Learning*. Albany, NY: State University Press of New York, 79–99.

Sunal, D.W., J. Hodges, C.S. Sunal, K.W. Whitaker, L.M. Freeman, L. Edwards, R.A. Johnston, and M. Odell (2001), "Teaching science in higher education: Faculty professional development and barriers to change," *School Science and Mathematics*, **101** (5), 246–57.

Walczyk, J.J., L.L. Ramsey, and P. Zha (2007), "Obstacles to instructional innovation according college science and mathematics faculty," *Journal of Research in Science Teaching*, **44** (1), 85–106.

Weimer, M. (2002). *Learner-Centered Teaching*, San Francisco: Jossey-Bass.

Wiggins, G., and J. McTighe (2005), *Understanding by Design*, Alexandria, VA: Association for Supervision and Curriculum Development.

APPENDIX 2A
Sample Participant Plan Prepared by Jennifer Kujawa Rhoads with Module Instructor Comments by KimMarie McGoldrick

1. Based on the One-Sentence-Summary Objective Setting Exercise, list one or two learning objectives you want your students to achieve as a result of implementing this cooperative learning exercise.

I want to develop my students' ability to interpret and communicate both sides of controversial health care policy issues during the 2008 presidential election. This will be done both in and out of class by facilitating group analysis and presentation of various health care issues currently being debated in the presidential campaign to help my students learn how to synthesize and communicate health care reform proposals.

> **Comment 1:** Nicely laid out, does a good job of keeping to learning skills and not focusing on specific content.
> **Comment 2:** From reading your full plan it looks like you also want them to locate the details of each plan as well.
> **Comment 3:** Is this based on the integration of individual components into a more comprehensive plan?

Do you simply want them to communicate or do you wish to add any evaluation, pro/con, etc?

2. List one or two content objectives you want your students to achieve as a result of implementing this cooperative learning exercise.

Students will understand and be able to evaluate the various issues in Senator McCain's and Senator Obama's health care reform proposals (i.e. health insurance mandates, pre-existing conditions, etc.).

> **Comment 1:** Will there be some set up exercise that students complete to understand which are the key issues? Or will you simply be providing these to the students? For example, if one looks at past presidential campaigns are the health care issues which received focus the same basic categories as for today? Can this also provide an interesting lesson for students? Perhaps a follow us exercise?

3. What category of cooperative learning exercises best fits your objectives? Briefly explain why this is the case.

The writing category with my addition of an oral presentation fits my objective of students being able to synthesize and communicate health care issues. The synthesis will happen with the group writing portion (written group worksheets) and the communication will happen with the oral group presentations.

Comment 1: Good choice, fits well with your objectives.

4. What specific type of cooperative learning exercise for the category noted in question 6 best fits your objectives? Briefly explain why this is the case.

Features of the round table exercise will be used for the writing portion. Students will be divided into groups of four and given an issue to research and present to the rest of the class. Group members will conduct individual initial research on their assigned issue and will then bring a completed individual worksheet to share with the rest of the group. Note that I believe this initial individual research will be necessary because the students will have limited knowledge about the health care issues. Group members will share their responses in a round table format. They will then work to synthesize their individual answers to produce a group version of the written worksheet.

Comment 1: I fully agree, it also promotes individual accountability.

5. Describing your cooperative learning exercise through the process of implementing and evaluating.

a. Preparations (Structuring the Task, Orienting Students): Please provide a description of the exercise you have developed. It should address how the task will be structured and how students will be oriented to cooperative learning.

Students will first be introduced to this project through a paragraph in the syllabus that includes a brief description of the forthcoming activity and the expected outcomes. The paragraph below is what will be included in the syllabus:

Comment 1: Good, I like how you have expectations for this project set up right from the start of the semester.

By utilizing the forthcoming presidential election, we will be examining and discussing specific issues pertinent to the U.S. health care system. We will do this through examination of the health care reform proposals of Senator McCain and Senator Obama. You will work in a small group to prepare a written outline of an oral presentation. Group members will be chosen at random to present the various sections of the presentation. As a capstone for this project each student will be responsible for writing a 6–8-page paper.

Comment 1: You might want to include a sentence prior to this which states that they will perform some preliminary research, use groups to refine their understanding and then also prepare the presentation.
Comment 2: Do you want to tell them "on what"?

The structure of the project that I have developed is threefold. There is an initial individual portion, a middle group cooperative portion and then a final individual portion. On September 29, the class will be broken up into groups of four and each group will be assigned a health care issue currently being debated during the presidential election. The initial individual portion of the project is that each student has one week to complete a worksheet for the assigned topic (see attachment 1). This worksheet includes a section for the student to provide some background information on the assigned issue, find or create examples that illustrate the issue, summarize how Senator McCain's policy addresses the issue, and summarize how Senator Obama's policy addresses the issue. This initial individual writing assignment is to ensure that each student obtains background knowledge of their topic before discussing it in a group.

Comment 1: Really nicely done. This is a very well thought out project.
Comment 2: How will groups be assigned? Randomly? If so, using what process? Since this is a substantial project, I would suggest that you not use a random draw but rather think carefully about how you might use student opinions to create diverse groups. Recall the line up and divide exercise at the workshop. Could you have students express an opinion on a topic and then create groups so you have a diversity of perspectives?
Comment 3: How will these be assigned? Does the process by which you assign particular issues to a specific group matter?
Comment 4: In question 1a, how detailed do you want them to be? Do you expect them to come up with some statistics supporting their background knowledge? Should you remind them to keep track of their citations in case they need them for their individual papers (avoid plagiarism!).

On October 6, the cooperative learning portion of the project will take place during class. The students will bring their individual worksheets to class and then meet in their small groups to discuss, synthesize and compromise until a group version of the same worksheet has been produced (see attachment 2). This written worksheet will serve as the basis of an oral presentation to the rest of the class, which the students will have one week to prepare. The presentations will cover the same four aspects of the health care issues included in the worksheet. On the day of the presentation, the group members will be chosen at random to present a portion of the presentation.

Therefore, each student will be presenting one section from the group's presentation but they will not know which one (i.e. background, McCain's proposal, etc.). These presentations will be on October 15 and 17.

Comment 1: Excellent link to the number of students in a group so that you can randomly call on them.
Comment 2: My students hear 'presentation' and think they MUST have a fancy PowerPoint presentation. To what extent will you expect this presentation to have audio/visual/etc. After all, it is possible for them to even add video links to the candidates speeches which help define their position. I know you suggest to them only 2 minutes per section, but do you want to address the level of formality too?

The final individual portion of the project is a written paper allowing the student to summarize and evaluate the information presented by all the groups. This paper should be 6–8 pages long and will be due roughly 3 weeks after the presentations are over (about November 3).

Comment 1: Good, this will provide them motivation to pay attention while other groups are presenting.

b. Set up (Introducing the Exercise, Forming Groups, Group Decision Making Strategies): Briefly describe how you will introduce this exercise to students, what method of group formation and of what size you have chosen, and the extent to which you will describe group decision making processes to your students.

When I introduce the project to the class on September 26, I will pass out a descriptive handout that outlines the process of the activity and deadlines (see attachment 3). I will form groups randomly using my alphabetical listing of the roster. I anticipate having 8 groups of 4 students. Groups will be instructed to continue discussing individual responses and review resources until they can all compromise on a group response to each question.

Comment 1: This is really well laid out for the students. I especially like the fact that you have them running against both of the candidates, forcing them not to rely on their republican or democratic tendencies but to work on the issues.
Comment 2: You will be almost a month into the course by the time this assignment starts. Will you have any more knowledge of the students on which to base this assignment? Consider diversity in forming groups… as suggested above, diversity in opinions or performance in the class to date.
Comment 3: You already have some components of the exercise that require each student to participate, at least initially when they share their individual worksheets. But could this be refined a bit. First, you might

find that a shy person will claim that what they had on their worksheet was basically the same as what others have said, even if this is not entirely true. You might want to be clear in the directions that each individual is to read aloud their answer to the section they are working on. Second, after this sharing is complete there is no mechanism that prevents a dominant person from taking over. Can you think of adding either roles or some processing suggestions to keep this from occurring? It may be enough to simply remind them that everyone must agree and understand since they will be randomly called upon to present each section.

c. Monitoring (Behaviors, Task Completion): Briefly describe how you will interact with groups during the exercise and what follow on activities you have developed for those groups finishing their task early.

I have scheduled a 50-minute class period to devote to in-class group work. I will be circling throughout the room to keep an eye on each of the groups to make sure they are on task, reinforce positive progress and be available to answer any clarifying questions about the project (not content). If a group finishes before the class period is over I will quickly review the group worksheet and either suggest areas needing improvement or direct the group to begin preparing the oral presentation.

Comment 1: Good, I think this is enough time for them to get through the worksheets, and potentially think about a presentation.
Comment 2: I wonder about this. In some ways it rewards those who have finished first in a way that other groups cant take advantage of. Typically, we like to have extension exercises as an add on to CL exercises so that it keeps students focused on the exercise without providing them an advantage over other groups.

d. Closure: (Quiet Signal, Providing Closure to the Exercise, Processing Group Functioning, Grading and Evaluation): Briefly describe your quiet signal, how you will bring closure to the exercise, the extent to which you will discuss group functioning with the class, and whether this exercise will be directly evaluated.

I typically bring a class back together after group work by standing in the front of the room and asking for their attention. This typically works, but if it doesn't then I will flick the lights on and off as a signal.

This activity will be evaluated for a grade. There will be an immediate formal reporting out activity in the form of a group worksheet that includes the synthesized responses of each group for its health care issue. The group is required to turn its completed worksheet in to me before leaving class on the in-class work day. I will grade the worksheets on the basis of correct content and completeness, and return them the next class period so the groups can use them to create their oral presentations.

Comment 1: I like this. Students are evaluated at the individual and group level, the evaluation is timely, and they get feedback before moving forward. Question: I assume you will be collecting the individual work as well… will you need to ask students to bring 2 copies, one for grading and one for group work? I suspect many of them will want to hold onto their individual sheets even after their group work as they continue to think about the project.

There will also be a delayed formal reporting out activity in the form of an oral presentation that will be graded for accurate content, clarity, knowledge of the material and effectiveness in conveying the information to the class. As mentioned above, the students will be chosen at random to present one section of their group presentation. This will promote students working hard together to ensure that each group member fully understands and can explain any section of the presentation.

Comment 1: Yes!

6. Briefly explain how each of the four key elements will be incorporated into this exercise.

e. Positive interdependence

Comment 1: Don't you also have resource interdependence? After all, the students bring individual research to the group and while some may overlap it is likely that each will have something unique in their contribution.

Output goal interdependence – each group must develop a single group worksheet and oral presentation.

Learning goal interdependence – group members will be chosen at random to present the various sections of the oral group presentation. Therefore, all members of the group need to be able to explain every section of the group's presentation.

f. Individual (and group) accountability

Individual accountability – Each student is responsible for preliminary research that he or she then shares with the group. In addition, after all of the groups have completed their presentations, each of the students is responsible for writing a 6–8-page analysis of all of the issues presented by the groups.

Group accountability – Each group will receive a group grade for its group worksheet and oral presentation.

g. Equal participation

Students will be required to do initial research on their group's assigned health care issue before actually working together as a group. Each student must find at least two resources to bring to class and complete a worksheet where he or she completes initial thoughts/preliminary answers to each of the four sections for the assigned issue. This ensures that the individual group members are prepared to participate in the round table exercise in class with their groups.

Comment 1: Yes, but note my comment above. While they are prepared, beyond initial sharing there is little incentive to continue to participate. They could simply take what the group decided and use it for the presentation. I am not suggesting you need to change something, just think about it.

Also, groups of four students will be formed and each group will be preparing an oral presentation of the four sections of their assigned issue (background and current state, examples illustrating the issue, McCain's position and Obama's position). Students will be chosen at random to present one of the sections from their group's presentation.

h. Simultaneous interaction

The students will work as a group to synthesize and revise their individual worksheet responses into a group worksheet which will be the basis for their oral group presentation. Since students are working in small groups, more than one student will be participating at any one time.

7. Now that you have fully described your cooperative learning exercise, please explain briefly how you will decide whether or not your students have met the objectives you outlined above. How will you evaluate whether you have met your instructional objectives? What evidence will you collect?

I will be assigning grades for the individual worksheets, group worksheets, oral presentations, and individual follow-up papers (see attachments 4–7). The grades from the cooperative learning portion of the project (group worksheets and group oral presentations) will show whether the students met my learning objective of being able to synthesize and communicate health care reform policies. The final written paper is an individual extension of the group work which will allow me to judge how well the students can not only communicate but also apply their new knowledge to formulate their own positions.

CHAPTER 3

Advancing the Scholarship of Teaching and Learning in Economics

KimMarie McGoldrick

Advancement of the disciplinary knowledge base regarding how and what economics students learn depends on instructor participation in the Scholarship of Teaching and Learning (SoTL). Scholars are likely to be familiar with SoTL activities that are associated with traditional, formal visions of scholarship such as academic paper presentations, faculty workshops, and submissions to peer-reviewed journals. A range of opportunities for participation in SoTL associated with each of these categories exist in economics. Both regional and the national economics conferences support sessions dedicated to economics education. Regional teaching workshops ranging from single- to multiple-day events including both invited plenary sessions and opportunities to submit papers are located on both coasts, as well as in between.[1] Publishing economic education research is made possible through a number of dedicated outlets including the *Journal of Economic Education* (*JEE*), *Perspectives on Economic Education Research* and *International Review of Economics Education*.

Although SoTL certainly includes these more familiar and formal activities associated with traditional visions of scholarship, it also supports a wide range of complimentary activities. SoTL activities are characterized by informed, purposeful reflection on teaching and learning and participation in the conversation among like scholars, via the teaching commons. Because the commons is intended to be a venue where individuals come together to exchange ideas, it includes informal SoTL activities such as networking, sharing innovative teaching strategies and supporting materials, and the documentation of student learning outcomes by individual faculty to be used for course enhancement. Such activities are likely to occur at regional and national conferences as well as teaching workshops which support more formal SoTL activities, but are also supported by teaching economics blogs[2] and listservs such as Tch-Econ.[3]

This chapter discusses SoTL, both in economics and more broadly, and describes how the Teaching Innovations Program (TIP) provided scaffolding for faculty participants to enhance disciplinary understanding of student learning in economics. Specifically, it describes how each of the phases of TIP has encouraged and supported these activities. The chapter begins with an overview of the definition and characteristics of SoTL, both generally and as applied in economics. Phases of TIP are then described and TIP alumni activities consistent with SoTL are provided as evidence of the impact of TIP. I conclude with a discussion of the long-run impact of this short-run program.

I. SoTL HISTORY AND PERSPECTIVES

SoTL developed out of the 1980s during which debates over teaching and research, their value and role in the institution, were in high gear. In 1990, Ernest Boyer introduced a broader definition of scholarship, one that moved beyond traditional scholarship of discovery by defining scholarships of integration, application, and teaching, launching a national debate regarding how the concept of scholarship was interpreted. In his brief discussion of what the Scholarship of Teaching entailed, he noted that "The work of the professor becomes consequential only as it is understood by others" (Boyer 1990, 23), and described teaching as a scholarly activity that begins with teachers who are "well informed, and steeped in the knowledge of their fields" and that teaching as an activity "builds bridges between the teacher's understanding and the student's learning. Pedagogical procedures must be carefully planned, continuously examined, and relate directly to the subject taught," alluding to both research processes and the discipline-specific nature which underlie the scholarship of teaching (pp. 23–24). He further argued that "faculty, as scholars, are also learners" (p. 24), and therefore contribute to a growing knowledge base. Yet Boyer's description was sufficiently general that it has led to many interpretations and modifications which are only now converging on two key characteristics:

- SoTL is not synonymous with excellent teaching
- SoTL necessitates public vetting of teaching and learning queries

Excellent teaching is a demonstration of understanding pedagogic techniques and implementing them in an effective manner, but it is not SoTL.

"It requires a kind of 'going meta,' in which faculty frame and systematically investigate questions related to student learning – the conditions under which it occurs, what it looks like, how to deepen it, and so forth – and do so with an eye not only to improving their own classroom but to advancing practice beyond it" (Hutchings and Shulman 1999, 15). Similarly, Darling (2003) argues that SoTL entails "work that encourages an empirical examination of teaching in relation to student learning. It is distinct from scholarly teaching in that it goes beyond teaching well, even superbly, to participating in a focused inquiry process and reflective practice about one's own teaching."

Advancing the practice of education implies that SoTL participants join in the community of scholars, contributing to conversations dedicated to understanding how students learn. In short, it is about making the often private teaching and learning queries associated with our own classes available to public scrutiny. Trigwell et al. (2000) present a model which describes the Scholarship of Teaching and Learning as having "four dimensions relating to the areas of (a) being informed about teaching and learning generally and in the teacher's own discipline; (b) reflection on that information, the teacher's particular context and the relations between the two; (c) the focus of the teaching approach adopted; and (d) communication of the relevant aspects of the other three dimensions to members of the community of scholars. All four dimensions are considered to be a necessary part of the scholarship of teaching" (p. 167). Similar arguments regarding the public sharing of ideas about teaching and learning have been adopted by Martin et al. (1999) and Witman and Richlin (2007), among others.

Boyer's original statements about the Scholarship of Teaching have led some to relegate SoTL output similarly to traditional scholarship, valuing only the published research article since it more clearly upholds the standards of public scrutiny. Measuring SoTL on the basis of journal publications alone leads to a dramatic understatement of the extent to which such activities take place. SoTL activities are characterized by active participation in and contribution to the conversation among like scholars, suggesting that participation in the teaching commons is a component of SoTL. The teaching commons is "a conceptual space in which communities of educators committed to inquiry and innovation come together to exchange ideas about teaching and learning and use them to meet the challenges of educating students" (Huber and Hutchings 2007). As such, the commons acts as a public clearinghouse of examples. Because the commons is intended to be an exchange of ideas, it "can include (at one end) studies with elaborate research designs and formal execution that go beyond a single classroom, program, or discipline, as well as (at the other end) quite modest efforts to document and reflect on one's teaching and share what one has learned" (Huber and Hutchings 2005, 4).

II. SOTL IN ECONOMICS

National surveys conducted over the past decade verify that economists continue to rely heavily on passive lecture-style teaching pedagogy, an instructional format that, according to Becker and Watts (1998b), has been "established by convenience, custom, and inertia rather than efficiency or, especially, by what represents effective teaching practices in today's undergraduate curriculum"[4] (p. 4). Other disciplines, particularly the science, technology, engineering and mathematics (STEM) disciplines such as physics, are moving more quickly than economics to replace lecture-based instruction with more active student-centered teaching methods. A recent survey by the *Chronicle of Higher Education* (2009), covering 22,562 faculty at 372 four-year colleges and universities nationwide, revealed that there has been an increase in the use of active learning pedagogies. For example, the percentage of faculty who stated they used cooperative learning in all or most of their classes increased from 48 percent in 2005 to 59 percent in 2008. In comparison, Watts and Becker (2008) find that the median proportion of class time dedicated to cooperative learning in economics is reported at only 6 percent. Although these two survey results are not directly comparable, they do suggest that economics lags behind other disciplines in the use of student-centered active learning pedagogies.

Some may argue that dominance of the lecture mode in economics results from a lack of discipline-specific research identifying positive impacts of alternative pedagogic approaches. This, again, stands in stark contrast to other disciplines which have developed a rich, cumulative knowledge base of effective teaching strategies and curricular resources grounded in the learning sciences[5] and empirically tested in the classroom. While much is to be learned from advances in these other disciplines, furthering the development of an understanding of how pedagogic practices enhance learning *of economics* necessitates advances in the scholarship of teaching and learning *in economics*: "there are many issues that cut across disciplines. But while historians, psychologists, and mathematicians may all explore how best to foster 'deep understanding' in their college classrooms, teaching and learning are, in the end, not the same across fields – nor, for that matter, are inquiry and exploration into these processes" (Huber and Morreale 2002, 2). Developing such discipline-specific evidence requires that more faculty adopt student-centered active learning pedagogies, and that they participate in the scholarship of teaching and learning (SoTL) to provide evidence of their effectiveness.

To determine the extent of support for SoTL in economics, one might consider two indicators: evidence of institutionalized scaffolding and explicit disciplinary discussions of SoTL. In the former case, greater opportunities for participating in the teaching commons through well-defined venues and processes should promote greater participation in SoTL. Broad discussions, including those that provide overviews of, set agendas, and define methods for SoTL in economics offer guidance for less-seasoned researchers to contribute.

Scaffolding can be signaled by the extent to which SoTL has "been integrated into and used by the various academic disciplines" and the existence of venues "available to professors within each of the disciplines to present and publish" SoTL research (Witman and Richlin 2007, 1). Witman and Richlin (2007) compare a wide range of disciplines in their quest to evaluate disciplinary support for SoTL, gathering evidence on activities such as dedicated conferences, sessions at meetings, and publication outlets associated with leading disciplinary organizations. For example, they analyzed the activities of the AEA, CEE, and *JEE* in comparison with other social sciences disciplines (sociology, political science, and psychology) and disciplines within humanities, natural sciences, and the professions. Their conclusions suggest that "as a group, the Natural Sciences and Professions seem to have most firmly adopted the SoTL, while the Social Sciences and the Humanities are somewhat less attached" (p. 14). More specifically, the lack of a nationally organized SoTL conference, the scarcity of SoTL sessions at the national meetings, and the relegation of SoTL research to a single association sponsored outlet (*JEE*) lead them to suggest that "there seems to be less of an emphasis on the SoTL in Economics than in some of the other disciplines" (p. 11).

Despite this apparent lack of structural support for SoTL in economics, recent projects have begun to build such structures as they develop teaching activities grounded in the learning sciences, and provide a venue for sharing new or revised practices. For example, the *Starting Point: Teaching and Learning Economics* site[6] introduces economists to teaching innovations both within and beyond the discipline, provides instructors with tools to begin integrating and assessing these innovations in their own classrooms, and encourages the sharing of teaching innovations. As an example of the teaching commons, the *Starting Point* site "provides a collection of documented examples, organized through an intentional framework... [including] comprehensive descriptions of learning objectives, instructional content, required pre-requisite knowledge, and assessment guidance, in addition to a description of the activity" (Maier, McGoldrick, and Simkins 2010, 3). Instructors come to the site not only to learn from others' examples, but also to contribute to the conversation through contributions of their own examples to the growing library.

Explicit discussions of SoTL in economics also are less common than in other disciplines. While many economic education studies are designed to shed light on specific teaching methods and student learning, very little has been written specifically addressing how economists participate in and view SoTL. Building off economists' comparative advantage in empirical research, it should come as no surprise that the conceptualization of SoTL in economics is one that leads to the development of new knowledge, is grounded in quantitative research processes, and is vetted publicly. Three key areas provide the basis for discussions of SoTL in the economics literature: background, agenda, and methods.

SoTL is grounded in an understanding of teaching and learning within one's discipline. This background knowledge encompasses goals of the discipline, what is taught and how it should be taught and the extent to which this differs across venues, and what we know about associated learning. In the past 20 years, a number of key economics publications have surfaced to provide a starting point for this understanding. Probably the clearest statement of the goals of the economics major can be found in Siegfried et al. (1991), who reviewed both the purpose and structure of the undergraduate major, and described what was meant by "thinking like an economist." Arguments of what this entails in the context of a liberal education are discussed in Colander and McGoldrick (2009). Becker (2000) conceptualizes economic education by providing an overview of "what we teach, how we teach, and the assessment of educational outcomes at the baccalaureate level" (p. 109). Johnston, McDonald, and Williams (2001) provide an introduction to seven articles originally presented at the 2000 SoTL in Economics conference held in Australia, the objective of which "was to bring attention to research being conducted in economic education at the tertiary level and to engage academic economists in discussion about the scholarship of teaching economics" (pp. 195–96). These articles cover the very basics of SoTL, complementing the work of Becker (2000), including answers to such questions as "Who should determine the curriculum?," "What should be taught?," and, "How should it be taught?" (p. 196). It is important to note that not all SoTL activities are relegated to understanding economic education at the college level. Walstad (2001) provides a broad overview of economic education in U.S. high schools including enrollments, content, testing methods and achievement, and teacher preparation, and concludes by setting an agenda for future research, identifying "issues where research findings might improve economic education" (p. 208).

While agendas for economic education research are often hidden in the conclusions of existing work, an important exception to this is Becker et al. (1991) which explicitly focuses on and outlines such an agenda for research at the college level. They argue that research in economic education should focus on three areas: defining, measuring, and evaluating learning outputs;

analysis at the level of the major to evaluate its structure; and replication of historical results to ensure applicability in current times.

Setting research agendas, at either the high school or college level, are moot unless accompanied by a supporting structure of methods for conducting such research. Economic education research is not unlike other research in economics in that its goal is to have an impact on practices by conducting analysis using the tools and methods associated with the discipline. As such, it should not be surprising that arguments abound for research to "be empirical and contextualized, i.e., built on sound knowledge of student learning products derived from experiential data in particular contexts" (Tang 2003, 157). In fact, Becker (2004) argues that what is missing from educational research, across all disciplines, is a quantitatively rigorous approach. He offers "specific criteria[7] for both conducting and exploring the strength of discipline-specific quantitative research into the teaching and learning process" (pp. 1–2). Currently, there is a project underway designed to provide even more quantitative guidance for employing appropriate research methods in economic education. Commissioned by the Council for Economic Education and the American Economic Association Committee on Economic Education, Becker (2009) has developed "four modules that will enable researchers to employ [techniques to deal with missing observations, missing variables, errors in variables, simultaneous relationships and pooled cross-section and time-series data] in their empirical studies of educational practices, with special attention given to the teaching and learning of economics" (p. 2).

Given that opportunities to participate in SoTL-related activities are relatively sparse in economics, although resources for the development of SoTL appear to be on the rise, how did TIP contribute to the advancement of SoTL? Historically, opportunities to participate in SoTL in economics came in the form of teaching workshops, national and regional meeting sessions and journal publications. These activities are generally passive, as participants act as receptors of knowledge rather than engage in the process of creating it. TIP differed from previous programs because it provided scaffolding which engaged faculty in the SoTL process, first providing participants with opportunities and encouragement to take part in the teaching commons, then nurturing them in the construction of their own innovations, and finally encouraging participants to expand the knowledge base by evaluating and sharing their work.

III. SOTL AND THE TEACHING INNOVATIONS PROGRAM

SoTL requires a careful consideration of the purpose, process, and outcomes of teaching activities. Instructors who are new participants in SoTL may not be as well versed in grounding teaching activities in learning and content objectives. They may not be aware of key structural pedagogic components which, for example, distinguish cooperative learning from group work. Methods of informal and formal assessment of learning that occur within the classroom need to accompany the implementation of teaching innovations to determine their success or areas for improvement in the next iteration.

SoTL moves private, classroom-confined activities into the public sphere. Yet much work needs to be done on the part of the instructor before their scholarship is ready for public review and the more traditionally recognized form of SoTL, the journal publication. Since few graduate programs offer a field in economic education, it is unlikely that most emerging SoTL participants are versed in the literature and methods for conducting this work. Bridging the gap between classroom practices and journal publications necessitates a wide range of venues for instructors to present their work, in all the stages of sophistication, ranging from the development of the exercise itself to the formal methodological evaluation of associated learning gains. It is only when such evidence of learning is rigorously documented that the knowledge base expands. TIP was structured in three phases, each providing support for key components in the development of SoTL: grounding understanding of pedagogic practice in existing knowledge base, providing support for purposeful development of and reflection on specific pedagogic practices, and participating in (both formal and informal components of) the teaching commons.

Preparation for SoTL (workshops and web-based instruction)

Phase 1 was participation in a three-day workshop. At the workshop, participants were introduced to interactive teaching strategies, shared examples of their own previously developed exercises, and began the planning process for developing an exercise based on the interactive strategies. Workshops were important for SoTL activities because they set the stage for practicing careful reflection and Findlow (2008) identifies, among others, the "time to network informally" as an innovation-enabling factor (p. 317). Each pedagogic practice was introduced using both objectives and key structural components, and was presented in the context of the existing knowledge base and expected learning outcomes. Workshops also dedicated an entire session to formative and summative assessment. Finally, all participants had two opportunities to exchange ideas about teaching and learning in economics. Participants worked in groups to identify and demonstrate the single most important thing an instructor can do that leads to increased learning (engagement, active, real world, etc.) and each participant was provided an opportunity to share his or her own favorite active learning activity with the larger group. TIP staff facilitated this sharing process, requesting that participants provide information about their own teaching context, a description of the activity they implemented, and a summary that linked the activity to enhanced learning. In short, Phase 1 of TIP provided the opportunity for all 335 participants, representing a wide range of U.S. colleges and universities, to be reflective about the methods and purpose of their own teaching and to share that with the larger community.

Phase 2 entailed participation in web-based instruction that occurred in the academic year following the workshop. Phase 2 steps supported SoTL activities by engaging and mentoring participants in the development of teaching innovations. "Research also shows that acquiring pedagogic content knowledge and developing methods different from what teachers themselves experienced as students requires learning opportunities for teachers that are more powerful than simply reading and talking about new pedagogical ideas (Ball and Cohen 1996)" (Major and Palmer 2006, 621). Like researchers conducting traditional discovery scholarship, teachers need opportunities to "learn through studying, by doing and reflecting, by collaborating with other teachers, by looking closely at students and their work, and by sharing what they see" (ibid.).

Participants in TIP completed modules designed to help them introduce interactive teaching strategies in a course they were teaching. This process began when the participant reviewed instructional materials providing a more in-depth narrative of the knowledge base underlying the pedagogic practice and key structural components of the interactive strategy. For example, the cooperative learning module introduced participants to the importance of grounding their exercise in both learning and content objectives, described the PIES structure which distinguishes cooperative learning from group work,[8] introduced objective-based categories of cooperative learning exercises and their associated formats, and addressed implementation issues of particular relevance to economists such as free riders and content coverage.

Based on their (new or enhanced) understanding of the pedagogic strategy, participants then reflected on their own teaching contexts as they developed an implementation plan using a format which mirrored key components of the interactive strategy. For example, participants developing a cooperative learning plan were required to describe how each of the PIES key structures was embedded in their exercise. Each plan for innovation also included an assessment of learning component, encouraging participants to be purposeful in their evaluation of the impact of the pedagogic practice with respect to stated learning and content objectives. Completed plans were then reviewed by module coordinators, individuals with extensive experience in implementing that particular pedagogic practice. A dialogue between the module coordinator and the participant ensured that revisions to the plan were consistent with achieving the objectives of the instructor and conformed to key structures of the pedagogic strategy.

During this interactive phase, the identification of goals and development of assessment procedures (key and difficult components of SoTL) were cited as an important focus of discussion. Participants were nurtured in the development of learning and content objectives in the cooperative learning module, for example, through a dedicated activity which generated a statement of objectives subsequently included in the implementation plan. When revisions of the plan were developed during the interaction phase with the module instructor, an enhanced understanding of these objectives was generated. Finally, after implementation, participants were asked to reflect on what they believed went particularly well in preparing and implementing the exercise and what they would do differently the next time they conducted a similar exercise. The emphasis on relevant knowledge base, objectives and reflective practice encouraged participants to think carefully about measurements of learning, and receive important formative feedback leading many participants to continue their contribution to SoTL via opportunities supported by Phase 3 of TIP.

Formal Participation in SoTL

Phase 3 was entirely dedicated to more formal scholarship activities, engaging TIP participants in a key characteristic of SoTL: public vetting of teaching and learning queries. The importance of this for expanding the knowledge base and changing teaching practices cannot be understated. Garet et al. (2001) identify a key structural feature of professional development experiences as "the extent to which the activity offers opportunities for active learning, such as opportunities for teachers to become actively engaged in the meaningful analysis of teaching and learning" (p. 920) including "the opportunity to give presentations, lead discussions, and produce written work" (p. 926). Participation in opportunities of this nature was shown to significantly enhance the self-reported knowledge and skills which in turn have a "substantial positive influence on change in teaching practice" (p. 934). The goal of Phase 3 of TIP was both to provide opportunities dedicated to TIP alumni and encourage their participation.

Three types of opportunities were developed to encourage TIP participants to engage in meaningful analysis of teaching and learning, each having a different level of sophistication for contributing to the existing knowledge base. It was at these venues that participants were able to share their ideas and receive feedback on their work from a larger audience.

TIP staff organized two types of sessions at national and regional association meetings. The first was a pedagogical innovation session consisting of a panel of TIP participants who described their unique implementations of a specific pedagogical technique. Presentations of this nature were not expected to be accompanied by empirical tests of the impact of this innovation. To accompany their presentation, participants were asked to prepare a brief paper (3–4 pages in length) explaining the technique or idea they had implemented, the context of the innovation (school, class level, class size, etc.), and advice and instructions for others who might want to try what they had done.

The second type of session included traditional pedagogical research papers in which learning associated with the pedagogical technique was empirically documented. Papers in this category were expected to include a review of related literature, the context of the innovation (school, class level, class size, etc.), details of the innovation, assessment of enhanced learning, and thoughts on enhancements of the innovation or measurement of learning.

The final SoTL opportunity developed for TIP alumni came in the form of a conference and this book volume. The goal of this activity was to develop a lasting product which, among other things, highlighted the work of a select group of participants. To support the development of the volume, a final conference was held in 2010 for contributors to present their work and receive additional feedback before finalizing their contributions. Each of the seven TIP module coordinators facilitated the development of a chapter, inviting TIP alumni to contribute detailed applications to complement their own overview of the associated pedagogic technique. For example, the choice of potential co-authors for the cooperative learning chapter was difficult as there were many TIP participants who successfully completed the module. In this case the decision was based on the extent to which the developed exercises were unique, how each might complement one another, and each participant's demonstrated enthusiasm for the Scholarship of Teaching and Learning (signaled by participation in one national or regional conference sessions described above).

Some SoTL Outcomes

Outcomes associated with opportunities coordinated by TIP staff are presented in this section to provide the reader with an overview of the extent to which TIP contributed to SoTL. It is important to note, however, that there are a number of reasons why such descriptions are likely to underestimate the impact of this program. Informal SoTL activities such as discussions with colleagues or changes to teaching practices are not easily observed or quantified. This is complicated by the fact that activities that constitute the scholarship of teaching (a là Boyer) also are not typically understood as scholarship. Thus, even when queried, faculty are likely to underestimate their participation. A key difference between the scholarship of discovery and SoTL activities is that advances in our understanding of teaching and learning are more likely to be grounded in private motivations (improving our students' learning) and may never be presented to larger audiences. Finally, although TIP staff facilitated SoTL opportunities for program participants, an informal survey revealed that some alumni took the initiative to engage in SoTL activities independent of the program. How extensive these spillover effects are is not known. Despite these tendencies to underreport, the description that follows suggests a substantial participation in SoTL. Outcomes are presented for each of the TIP-organized, formal output venues described above as well as for participant-initiated activities and journal publications. (Appendix 3A provides a summary of all identified SoTL activities.)

Twenty-seven percent of TIP alumni (91 out of 335) participated in TIP-organized sessions at regional or national meetings. Thirty percent of these (27 out of 91) served on panels in the pedagogic innovation sessions held at the Southern Economic Association meetings in 2009 and 2010. Another thirty-six percent of TIP alumni (33 out of 91) presented papers in traditional research sessions, 14 at the national ASSA meetings with the remainder at the Southern Economic Association (8) and Western Economic Association (11) meetings between 2006 and 2011. Although experiments and cooperative learning were the most popular innovations presented in these venues (14 and 13 times respectively), all pedagogic practices were represented by at least one presentation. Thirty-four percent (31 out of 91) served as discussants in these sessions.

As noted above, each module coordinator chose three TIP alumni to co-author one of the pedagogic technique chapters in this volume, each describing the innovative practice they developed in conjunction with this program. In support of this volume, TIP staff coordinated a full day conference to provide participants with the opportunity to share their innovations and receive feedback from fellow program alumni. The conference program was designed to showcase the innovations developed by program participants and 21 TIP alumni presented their innovations. Discussion time was built into each pedagogic topic session to allow for the exchange of new ideas about teaching and learning, in support of the teaching commons.

Although this volume supports the goal of making innovative materials more widely available, it was not the sole publication outlet for TIP researchers. TIP alumni also have published four papers and an additional two are forthcoming (see Appendix 3A for details). While some may argue that a less than 2 percent (6 out of 335) return on one's investment is very small, one must take into consideration that conducting research is a lengthy process. This is especially true of SoTL since most faculty are not trained in the field of economic education and documenting learning outcomes requires that researchers develop a viable innovation, implement the innovation, gather learning outcomes data, and then author a paper. Further delays occur in the review process, from receiving the first round of reviews to revising the paper and waiting for a final decision. This is followed by further delays in the time to print. Given that TIP held its first workshop in 2005, six accepted publications is arguably a substantial and lasting impact over a five-year time period.

Finally, two other outcomes provide evidence of the impact of TIP on SoTL in economics. TIP alumni also took the initiative to participate in scholarship activities not organized by program staff. These include six poster presentations at the 2010 ASSA meetings, thirteen presentations in non-TIP organized sessions or at conferences other than regional and national meetings, four presentations at teaching conferences, and one plenary presentation. Additional positive impacts occurred as participants were motivated to participate in SoTL activities beyond the module content supported by TIP. For example, when asked about the extent to which they engaged in presentations or article development, one TIP participant noted that one of her publications was "not based on the teaching modules I worked [on] with TIP, but I know that I would have never taken the initiative of writing [it] if I had not been part of TIP." Another participant noted similar positive externalities of the TIP program: "While they weren't directly TIP-driven, I've published two papers and given two poster sessions in the past few years that drew on inspiration from TIP."

IV. CONCLUSIONS

The goals of the Teaching Innovations Program were to enhance student learning by engaging instructors in the use of innovative pedagogic practices, and providing support for them to share experiences and participate in the scholarship of teaching and learning. The only way to escape the status quo of lecturing and expand usage of active learning pedagogic practices without reinventing the wheel each time, is to treat teaching like a true scholarly activity. Teachers "must start to talk about teaching… become familiar with the scholarly literature on teaching… learn what others have discovered about teaching in the discipline… and share their own teaching experiences and insights by publishing in the open literature" (Michael 2007, 46).

TIP designed specific phases to aid instructors in becoming consumers and producers of pedagogic innovations. Unlike previous programs, this process was not “viewed as separate bits of inquiry, valuable to specific courses and their instructors only” (Schroeder 2007, 1). The recognition that, “[m]uch SoTL work occurs in isolation, undertaken by one or a small number of faculty members within a department, often working alone” (McKinney 2004, 7) served as motivation to develop scaffolding for instructors to participate in the teaching commons. Throughout all phases of TIP, participants learned about the existing knowledge base, reflected on their own practices and contexts, developed innovations which included an assessment of learning, and shared their work with the broader community of scholars. TIP provided a structure and support for SoTL in economics, developing communities of scholars, combating the isolationism and sharing work to advance understanding of learning in economics. While it is too early to measure the full impact of TIP on advances in economic education, as research takes time to develop and mature into a final public product, the supporting structures provided by TIP substantially increased the number of individuals actively participating in the Scholarship of Teaching and Learning.

NOTES

1. These include workshops held at institutions including Bowling Green University, Florida State University, Robert Morris College, University of Kentucky, University of North Carolina at Wilmington, and others sponsored by the Gulf Coast Economics Association.
2. See, for example: http://economicsforteachers.blogspot.com/.
3. http://org.elon.edu/econ/tch-econ/.
4. See also Becker and Watts (1996; 1997; 1998a; 2001; 2007), Siegfried et al. (1996), and Benzing and Christ (1997).
5. Learning science research includes identifying and challenging student misconceptions, developing novice learners into expert learners, promoting the transfer of learning to new situations, and metacognition.
6. http://serc.carleton.edu/econ/index.html
7. 1) Statement of topic, with clear hypotheses; 2) Literature review, which establishes the need for and context of the study; 3) Attention to unit of analysis with clear definition of variables and valid measurement; 4) Third-party supplied versus self-reported data; 5) Outcomes and behavioral change measures; 6) Multivariate analyses; 7) Truly independent explanatory variables; 8) Attention to non-randomness, including sample selection issues and missing data problems; 9) Appropriate statistical methods of estimation, testing, and interpretation; 10) Robustness of results; 11) Nature and strength of claims and conclusions.
8. Positive interdependence, Individual accountability, Equal participation, and Simultaneous interaction (Kagan 1992).

REFERENCES

Ball, D.L., and D.K. Cohen (1996), "Reform by the book: What is – or might be – the role of curriculum materials in teacher learning and instructional reform?," *Educational Researcher*, **25** (9), 6–8.

Becker, W.E. (2000), "Teaching economics in the 21st century," *Journal of Economic Perspectives*, **18** (1), 109–19.

Becker, W.E. (2004), "A critique of the quantitative research on teaching: which methods work," in W.E. Becker and M.L. Andrews (eds), *The Scholarship of Teaching and Learning in Higher Education: Contributions of Research Universities*, Bloomington, IN: Indiana University Press, 265–310.

Becker, W.E. (2009), *Introduction to an Online Handbook for the Use of Up-To-Date Econometrics in Economic Education Research*. Available at: http://www.vanderbilt.edu/AEA/AEACEE/Econometrics_Handbook/index.htm

Becker, W.E., R. Highsmith, P. Kennedy, and W. Walstad (1991), "An agenda for research on economic education in colleges and universities," *Journal of Economic Education*, **22** (3), 241–50.

Becker, W.E., and M. Watts (1996), "Chalk and talk: A national survey on teaching undergraduate economics," *American Economic Review*, **86** (May), 448–53.

Becker, W.E., and M. Watts (1997), "Teaching economics to undergraduates," *Journal of Economic Literature*, **35** (September), 1347–73.

Becker, W.E., and M. Watts (eds) (1998a), *Teaching Economics to Undergraduates: Alternatives to Chalk and Talk*, Cheltenham, UK and Lyme, USA: Edward Elgar.

Becker, W.E., and M. Watts (1998b), "Teaching economics: What was, is, and could be," in W.E. Becker and M. Watts (eds), *Teaching Economics to Undergraduates: Alternatives to Chalk and Talk*, Cheltenham, UK and Lyme, USA: Edward Elgar, 1–10.

Becker, W.E., and M. Watts (2001), "Teaching economics at the start of the 21st century: Still chalk and talk," *American Economic Review*, **91** (May), 446–52.

Becker, W.E., and M. Watts (2007), *A Little More Than Chalk and Talk: Results from a Third National Survey of Teaching Methods in Undergraduate Economics Courses*. Available at: http://mypage.iu.edu/~beckerw/working_ papers.htm.

Benzing, C., and P. Christ (1997), "A survey of teaching methods among economics faculty," *Journal of Economic Education*, **28** (Spring), 182–88.

Boyer, E. (1990), *Scholarship Reconsidered: Priorities of the Professoriate*, The Carnegie Foundation for the Advancement of Teaching, San Francisco, CA: Jossey-Bass.

Chronicle of Higher Education (2009), "Data points: More faculty members adopt 'student centered' teaching," October 18. Available at: http://chronicle.com/article/Chart-More-Faculty-Members/48848/.

Colander, D., and K. McGoldrick (2009), *Educating Economists: The Teagle Discussion on Reevaluating the Undergraduate Economics Major*. Cheltenham, UK and Northampton, MA, USA: Edward Elgar.

Darling, A.L. (2003), "Scholarship of teaching and learning in communication: New connections, new directions, new possibilities," *Communication Education*, **52** (1), 47–49.

Findlow, S. (2008), "Accountability and innovation in higher education: A disabling tension?," *Studies in Higher Education*, **33** (3), 313–29.

Garet, M.S., A.C. Porter, L. Desimone, B. Birman, and K.S. Yoon (2001), "What makes professional development effective? Results from a national sample of teachers," *American Educational Research Journal*, **38** (4), 915–45.

Huber, M.T., and P. Hutchings (2005), *The Advancement of Learning: Building the Teaching Commons*, Stanford, CT: Jossey-Bass.

Huber, M.T., and P. Hutchings (2007), *The Advancement of Learning: Building the Teaching Commons*, The Carnegie Foundation for the Advancement of Teaching, San Francisco, CA: Jossey-Bass. Available at: http://www.carnegiefoundation.org/perspectives/sub.asp?key=245&subkey=800 (accessed May 1, 2007).

Huber, M.T., and S.P. Morreale (eds) (2002), *Disciplinary Styles in the Scholarship of Teaching and Learning: Exploring Common Ground*, Washington, DC: American Association for Higher Education and the Carnegie Foundation for the Advancement of Teaching.

Hutchings, P., and L.S. Shulman (1999), "The scholarship of teaching: New elaborations, new developments," *Change*, **31** (5), 10–15. http://www.carnegiefoundation.org/publications/sub.asp?key=452&subkey=613 (accessed October 19, 2009).

Johnston, C., I. McDonald, and R. Williams (2001), "The scholarship of teaching economics," *Journal of Economic Education*, **32** (3), 195–201.

Kagan, S. (1992), *Cooperative Learning*, San Juan Capistrano, CA: Resources for Teachers, Inc.

Major, C., and B. Palmer (2006), "Reshaping teaching and learning: The transformation of faculty pedagogic content knowledge," *Higher Education*, **51**, 619–47.

Maier, M., K. McGoldrick, and S. Simkins (2010), *Starting Point: Pedagogic Resources for Teaching and Learning Economics*, Paper presented at the ASSA meetings, January, Atlanta, GA.

Martin, E., J. Benjamin, M. Prosser, and K. Trigwell (1999), "Scholarship of teaching: A study of the approaches of academic staff," in C. Rust (ed.), *Improving Student Learning: Improving Student Learning Outcomes*, Oxford, UK: Oxford Centre for Staff Learning and Development, Oxford Brookes University, 326–31.

McKinney, K. (2004), "The scholarship of teaching and learning: Past lessons, current challenges, and future visions," *To Improve the Academy*, **22**, 3–19.

Michael, J. (2007), "Faculty perceptions about barriers to active learning," *College Teaching*, **55** (2), 42–47.

Schroeder, C.M. (2007), "Countering SoTL marginalization: A model for integrating SoTL with institutional initiatives," *International Journal for the Scholarship of Teaching and Learning*, **1** (1), 1–9.

Siegfried, J.J., R.L. Bartlett, W.L. Hansen, A.C. Kelley, D.N. McCloskey, and T.H. Tietenberg (1991), "The status and prospects of the economics major," *Journal of Economic Education*, **22** (3), 197–224.

Siegfried, J.J., P. Saunders, E. Stinar, and H. Zhang (1996), "How is introductory economics taught in America?," *Economic Inquiry*, **34** (January), 182–92.

Tang, T. (2003), "Understanding students' misunderstanding in economics," *Economic Analysis and Policy*, **33** (1), 157–71.

Trigwell, K., E. Martin, J. Benjamin, and M. Prosser (2000), "Scholarship of teaching: A model," *Higher Education Research and Development*, **19** (2), 155–68.

Walstad, W.B. (2001), "Economic education in U.S. high schools," *Journal of Economic Perspectives*, **15** (3), 195–210.

Watts, M., and W.E. Becker (2008), "A little more than chalk and talk: Results from a third national survey of teaching methods in undergraduate economics courses," *Journal of Economic Education*, **39** (3), 273–86.

Witman, P.D., and L. Richlin (2007), "The status of the scholarship of teaching and learning in the disciplines," *International Journal for the Scholarship of Teaching and Learning*, **1** (1). Available at: http://www.georgiasouthern.edu/ijsotl/v1n1/essays/witman/IJ_witman.pdf.

APPENDIX 3A
Phase 3 SoTL Outcomes

Conference Participation

	Conference	Year	Paper Authors	Poster or Panel Presen-tation	Discussants
TIP-Organized Sessions	ASSA	2011	3		4
		2010			4
		2009	4		4
		2008	4		4
		2007	3		3
	SEA	2010	4	11	5
		2009		16	
		2006	4		3
	WEA	2010	3		4
		2007	8		4
	TIP	2010	21		
Participant Initiated Presentation	ASSA	2010		6	
	Other	Various	13		
	Teaching Workshop	Various	4		
	Invited	2008	1		
TOTALS			72	33	31

Publications

Davis, L.S. (forthcoming), "Teaching the economics of sin," *Teaching Ethics*, Special Issue on Ethics Across the Curriculum.

Madden, K. (forthcoming), "Engaged learning with the inquiry based question cluster discussion technique: Student outcomes in a history of economic thought course," *Southern Economic Journal*.

Mitchell, D., R. Rebelein, P. Schneider, N. Simpson, and E. Fisher (2009), "A classroom experiment on exchange rate determination with purchasing power parity," *Journal of Economic Education*, **40** (2), 150–65.

Rousu, M. (2008), "A football play-calling experiment to illustrate the mixed strategy Nash equilibrium," *Journal of the Academy of Business Education*, **9**, 79–89.

Vazquez-Cognet, J.J. (2008), "The production of mathematical problems: A diminishing marginal returns experiment," *International Review of Economic Education*, **7** (1), 103–16.

O'Brien, M., and D. Doorn (2007), "Assessing the gains from concept mapping in introductory statistics," *International Journal for the Scholarship of Teaching and Learning*, **1** (2), 1–19.

Grove, W.A., and T. Wasserman (2006), "Incentives and student learning: A natural experiment with problem sets," *American Economic Review*, **96** (2), 447–51.

CHAPTER 4

Making Cooperative Learning Effective for Economics

KimMarie McGoldrick
Robert Rebelein
Jennifer K. Rhoads
Sue Stockly

Cooperative learning is one of the most versatile and researched interactive learning techniques. Well-constructed cooperative learning exercises have been demonstrated to be more effective than individual learning and, by appealing to a broader set of students, have the potential to increase diversity within the economics major. Students participating in cooperative learning exercises earn higher grades and better scores on tests for both volume and accuracy of material, long-term retention, and problem-solving and higher reasoning abilities (Johnson, Johnson, and Smith 1998).[1] In economics, Yamarik (2007) found that students scored four to six points higher on exams compared to students in a traditional, lecture format class after controlling for classroom, demographic and academic factors. Yamarik argues that this gain in scores can be linked to greater instructor–student interaction, greater likelihood of group studying, and enhanced interest in economics.

Despite these potential gains, cooperative learning still is not widely practiced in economics. Watts and Becker (2008) report that the median proportion of class time dedicated to cooperative learning is only 6 percent. This chapter's objective is to promote increased use of cooperative learning in economics by reducing implementation costs through describing key structures for success and methods for choosing among the wide variety of exercise formats. Three detailed examples then follow, showcasing various choices made with respect to objectives, formats and logistical considerations within the cooperative learning structure, providing a glimpse into the versatility of cooperative learning.

I. STRUCTURES

Cooperative learning exercises entail more than simply placing students into groups and having them work together on a problem. Poorly structured group exercises are likely to promote free-rider behavior, allow for participation of underprepared students and result in disgruntled students. Although cooperative learning experts differ in their specific descriptions of effective structures, a number of key elements consistently surface.

- *Positive interdependence* is achieved when individual and group successes are positively correlated (Kagan 1992, 4). Individuals are motivated to contribute to the group because their success is enhanced when the group achieves its goals. Ways to promote positive interdependence include: (1) having a single product produced by the group; (2) ensuring that each member of the group can explain the group's product; (3) having group members share resources to complete the task; and (4) assigning members distinct roles that are key to group functioning. (Smith and Waller 1997, 202)
- *Individual (and group) accountability* implies that both individual contributions and overall success of the group are evaluated. Typically, group members are assessed individually; however, the degree to which the group has achieved its goal has been shown to positively impact individual achievement (Webb 1983; 1991).
- *Equal participation* is achieved when each group member is encouraged to contribute during a cooperative learning exercise (Smith 1996, 74–76).
- *Simultaneous interaction* occurs when more than one participant is active at a time, as students within different groups contribute during the exercise, leading to more time per student for active participation.

Choosing a Cooperative Learning Format

Cooperative learning is "one of the most thoroughly researched of all instructional methods" (Slavin 1990, 52) in part because of the many forms it can take, ranging from quick and informal formats to formats encompassing entire class periods (or more) with very formal components. Determining which format is most appropriate for a given set of circumstances requires matching objectives with appropriate cooperative learning exercise formats. Thus, a key step in the cooperative learning exercise development process calls for instructors to first identify their learning (skills) and content objectives for the course and then choose specific cooperative learning formats that will best achieve the specified objectives.[2]

Cooperative learning activities can be loosely categorized by content to be mastered or by the learning objective that each enhances. While such a method of classification is by no means strict (as some cooperative learning exercises are flexible enough to enhance a wide range of skills), it provides a starting point for developing cooperative learning exercises grounded in identified objectives. For example, Barkley, Cross, and Major (2005) organize cooperative learning exercises by learning objectives, identifying categories of discussion, graphic organizers, writing, reciprocal teaching, and problem solving. A brief description of each category accompanied by a specific cooperative learning format and example that supports the learning objectives in that category follows. Three of the described formats (round table for writing, learning cell for reciprocal teaching, and send-a-problem for problem solving) are then exemplified in greater detail.

One of the most commonly used and simple of all the cooperative learning formats falls within the discussion category. The think–pair–share format enhances discussion-related skills such as formulating ideas, practicing communication and developing listening skills. The think–pair–share exercise begins with students thinking independently about a problem or question. Each student then pairs up with another student and, taking turns, shares their thoughts. Students experience a low-threat environment in which to share their initial solutions and have the opportunity to reevaluate after hearing their partner's reflections before participating in the larger class discussion. Consider the following as a specific example of a think–pair–share exercise designed for the principles level course:

> "After a lecture on sunk costs, the instructor raises the question: *You bought a ticket for a movie, and now discover that you lost it. Should you buy a second ticket, or should you go home?* Students first consider their answer individually, and everyone votes by showing thumbs up (buy the ticket) or thumbs down (go home). After viewing the distribution of responses, students are given two minutes to pair up and take turns explaining the reason for their answer to their partner. Students reconsider their answer based on this discussion, followed by a re-polling of the class. A small sample of students may be asked to share their reasoning with the class. Learning is reinforced by formally connecting their responses to the economic concept of sunk costs" (Maier, McGoldrick, and Simkins 2010, 159).

Graphic organizers provide students with a visual display that organizes and classifies information. Participating in a cooperative learning exercise of this nature helps students to discover patterns and relationships that might not otherwise be made explicit. The sequence chain format requires groups to determine and depict a series of events, actions, or decisions. The instructor provides the initial change and the ultimate outcome to be determined. Students begin with the initial event and show the logical progression of events, actions, and decisions that lead to the final outcome. Employing the sequence chain format in an introductory macroeconomics course, for example, provides a visual representation that fully identifies the chain of events that link an open market operation with changes in aggregate output: open market purchase $\rightarrow \uparrow$ money supply $\rightarrow \downarrow$ interest rates, etc. Students can then use this graphic organizer to frame their discussion of the impact of a monetary policy change.

The reciprocal nature of cooperative learning exercises encourages students to demonstrate understanding by presenting material to their peers, creates an opportunity to receive feedback on their exposition of this understanding, and generates multiple lenses through which to interpret material. Reciprocal teaching exercises create opportunities for students to learn from one another as facilitated through structured formats such as the learning cell. In preparation for this cooperative learning exercise, students read materials prior to class. During or prior to class, students are asked to (independently) prepare three questions (and answers) that address the main points of the reading. While some can be factual questions, at least one should be interpretive (see Chapter 6). In the cooperative component of the exercise, students share their questions with group members who work together to develop an answer until the question author is satisfied. This process continues with the next student's questions until all students have participated. A learning cell example is described in Section II.

Cooperative learning exercises developed in conjunction with writing assignments promote skills that enhance clarity of thought and the ability to organize and synthesize information. Using a round table format, for example, members of a group sequentially respond to a question. The first student begins the response with a written point or two before describing these aloud and passing the question to the next student who repeats the process. After all students have responded, the group evaluates all responses, reorders, refines, etc., until their listing is complete. As described later in Section III of this chapter, an alternative specification of the round table format can be integrated into a more comprehensive course project as students bring individually completed research topic worksheets to the group which then sequentially vets each member's worksheet content, synthesizing and enhancing related points of research, ultimately generating a single comprehensive output on which further project components are based.

Successful problem solving necessitates that students learn to develop strategies, recognize and understand applications, and critically analyze solutions. Cooperative learning exercises can implicitly develop these skills using multiple problems or do so explicitly by incorporating the identification of problem-solving steps into problem solutions. The send-a-problem format uses multiple problem solving which begins as each group is provided a different problem affixed to the outside of an envelope. The group works to solve the problem until time is called and they place their answer in the envelope and pass it to the next group. The second group attempts to answer the problem without looking at the first solution. When time is called, the second group's solution is added to the envelope and it is passed on to the third group. In the last stage of the exercise, the third group opens the envelope and evaluates both solutions, compiling a final solution which is then reported to the class (McGoldrick 2005). An example of this send-a-problem application for an intermediate microeconomics distance learning course is described in Section IV. Maier, McGoldrick, and Simkins (2010, 163–64) describe an alternative send-a-problem format in which a sequential problem-solving process is employed as students begin by completing the first stage of a problem, with subsequent groups building off this answer until all components are complete. For example:

Problem: The country of Econation is operating at full employment but policy makers believe the current inflation rate of 10 percent is too high to be consistent with economic efficiency and long-term economic growth.

1. *First group:* Provide a graphical presentation (along with a brief explanation) of current economic conditions in Econation.
2. *Second group:* You have been charged with recommending a policy change that would rectify the problem noted by policy makers. Provide a description of this change and a justification for using this as opposed to an alternative policy.
3. *Third group:* Show (and explain) this policy change using the graph completed by the first group.

Understanding the opportunities for cooperative learning in economics necessitates more than a discussion of structures, objectives, and exercise formats; it is best demonstrated through examples that illustrate these components. What follows are three examples that showcase choices made about objectives, formats, and logistical considerations within the cooperative learning structure. They vary in application from principles to electives, in-class to distance learning, and in intensity of required resources (time).

II. UNDERSTANDING ECONOMIC POLICY USING LEARNING CELLS
Robert Rebelein

This exercise was developed for Introduction to Macroeconomics at Vassar College, a small, selective liberal arts college where enrollment averages 25–30 students per section. By the time I use this exercise, we have covered the basics of the business cycle including cyclical behaviors of GDP, inflation, and unemployment, and have constructed the AD–AS model to help students understand how these aggregate quantities are related to each other. We also have discussed basics of monetary and fiscal policy tools. Students will have seen some textbook examples of how to use monetary and fiscal policy tools and of their effects but, in my experience, most students do not yet have a full understanding of relationships between various macroeconomic aggregates and generally do not have a thorough understanding of how different policy tools will impact different aspects of an economy. This exercise is intended to help students develop their understanding of the richness of these concepts.

A key learning objective I have for students in this course is to learn to critically evaluate articles they might read in the popular press. My experience is that traditional teaching methods do not equip all students with the ability to perform this type of analysis. Working together in a cooperative process, however, enables them to learn from each other so that they can (hopefully) perform this type of analysis on their own in the future. The specific learning objectives for this exercise are for students to learn to:

1. identify and interpret economic content of statements made in press articles; and,
2. evaluate policy remedies for different types of economic situations.

Description of the Innovation

This exercise utilizes both independent and group activities. The group activity encourages reciprocal teaching through a "learning cell" in which students work together to answer a series of questions. The exercise proceeds in three phases, described in detail below; two occur outside the classroom and the third is conducted in class. The first phase requires the instructor to identify several relevant readings. The second phase requires students to read each article, select one, and prepare several insightful questions on that article. The third phase requires students to work together in small groups to answer questions written by their peers. It is worth mentioning that I do not otherwise have students read articles for this course. Students are encouraged to pay attention to current events, and significant events are discussed in class, but this exercise provides students their first opportunity to receive feedback on their ability to critically evaluate popular press articles.

Phase 1 – Instructor preparation

The first phase required identification of three articles appropriate for students to read. Ideal articles are from one to three pages long and do more than simply report facts. I selected an article about continued high inflation in India, an editorial recommending that the U.S. President and Congress focus on long-term economic policy goals, and an article describing steps taken by the European Central Bank to increase its key lending rate.[3]

Key to their usefulness for this exercise, each article discussed either government actions taken to address the issue or the issue's economic implications. The first article provided a recent history of inflation in India and reported steps already taken, and those being contemplated, by the Indian government to address the problem; it also reported specific consequences of persistent high inflation. The second article identified specific problems in the U.S. economy at that time and offered relevant policy recommendations. The third article described stresses that were then confronting European Monetary Union countries and how raising interest rates might affect those stresses. In each article, the author(s) provided some, but not all, potentially useful information, and described some, but not all, implications of the discussed policy. Inclusion of some analysis showed students connections between economic policy and economic outcomes while omission of other details allowed students to use their course learning to explore the possibility that news reports often leave out potentially significant points.

Phases 2 and 3 required student participation, so I prepared an instruction sheet to provide them information necessary to complete the exercise. This instruction sheet included details about what students were expected to do during each part of the exercise, including relevant deadlines. (Appendix 4A presents a sample instruction sheet.)

Phase 2 – Individual tasks

The second phase began with distribution of the instruction sheet, which was then reviewed to ensure everyone understood the assignment. Each student was expected to read all three articles and then choose one to focus on for this phase. Using their selected article, students were asked to develop one question in each of the following categories:

- Factual – a question that can be answered objectively using information available in the article. An example of a student-generated factual question for the first article is: "According to the article, *why* has inflation jumped to a record level recently?"

- Interpretive – a question that requires analysis of information available in the article. An example of a student-generated interpretive question for the second article is: "The author states that the two most pressing issues currently facing the economy are the deflation in housing prices and the decline in the industrial sector. To what extent does the author believe the government's current policy of tax cuts and high federal spending address these issues?"
- Connecting to other course material – a question that requires students to apply concepts learned in the course to the situation described in the article. An example of a student-generated connecting question for the third article is: "'Higher [interest] rates typically strengthen a currency by attracting investors;' how would one go about substantiating this statement using the concepts and ideas we have learned in class?"

My introduction to the exercise included guidance for constructing questions in each category. Students also were asked to prepare sample responses, as if the questions had been asked on a homework assignment or exam, and to submit both questions and answers to me at least 24 hours before the third phase. I emphasized that they needed to read all three articles carefully even though they were focusing on just one article for this phase.

At the end of this phase I reviewed submitted questions and identified those I believed would best suit the learning objectives identified above. My goal was to have several questions from each category (factual, interpretive, and connecting to course material) for each article. Because a greater number of questions were submitted than were needed for the third phase, this exercise also generated a set of questions suitable for future homework assignments, quizzes, or exams.

In preparation for the in-class exercise component, I divided the class into groups of three and assigned each a set of three questions, one from each category, for a single article. To broaden student learning, students were assigned a different article than the one for which they wrote questions. This required a little logistical coordination but, because several students developed questions for each article, it was not a problem to form such groups. In addition, when assigning students to groups, I sought to increase heterogeneity within groups by also considering economic skill levels of students and (to the extent known) their social skills.

Phase 3 – In-class component

The in-class component began with a review of instructions, followed by group assignments and distribution of questions. I emphasized that each student was expected to know and understand all their group's answers. To reinforce this expectation, I told them I would randomly choose a member to report their group's answers to the class. The possibility that any of them could be called upon to share their group's answer increased positive interdependence. To ensure sufficient time for class discussion, I allowed only 20 minutes to develop answers.

The students separated into groups and began their work. Each group recorded an answer for each of their assigned questions and, to encourage students to think carefully about their answers, was required to turn in written responses at the end of the exercise with the implication that these would contribute to their grade.

During the group work, I circulated to observe and listen to each group, evaluating how each group was functioning and the progress they were making. If a group seemed to be doing fine, I moved on. If a group was headed in a wrong direction or was considerably behind other groups, or if a group member was dominating (or not participating), I intervened. This intervention took different forms including asking leading questions, asking students directly what they thought (particularly useful when there is a nonparticipating group member), or asking other group members if they had solicited everyone's opinion. Groups that finished their task early were asked to develop a diagrammatic illustration of their answers.

After about 20 minutes (and a time warning), I brought the class back together for the final exercise component, during which each group reported its answers to the class. I selected an article and randomly called on representatives of groups with questions on that article to recite their answers to the class. To stimulate discussion among students, I invited other students to comment on the answers and I asked questions designed to get students thinking about each other's answers. For example, I asked one student her opinion (accurate or not, complete or not) of the analysis reported by another group. Her group had answered questions on the same article, so she was familiar with the issues even though her group had different questions than the reporting group. Sometimes I asked the question's author to comment on the group's answer and to compare it to his or her sample answer. If there was disagreement between the author and reporting group, I would turn back to the group for a defense of their answer. As the exercise progressed and students realized I really did want to hear their thoughts on the issues, they became more willing to speak up and express their views. Eventually, students were talking more to each other than to me – something I had hoped would happen because it was more likely to lead to continued discussions outside the classroom.

I found that different groups tended to reach similar conclusions, even though they had different questions to answer. However, sometimes groups emphasized different aspects of the situation in reaching their conclusions, which presented an opportunity for discussion. For example, one group focused on a policy's effect on consumers while another group focused on the effect on producers; because some policies that help consumers harm producers and vice versa, this provided an opening to discuss appropriate goals of government policies.

Lessons Learned and Teaching Notes

The exercise can be used in any course requiring students to synthesize significant amounts of information, as is typical in policy applications associated with international trade, money and banking, or public finance. The exercise is best conducted after students have a basic understanding of concepts and theories required for the course. Incorporating the exercise near the course conclusion helps students understand how to use concepts they have learned. Students reported learning a lot and enjoying discussion of real-life applications and that part of the benefit came from hearing other students' thoughts about the articles and the questions they had written.

This exercise need not be run in exactly the manner described above. An instructor must consider his or her course objectives and student abilities and tailor the exercise to their specific situation. The following are some things to think about when preparing to use this exercise.

- Each article must describe some aspect of an economic situation in a country, a possible fiscal, monetary, or regulatory action the government might take, and at least suggest the expected results of that action.
- Most often, appropriate articles can be drawn from the popular press; other possible sources include policy think tanks or *The Economist's Voice*.
- Choosing three articles provides sufficient topical variety for students to choose one of interest, whereas using more articles can become difficult to manage in later phases.
- The articles do not have to be about the U.S. economy. In fact, it can be helpful to show students that principles learned apply to other economies and many students enjoy learning about other countries.
- The choice of three students per group was motivated by a desire to keep group size small to reduce the potential for free-riders while also wanting groups large enough to generate a diversity of ideas and opinions.
- To minimize the risk of free-riding, each student could be assigned a role, such as scribe, taskmaster, and time-keeper.
- It is important to limit the amount of time allotted to small-group work so as to allow sufficient time for each small group to report answers

and to have time for discussion. Twenty minutes usually will be sufficient for groups to formulate good answers.

- A more sophisticated version of this exercise would require students to locate appropriate articles. This would require that students be provided guidance about what to look for in selecting articles, which could be done as part of an earlier exercise.
- Variants on the timing of when students submit and answer questions are also possible. For example, students could submit their phase two questions further in advance of phase three. The instructor could then distribute all questions to all groups prior to phase three. Providing all questions to everyone encourages students to come prepared for the broader class discussion without reducing the actual cooperative group component.
- Because groups work at different speeds, it is best to have a complementary task available for groups that finish quickly. Having students illustrate answers graphically often works well.
- All questions and student answers can be posted online for the entire class to see. If desired, the instructor could add comments to incorrect or incomplete answers.

One challenge of using cooperative learning techniques is determining whether or not students achieved the desired learning objectives. An advantage of this learning cell exercise is that it generates a number of sources for assessment, including questions and model answers written by students, answers generated by groups, and observations of group functioning. A primary criterion for determining the success of the exercise should be the quality of student answers. These answers can be evaluated based on their thoroughness, including the use of article evidence, and the degree to which they incorporated theories and concepts discussed throughout the semester. Group answers should be more comprehensive than individual answers because they reflect the work of several people.

III. INVESTIGATING HEALTH CARE REFORM USING A ROUND TABLE EXERCISE[4]

Jennifer K. Rhoads

The months leading up to the 2008 United States presidential election were filled with extensive debates between the principal political party nominees, Republican Senator John McCain and Democrat Senator Barack Obama, over topics including immigration and the war in Iraq. Another topic that attracted heightened interest during this campaign was U.S. health care reform. Given that concerns about the existing health care system and proposed changes were complex and often controversial, it seemed likely that this discussion would persist for years into the future regardless of who won the election. To help students become educated participants in the ongoing discussion, the health care reform debate was integrated into my health economics course during the fall semester of 2008 at the University of Illinois at Chicago (UIC). The course was an elective taken primarily by seniors and economics majors. To capture the many interrelated issues involved in the topic of U.S. health care reform, a cumulative project was developed as a substantial part of the course. This project interwove cooperative and individual learning activities over a five-week period with both in-class and out-of-class components.

The first step in developing this project was to carefully consider the desired learning and content objectives. Since the U.S. health care reform debate was likely to evolve over time, it was important for students to go beyond simply identifying current key points of Senators McCain's and Obama's reform proposals, although this was an important content-centered objective. They also needed to develop skills associated with researching key facts, synthesizing arguments, and communicating multiple positions on an issue. The round table cooperative learning format, which falls within the writing category of cooperative learning exercises, was selected as a starting point for developing this project since it provides a process for groups of students to organize and synthesize complicated information. This exercise was enhanced through the addition of other project components including individual research and writing, and group oral presentations.

Description of Innovation

A brief overview of the project components and objectives was included in the course syllabus (see Appendix 4B) to set expectations of both time commitment to and quality of the project (signaled by 20 percent of the course grade allocated to the project). A more detailed handout distributed on the first day of the project outlined each step and associated deadlines. The class of thirty-nine students was divided into nine groups of four or five. Each group was assigned one of the following health care reform debate issues: pre-existing conditions, portability, insurance mandates, public health care programs, tax credits and subsidies, medical malpractice jury awards, electronic medical records, government-sponsored insurance pools, and pharmaceuticals. At the beginning of the semester students indicated their political party affiliation (if any) on a pretest. Formal cooperative learning groups were created using this information to ensure that a wide range of political perspectives were represented within a group and that the subsequent analysis would include all viewpoints.

This U.S. health care reform project was designed using three sequential phases: individual, cooperative group, and then individual again. The first phase required students to work individually for one week to complete a worksheet compiling information about their assigned issue (see Appendix 4C). This worksheet included sections for key background information, illustrating examples, and summaries of how Senators McCain's and Obama's proposed policies addressed the issue. This first phase of the project promoted individual accountability by ensuring that each student was prepared with adequate background knowledge before participating in the second, cooperative, phase of the project.

The round table exercise in the cooperative phase of the project was conducted during a fifty-minute class period devoted to in-class group work. In addition to completing the fact-gathering worksheet, each group member was required to bring at least two resources to class to share with the other group members. This aspect of the project enhanced positive interdependence through the use of shared resources. Students met in small groups to discuss, synthesize and compromise until they had generated a group version of their individually drafted worksheets. Specifically, the round table format required group members to begin by sequentially sharing research contained in the background information section of the worksheet. The group then evaluated and synthesized the responses and referred to their additional shared resources to resolve inconsistencies until a consensus was reached. This process was repeated for the remaining examples and policy sections of the worksheet. This round table exercise simultaneously enhanced positive interdependence (through roles) and equal participation because each group member served as leader for one section while the other group members sequentially shared their responses for each section.[5] While the groups were working, I circled the room to assess each group's level of activity. When the students were actively involved in the round table process, I simply made my presence known in case there were any questions. If the process seemed stalled or the discussion was off task, I reiterated how the round table format should be conducted and prompted the students to engage in the relevant discussion.

At the end of the class period each group submitted a single group worksheet, which I reviewed and provided groups with feedback that identified elements for improvement or elaboration. Groups then had one week to work together outside of class to further develop their responses and to create an associated ten-minute oral presentation. Group members were assigned at random to present information associated with each worksheet section.[6] Since students did not know in advance which section they would present and the group's grade was based on the presentation as a whole, each group member had an incentive to ensure that all members fully understood material associated with every worksheet section. This arrangement promoted strong positive interdependence (output goal and learning goal interdependence) and group accountability while promoting equal participation and individual accountability.

The final, individual, project phase provided students the opportunity to demonstrate their mastery of learning and content objectives through a comprehensive paper. The unique aspect of this project phase was that students were required to synthesize and evaluate information presented by all groups. Students were asked to put themselves in the role of a third party presidential candidate and to discuss their position on each health care reform issue presented by groups in phase two of the project. Given that students were required to write about all issues presented but had only researched one issue intensely, they had to rely heavily on information presented by other groups. This project design helped students understand the importance of creating effective presentations and of paying close attention to peer presentations. Students also were motivated to ask clarifying questions after each group's presentation. Therefore, this project not only emphasized positive interdependence among group members within a group, but also among groups.

Student performance was assessed on the individual worksheet, group worksheet, oral presentation, and final paper. Allocation of the 100 project points reflected the cumulative nature and increasing expected quality of the students' work as follows: individual worksheet (10 points), group worksheet (20 points), oral presentation (20 points), and final paper (50 points). Overall, the students' performance revealed that they met quality expectations and achieved the learning and content objectives set for this project. For example, in the final phase, students effectively utilized information presented by other student groups to write thoughtful and cohesive individual papers defending their positions on each issue, demonstrating mastery of the objective to communicate key aspects of health care reform issues. Further, discussions went beyond restatements of facts and were generally of equal quality for a student's assigned issue and for issues presented by other groups, illustrating that students understood and could explain economic reasoning behind each of the issues. Finally, most students selected positions that were not consistently aligned with a particular political party, indicating that they were able to evaluate the issues by applying their own knowledge rather than defaulting to a particular political party's stance.

As an additional mode of assessment, pre- and post-tests measured changes in students' knowledge of the health care reform issues and interest level. Although this was optional and did not count toward the students' course grades, every student in the class completed both the pre- and post-tests. Results provide further evidence of the positive impact on student outcomes. The class mean score for the content portion of the tests increased significantly, from 64 to 86 percent. Further, 90 percent of students in the class responded that their interest in health care reform policy increased as a result of the project.[7]

Written feedback from students helps illustrate benefits from the student perspective. Students felt they learned a great deal about issues involved in health care reform, and were pleasantly surprised at how much they learned from their classmates. Students wrote that the project was a way to "learn more and retain it instead of only memorizing for a test" and that "the project helped me make an informed decision on who [sic] to vote for." In terms of project design, one student noted that "worksheets helped me organize my thoughts" and another stated that "every portion was a step towards understanding more about the topics." Further, one student commented that the most beneficial aspect of the project was that he "learned new relevant information from fellow students" which for him was "something new." This last comment especially highlights the value of cooperative learning from a student's perspective.

Lessons Learned and Teaching Notes

Although this project was designed within the context of the 2008 U.S. presidential election and health care reform, it is flexible enough to implement in a wide range of course and classroom contexts. For example, this project design could be implemented in an economics of education course in which groups could discuss the use of vouchers, charter schools, teacher pay and incentives, or effects of increased funding on student performance. Alternatively, consider a law and economics course where each student group is assigned a case, and presentations focus on background facts, results or final ruling, and the economic reasoning used in the case. Generally speaking, any topic with multi-faceted issues would lend itself well to this project design.

Additionally, this project could be modified to accommodate a wide range of class sizes. The most straightforward adaptation would be to expand or contract the number of groups (and thus issues covered). Alternatively, the number of worksheet sections (and resulting length of each presentation) could be expanded or contracted. Regardless, to uphold underlying mechanics of this project, the number of groups must match the number of issues assigned for analysis. Also, group size must match the number of sections in worksheets (and thus the number of sections in subsequent oral presentations).

This project was conducted over a five-week period, with roughly one week for independent research, one week for group research and presentation preparation, one week for in-class presentations, and two weeks for writing final individual papers. The time frame for this project is flexible and can easily be altered to allow for increased time within or between any project phases. When determining project deadlines it is important to consider the complexity of the topic being researched and logistical considerations faced by your students. Since U.S. health care reform is a complicated topic and many UIC students commute rather than live on campus, the time frame used for this iteration of the project may have been too condensed. For example, since meeting outside of class is more difficult to arrange among students who commute, allocation of more than one week to prepare for group presentations would likely have been helpful. This was reinforced by post-project feedback where some students indicated that they needed more time to prepare for presentations. Further, due to the intricate nature of issues researched, groups may have benefited from more in-class time working on group worksheets in the round table exercise. Finally, students indicated they would have preferred more time to work on their final individual papers.

Because so much of the final paper depends on oral presentations of other groups, this aspect of the project would be enhanced by adding a "group check-in" with the instructor during the project phase when group members are working together outside of class to prepare presentations. Arranging a short group meeting would allow the instructor to assess how well group members were working together, and help mediate or redirect the group if necessary. In fact, one of nine groups performed poorly in the oral presentation. It was apparent that group members did not communicate clearly and that they tried to minimize preparation time by dividing the work without any group feedback or collaboration. This group's attempt to ignore the cooperative nature of the project ultimately inhibited performance. Meeting with groups would have revealed these challenges and provided the opportunity to assist the group in developing a plan for working together to produce a more effective oral presentation.

Many economic topics, such as U.S. health care reform policy, can be daunting for students. This project provided a unique learning experience where students shared the burden of research, learned how to synthesize complicated issues within a small group, became experts on a particular issue, and developed their ability to communicate this information to their peers. As a capstone for this project, students used their newly acquired knowledge to evaluate and effectively defend their chosen positions for each of the U.S. health care reform issues included in the project.

IV. LEARNING INTERMEDIATE MICROECONOMICS WITH A SEND-A-PROBLEM EXERCISE
Sue Stockly

Fostering active student engagement presents special challenges within a distance-learning environment. Students taking courses through remote broadcasts are physically separate from the instructor and from the majority of their classmates. Opportunities to participate in class discussions and in group work are limited and lack of structure can lead to distractions from the lecture. The following offers an example of how cooperative learning techniques can be implemented in classrooms where some students are enrolled in off-campus sites.

This particular exercise was conducted at Eastern New Mexico University (ENMU) in an intermediate microeconomics course delivered to students in the classroom and in two remote sites. The main ENMU campus in Portales serves a large rural area and relies on instructional television (ITV) to broadcast lectures to students in other towns, some as far as 200 miles away. The delivery technology allows for only one camera view at a time. Students in remote sites see either the instructor or lecture slides, but never both simultaneously. These students can hear the lecture and can be heard by activating microphones in their respective remote-site classrooms. Thus, audio is two-way and video is one-way.

The audio configuration in remote sites, however, is not conducive to engagement in classroom activities. Students cannot be heard unless they intentionally activate individual microphones. Though they are encouraged to ask (or answer) questions during lectures, students are reluctant to do so because it entails interrupting the instructor. In addition, there are significant lags as sound is relayed through the broadcast system. As a result, remote-site students rarely participate in any type of classroom dialogue.

Moreover, instructors have the general perception that students in ITV sites take the lecture less seriously than students in regular classrooms. Facilitators in remote sites report that the fact that students cannot be heard by the instructor leads to lots of conversations unrelated to class materials. On average, students who take courses off-campus earn lower grades than those in the regular classroom.

The microeconomics course in which cooperative learning was integrated was non-calculus-based and offered via ITV. I introduced cooperative learning techniques with the goal of more fully engaging students from remote sites with course material and with other students. Course enrollments consisted of 13 students in the on-campus classroom, three in one off-campus site (Remote Site 1) and four in another off-campus site (Remote Site 2). Six cooperative learning groups were formed: four in the classroom and one in each remote site. Throughout the semester students were frequently asked to work problems in groups. What follows is a description of one such activity that was formally structured as a cooperative learning exercise.

Planning the Exercise

Development of this innovation began with formulation of a learning objective centered on problem-solving skills needed to succeed in intermediate microeconomics. The exercise was implemented two-thirds of the way through the semester with a focus on having students help each other understand basic steps needed to use an economic model. They were to demonstrate that understanding through mathematical calculation, graphical illustration, brief written descriptions and oral presentations. During previous semesters, I found that students struggled with production optimization problems and thus chose this material as the basis for the following content objectives. Using numerical data, students were expected to learn how to:

- Sketch an isoquant map and corresponding isocost curves,
- Identify optimal levels of production,
- Trace a long-run expansion path,
- Trace a short-run expansion path that a firm would take to move from one point on the long-run path to another, and
- Summarize the relationship between the long run and the short run depicted.

In order to promote interaction within and among groups (and thus engage students in the remote sites) the send-a-problem format (associated with the problem-solving category) was chosen as the framework for this cooperative learning exercise. Implementation of the send-a-problem activity would allow all students, including those in remote sites, equal participation and simultaneous interaction – introducing key elements of cooperative learning into an environment that did not previously foster this level of student engagement.[8] Barkley, Cross, and Major (2005) suggest that this form of exercise is particularly useful in helping students to develop strategies, understand applications and produce critical analysis of solutions.

"Sending" the problems was feasible because classroom and broadcast sites had fax machines, telephones and a facilitator who could coordinate the sending of problems among groups. Thus students in remote sites and on campus could send and receive problems as well as offer and receive feedback in a timely manner.

A number of preparatory steps were taken to ensure a smooth facilitation process. Three similar problems were developed – A, B and C. The problems were designed to help students practice using budget constraint and isocost equations to solve for unknown input prices, input quantities or costs and to sketch short-run and long-run expansion paths. Also required were brief written explanations of expanding production in the short-run and long-run returns to scale.

Envelopes were prepared that contained one problem and three answer sheets for students to use in each of three rounds. Facilitators in remote sites were provided three separate envelopes – one with problem materials for each round. They were also given instructions as to which faxed solution was to be placed in which envelope before it was given to remote site students. Fax connections were tested by facilitators to ensure proper operation and telephone conversations clarified each person's role in the exercise. Because of the nature of coordinating across three sites, providing clear guidance to students and facilitators was critical to the successful operation of the exercise. Appendix 4D includes a handout with step-by-step instructions used while the exercise was in progress.

Group formation necessitated oversight only in the regular classroom since each remote site was constrained by student enrollment. The four campus groups were constructed to ensure some skill heterogeneity. One more-advanced skill student, as determined by performance to date in the class, was allocated to each classroom group. Fortunately, there also happened to be at least one more-advanced student at each remote site.

To further prepare students for the activity, the previous class included an introduction to these types of problems. One problem was demonstrated step-by-step and students were asked to include these steps in their notes. A similar problem was assigned for homework with the stipulation that it was to be turned in at the beginning of the send-a-problem class.

Implementing the Exercise

On the send-a-problem class day, students were directed to turn in their homework and to sit with their groups; remote-site students handed the facilitator their assignment to be faxed to the instructor later. Each group was asked to assign the role of scribe to one group member.

Table 4.1 lays out the distribution of problems and their progression among groups during the exercise. For example, in round one, on-campus Groups 1 and 1a received problem A. The other two problems were distributed among remote sites and the remaining on-campus groups. Note that each of the three problems was distributed to two groups in each round. Restricting the number of problems to match the number of rounds ensured that each group had the opportunity to work on all three problems prior to the full class discussion. Making only one copy available to each group also enhanced positive interdependence.

Table 4.1: Send-A-Problem Progression

Group	Site	Round 1	Round 2	Round 3
1	On campus	A	C	B
1a	On campus	A	C	B
2	Remote site 1	B	A	C
2a	On campus	B	A	C
3	Remote site 2	C	B	A
3a	On campus	C	B	A

The classroom camera was turned toward students during each round to better observe student work during the exercise. This also enabled an end-of-round time signal by reorienting the camera back to the instructor. Sound in the classroom was not broadcast while students were working on problems (although remote-site students were able to activate their microphones and ask questions at any point). While students worked on problems, the instructor circulated among classroom groups to answer questions. Students in the remote-site groups were contacted by telephone to check if there were any questions. During each problem-solving round, all students in the class appeared fully engaged in the activity and were on-task the entire time. It was more difficult to assess the level of engagement for remote-site students, although each time the instructor called, students in those groups stated that the problem solving was going well and that there were no questions.

At the end of round three, one classroom group and both remote site groups presented final solutions for each of the problems. All group members contributed to their presentations, fielding a variety of questions from students across all sites.

Overall, student participation in every step of the send-a-problem activity, regardless of location, indicated a good level of positive interdependence.

Evaluating the Exercise and Summary of Lessons Learned

Various assessment formats were designed to measure the impact of this innovation. Although the small class size did not allow for tests of statistical significance, the instruments used are described to provide the reader with a range of potential evaluation techniques.

The homework problem provided a benchmark against which final group solutions at the end of round three of the exercise could be compared, thus insuring both individual and group accountability. Individual homework and the three group problems were assigned a total of 20 possible points. When these were graded, 92 percent of students on campus and 57 percent of ITV students earned higher group scores compared to individual scores.

Immediately after the cooperative learning exercise, students were required to complete and submit an evaluation form by email. Two of the questions asked them to rank how well they understood the material before coming to class and how useful they felt the exercise was. Seventy-five percent of students on campus and 57 percent of remote-site students had higher scores on the second question than on the first question, indicating that students perceived their learning was enhanced by participating in the activity. The evaluation form also included a question designed to measure general interest in this active learning format, asking if students would like the class to include other exercises during the semester. All the students on campus answered "yes" to this question (100%) compared to 57 percent of the remote-site students.

A final assessment compared performance of students who participated in the collaborative learning activity to students who took the course one semester earlier. The percent of correct answers on similar exam problems for in-class students was 80 percent the previous semester and 88 percent after the send-a-problem exercise; correct answers for remote-site students increased from 73 percent to 84 percent.

Evidence provided by these assessment strategies was mixed. The first three measures indicated that remote-site student perceptions about the exercise were less positive than those of on-campus students. Nonetheless, a majority of students, especially those in remote sites, did show improvement on graded exam problems.

There were several lessons learned through implementation of this specific cooperative learning format within a distance-learning framework. Student comments revealed that technical details were not entirely clear in the remote sites; these students might need additional instructions or checks on their understanding prior to implementation of cooperative learning activities. In general, the exercise did demonstrate that it is possible to use the send-a-problem activity within an ITV delivery system. Giving students the opportunity to work on problems and to present solutions in groups did result in higher levels of active learning – especially for students in remote sites who were accustomed to very low levels of engagement during class.

This cooperative learning exercise was feasible due to the specific distance education delivery system in place as remote students were able to fax solutions to other sites and to give presentations to the entire class. Delivery systems vary quite a bit from institution to institution ranging from online-only courses that use classroom management systems such as Web-CT or Blackboard, to video conferencing with two-way video and audio, to digital recordings of lectures subsequently posted online, to desktop web-conferencing programs such as WIMBA or WebX. The send-a-problem activity could be modified for implementation in any of these delivery systems. For example, students could be assigned to groups that communicate with each other through email or discussion boards and problems could be sent asynchronously with deadlines set for each round. A synchronous activity could require students to "attend" class through personal computers in campus computer labs, public libraries or from home. Group work and presentations could be completed using email, discussion boards, chat rooms or web-cams. My experience has been that implementation of cooperative learning techniques in a distance education environment is no more time-consuming than in traditional classrooms and that the benefits of enhanced learning through increased student engagement are well worth the costs.

V. FURTHER CONSIDERATIONS

As is both implicit and explicit from these three examples, constructing and planning a cooperative learning exercise requires more than just identifying objectives and selecting a category and format. Attention to logistical details and ensuring the exercise adheres to key structures described above enhance probability of success. Special attention should be paid to introducing the exercise, creating groups, assigning roles, monitoring student work, providing closure, and choosing assessment tools.

Introducing the exercise to students involves describing the activity itself, identifying objectives, providing key definitions, outlining procedures, giving examples, and then questioning to verify student understanding (Johnson, Johnson, and Smith 1991, 64–65; Barkley, Cross, and Major 2005, 69–70). Cooperative learning exercises often include both descriptive and informative handouts. Descriptive handouts reinforce the exercise introduction and can be an excellent guide for groups to remain on task. Informative handouts include key content-driven materials necessary to complete that specific exercise. Positive interdependence can be encouraged by distributing only one copy of the descriptive handout per group and/or providing different, complementary informative handouts to each group member (Johnson, Johnson, and Smith 1991, 62).

After a clear understanding of the exercise is achieved, the class is broken up into cooperative learning groups. There are three group types: informal (quickly formed, single concept addressed, non-repetitive pairings), formal (more careful formation, more complex topic, membership consistent for any single exercise but may change across exercises), and base (very careful formation, multiple topics over entire semester, membership constant over all topics). Objectives and exercise format choice can help define which group type is most appropriate. For example, instructors who wish to pursue the objective of enhancing students' communication and listening skills might use informal groups to implement a think–pair–share exercise. Alternatively, if the objective is to develop students' ability to demonstrate understanding or receive feedback on their exposition of this understanding, a learning cell exercise with formal or base groups might be more appropriate.

In forming groups (particularly formal and base groups) instructors need to consider the extent and form of member heterogeneity, group size, and the process of group creation. Research on the effectiveness of cooperative learning exercises suggests that heterogeneous groups (based on academic ability and individual characteristics such as attitudes, ethnicity, gender, etc.) generate "more elaborative thinking, more frequent giving and receiving of explanations, and greater perspective taking in discussing material…all of which increase the depth of understanding, the quality of reasoning, and the accuracy of long-term retention" (Johnson, Johnson, and Smith 1991, 60–61). While there is no hard and fast rule for group size, typically three to five members are recommended (Millis and Cottell 1998, 49). Larger groups require more resources (such as time) in completing tasks and may not be appropriate for less complicated exercises. Smaller groups may not lead to as rich an outcome as one member might dominate. Barkley, Cross, and Major (2005, 45–50) describe a number of processes for constructing groups such as random selection (e.g., odd–even, count off, and playing cards) or instructor selection (including student sign-ups, data sheets used to collect student characteristics or skills, test scores, and learning styles).

Once groups are formed, the instructor can ensure incorporation of many of the key elements of cooperative learning exercises through the assignment of individual roles. Commonly used roles include that of facilitator, recorder, reporter, and time keeper. For larger groups, additional roles of summarizer or encourager could be developed. Each role provides the opportunity for students to participate actively, keep the group on task, and reinforce positive contributions. Furthermore, assigning specific roles helps to filter out less constructive behaviors. Instructors incorporating cooperative learning exercises into their courses for the first time could begin by assigning the roles of recorder and/or reporter, and then introduce additional roles as they increase the degree of exercise complexity.

Once students are set on task, the instructor's role as "sage-on-the-stage" changes to "guide-on-the-side." Monitoring groups during a cooperative learning exercise is active work requiring the instructor to gauge the degree of necessary interaction, and providing direction and reflection for different groups, depending on how they are progressing. Students (and to a large degree, instructors) are accustomed to and comfortable with the instructor authority role, but for cooperative learning exercises to be successful, students must rely on one another and instructors should limit comments to clarifying instructions and goals, providing positive reinforcement as to progress achieved and raising questions to motivate further progress. Kagan (1992) suggests using the "three before me" strategy, requiring students to interact with three other sources before asking the instructor, as one method of reinforcing equal participation. Instructors also should monitor for group dynamic problems such as no leader, too many leaders, inequitable participation and general off-task behaviors. Upon encountering such problems, instructors should play the role of mediator (as opposed to director) to promote a collaborative effort that will build equal participation. Successfully monitoring groups and giving appropriate feedback are skills most instructors will need time to develop and hone.

Providing students with a predetermined 'quiet signal' (such as flickering classroom lights) facilitates the end of the group discussion but not the exercise. Cooperative learning exercises include a reporting out of group results/conclusions. Such activities can be immediate (in class directly after the exercise) or delayed (at the start of a future class meeting), informal (conversational sharing) or formal (written or oral report) and graded (at the individual or group level; by the instructor, peers, or self) or not. Regardless of the structure, reporting out provides opportunities to reinforce positive interdependence and both individual and group accountability.

Examples of potential reporting out techniques are too numerous to provide a detailed account here.[9] Note, however, that during reporting out students share their findings and conclusions, obtain feedback on their work, and participate in a summarization of learning achieved. For example, the three-stay, one-stray technique facilitates informal reporting out across cooperative learning groups. In a group of four, one student would rotate to a new group, report conclusions of their work, obtain feedback and then communicate a summary of this interaction back to his or her original group. Alternatively, a randomly chosen student could formally represent his or her group in a report to the whole class. While this group-by-group report may consume more class time, it allows for more collective interaction and instructor intervention.

Assessment is another important component of designing cooperative learning exercises. Not all activities need be directly assessed if there is a clear indication how they contribute to learning and thus to grades achieved through other activities (quizzes, exams). That said, it is not always easy to convince students of this value and instructors may choose to grade cooperative learning exercises more comprehensively when first introduced. Individual assessment tools can include worksheets completed during the exercise, a closely related follow-up homework assignment or a quiz in a subsequent class period. Grading comprehension at the group level can rely on traditional techniques applied in more creative ways. For example, to motivate students to contribute to effective group learning (positive interdependence), bonuses can be provided to all members of a group if individually they all meet some minimum standard level of performance on follow up assignments or quizzes. Alternatively, Bartlett (1995) suggests randomly choosing an individual from each group to be assessed; the grade earned by one is earned by all in the group.

It is important to provide opportunities for students to raise unanswered questions. Students could even record questions raised during the exercise for use in subsequent discussion, encouraging students to recognize the validity of their questions. It also is useful for instructors to point out common errors in the graded component of the exercise and to summarize key material. Finally, linking material to past and future lessons as well as more broadly defined course objectives serves to reinforce the importance of the cooperative learning exercise.

Paying careful attention to these logistical details, in addition to key structures that underlie cooperative learning exercises, will help ensure that the economic exercises developed by the instructor are more effective in meeting identified objectives. The wide range of potential cooperative learning exercises allows for both incremental implementation and the ability to adopt in all economics courses. Instructors may initiate their use of cooperative learning with the more basic think–pair–share format, gaining experience before moving towards a more involved format such as the send-a-problem exercise. Examples provided herein demonstrate the versatility of this active learning technique as it may be incorporated into a wide range of economics courses from introductory to intermediate to elective courses.

NOTES

1. Johnson and Johnson (1990, 32), in a meta analysis of nearly 200 studies over 50 years find that "cooperative learning promotes higher individual achievement than do… individualistic ones (effect size = 0.53). Effect sizes of this order describe significant, substantial increases in achievement. They mean, for example, that…students who would score at the 53rd percentile level when learning individualistically will score at the 70th percentile when learning cooperatively."

2. For those unfamiliar with learning theories or how they help instructors develop course objectives and improve their teaching, see Saunders (1998) and Gronlund (1995).
3. The specific articles used were: "Inflation Continues to Rise," in *The Times of India*, February 15, 2007 (http://timesofindia.indiatimes.com/articleshow/1617538.cms); "Investing wisely; Bush and Congress have a chance to focus on long-term economic policy. They should seize it." Editorial, *Los Angeles Times*, January 4, 2007, p. A14; "European Central Bank Raises Key Rate," by Joellen Perry, *Wall Street Journal*, March 9, 2007, p. A2.
4. Full details including student handouts and worksheets for this project can be found on the Starting Point: Teaching and Learning Economics website (http://serc.carleton.edu/econ/index.html).
5. Groups with five members were instructed to choose one section from the worksheet to break into two parts so there were five sections to discuss.
6. Groups of five members were instructed to break one section of the presentation into two parts so that there were five sections in the group presentation.
7. For a full discussion of the pre- and post-test results, the reader is directed to the working paper entitled, "Cooperative Learning in a Health Economics Course: 2008 U.S. Presidential Campaign and Health Care Reform," on the University of Illinois at Chicago Center for Economic Education website (http://cee.econ.uic.edu/ workingpapers.html).
8. See the fifth page of this chapter for the instructions for the send-a-problem activity.
9. For examples, see Barkley, Cross, and Major (2005, 79–80), Mills and Cottell (1998, 105–109), and Kagan (1992, 12:5–12:6).

REFERENCES

Barkley, E.F., K.P. Cross, and C.H. Major (2005), *Collaborative Learning Techniques: A Handbook for College Faculty*, San Francisco, CA: Jossey-Bass.

Bartlett, R.L. (1995), "A flip of the coin – A roll of the die: An answer to the free-rider problem in economic education," *Journal of Economic Education*, **26** (2), 131–39.

Gronlund, N.E. (1995), *How to Write and Use Instructional Objectives* (5th ed.), Englewood Cliffs, NJ: Merrill/Prentice-Hall.

Johnson, D.W., and R.T. Johnson (1990), "Cooperative learning and achievement," in S. Sharan (ed.), *Cooperative Learning: Theory and Research*, New York: Praeger, 23–38.

Johnson, D.W., R.T. Johnson, and K.A. Smith (1991), *Cooperative Learning: Increasing College Faculty Instructional Productivity*, ASHE-ERIC Higher Education Report No. 4, Washington, D.C.: The George Washington University, School of Education and Human Development.

Johnson, D.W., R.T. Johnson, and K.A. Smith (1998), "Cooperative learning returns of college: What evidence is there that it works?," *Change*, **20** (4), 26–35.

Kagan, S. (1992), *Cooperative Learning*, San Juan Capistrano, CA: Resources for Teachers, Inc.

Maier, M., K. McGoldrick, and S. Simkins (2010), "Implementing cooperative learning in introductory economics courses," in B. Millis (ed.), *Cooperative Learning in Higher Education: Across the Disciplines, Across the Academy*, Sterling, VA: Stylus Press, 157–79.

McGoldrick, K. (2005), "Cooperative learning categories and exercises," Teaching Innovations Program documents.

Millis, B.J., and P.G. Cottell, Jr. (1998), *Cooperative Learning for Higher Education Faculty*, Phoenix, AZ: American Council on Education and Oryx Press.

Saunders, P. (1998), "Learning theory and instructional objectives," in W. Walstad and P. Saunders (eds), *Teaching Undergraduate Economics: A Handbook for Instructors*, Boston: Irwin McGraw-Hill, 85–108.

Slavin, R.E. (1990), *Cooperative Learning: Theory, Research and Practice*, Boston, MA: Allyn and Bacon.

Smith, K.A. (1996), "Cooperative learning: Making 'group work' work," in T.E. Sutherland and C.C. Bonwell (eds), *Using Active Learning in College Classes: A Range of Options for Faculty. New Directions for Teaching and Learning, No. 67*, San Francisco: Jossey-Bass, 71–82.

Smith, K.A., and A.A. Waller (1997), "Cooperative learning for new college teachers," in W.E. Campbell and K.A. Smith (eds), *New Paradigms for College Teaching*, Edina, MN: Interaction Book Company, 183–209.

Watts, M., and Becker, W.E. (2008), "A little more than chalk and talk: Results from a third national survey of teaching methods in undergraduate economics courses," *Journal of Economic Education*, **39** (3), 273–86.

Webb, N. (1983), "Predicting learning from student interaction: Defining the interaction variable," *Educational Psychologist*, **18**, 33–41.

Webb, N. (1991), "Task-related verbal interaction and mathematics learning in small groups," *Journal of Research in Mathematics Education*, **22**, 366–89.

Yamarik, S. (2007), "Does cooperative learning improve student learning outcomes?" *Journal of Economic Education*, **38** (3), 259–77.

APPENDIX 4A
Policy Applications Exercise

Governments have a variety of fiscal and monetary policy tools that they can use to influence the economy. Now it is time to see how those tools are used in practice. A great deal of discussion goes into deciding what policy is the right one for a government to use in each particular situation. This exercise will help you to determine what issues should be addressed in such discussions, and to evaluate an example of this kind of discussion. The assignment is broken into two parts. In the first part, your task is to read each of the articles from the popular press listed at the bottom of the page. Next, choose one of the articles and develop several insightful questions on that article. You are to develop one question in each of the following categories:

- Content-based
- Interpretive
- Connecting to other course material

Note that the categories involve increasing degrees of complexity. After writing your questions, you are to construct model answers for each of your questions. Your questions and model answers should be submitted to me via email no later than 11am on (the day before the exercise).

The second part of this exercise will occur in class. I will divide the class into groups of three students. Each group will be given three questions to answer on one of the articles listed below. These questions will be drawn from those submitted by students. Each group will formulate its own answer to each of the questions. These answers will then be shared with the class and compared to the model answer submitted with the question.

Each student is expected to contribute to and understand each of the group's answers. I will randomly select one student from each group to report their answer(s) to the class. Answers will be evaluated on their thoroughness and on their proper use of the economic concepts discussed during the semester. Students will also be evaluated on their individual knowledge of the answers to the questions their group received.

The following articles are used for this activity:

"Inflation Continues to Rise," in *The Times of India*, February 15, 2007, available at http://timesofindia.indiatimes.com/articleshow/ 1617538.cms.

"Investing wisely; Bush and Congress have a chance to focus on long-term economic policy. They should seize it." Editorial, *Los Angeles Times*, January 4, 2007, A14.

"European Central Bank Raises Key Rate," by Joellen Perry, *Wall Street Journal*, March 9, 2007, A2.

APPENDIX 4B
U.S. Health Care Reform Project: Introduction Included in the Syllabus

By utilizing the forthcoming presidential election, we will be examining and discussing specific issues pertinent to the U.S. health care system. We will do this through examination of the health care reform proposals of Senator McCain and Senator Obama. You will perform preliminary independent research on one health care reform issue being currently debated. You will then work in a small group to prepare an oral presentation that showcases your group's refined understanding of its health care issue. Group members will be chosen at random to present the various sections of the presentation. As a capstone for this project you will be responsible for writing a 6–8 page paper. For this paper you will be asked to consider yourself a new presidential candidate and then choose and defend your position on each of the health care issues presented in class.

This project will be worth 100 points and will count as 20 percent of your overall grade. Since this project has the same weight as an exam in your overall grade, a significant amount of time and effort is expected. Below is a list of the pertinent dates for this project. Your attendance is mandatory on these days in order to satisfy the requirements of the project: September 29 – Introduction and group formation; October 6 – Group work in class; October 15, 17 – Group presentations; November 3 – Final paper due

APPENDIX 4C
U.S. Health Care Reform Project: Sections Included in Individual/Group Worksheets

Section 1: (1) Define and explain your issue. Provide some background knowledge about your issue. Why is it important? Who does it affect?; (2) Describe the current status of your issue in the U.S. health care system. For example, is it already present in the current system? If yes, to what extent? Include statistics if possible.

Section 2: Provide 2 examples that illustrate your issue. These can be actual cases that you find in your research or hypothetical examples.

Section 3: Discuss how Senator McCain's health care reform proposal addresses this issue. Who would be affected by this proposal and in what way?

Section 4: Discuss how Senator Obama's health care reform proposal addresses this issue. Who would be affected by this proposal and in what way?

APPENDIX 4D
Send-A-Problem Process Instructions
(75-Minute Class)

Beginning of class (10 minutes):

- Students sit in groups as they come in to class
- Students turn in problems to instructor or to facilitators to fax to office
- Each group assigns scribe with blank paper and pen

Round 1 (15 minutes):

- Hand out problems
- Students have 10 minutes to complete a faxable copy of solution
  - At end of Round 1
    - Group 1 gives A to instructor, Group 2 opens A
    - Group 1a sends A to Group 2a
    - Group 2 faxes B to classroom, Group 3 opens B
    - Group 2a sends B to Group 3a
    - Group 3 faxes C to instructor to include in envelope to Groups 1
    - Group 3a sends C to Group 1a

Round 2 (15 minutes):

- Facilitators hand out problems in the remote sites, plus Group 1 opens C
- Students have 10 minutes to complete faxable copy of solution
  - At end of Round 2
    - Group 1 faxes C to Group 2
    - Group 1a sends C to 2a
    - Group 2 faxes A to Group 3
    - Group 2a sends A to Group 3a
    - Group 3 faxes B to Group 1
    - Group 3a sends B to Group 1a

Round 3 (15 minutes):

- Students have 10 minutes to review solution and complete faxable copy
- Group 2 faxes C to classroom
- Group 3 faxes A to classroom

Presentations (15 minutes):

- Problem A by Group 3 Input from Group 3a
- Problem B by Group 1 Input from Group 1a
- Problem C by Group 2 Input from group 2a

  Note: Instructor projects Group 2 and Group 3 solutions while students in remote sites explain their answers. Students in Group 1 project and explain solutions in the classroom.

Wrap-up and preview of the next class (5 minutes)

CHAPTER 5

Conducting Experiments in the Economics Classroom

Denise Hazlett
Kathy A. Paulson Gjerde
José J. Vazquez-Cognet
Judith A. Smrha

A classroom experiment puts students in a controlled environment and asks them to make economic decisions. Their decisions become data the class later analyzes. Participating provides an insider's perspective on economic behavior, often in situations students have not yet encountered in their regular lives. For instance, an experiment can provide first-hand experience with an unfamiliar economic role, such as that of a lender or a producer. Analysis of the experimental results allows students to compare their behavior with theoretical predictions. They draw specific conclusions about the power of economic theory in this special case, and more general conclusions in the abstract. The laboratory experience produces a concrete example that makes tools such as supply and demand easier to understand and to use, bringing these abstract concepts to life.

Participating in experiments and analyzing the results transforms students into investigators who demonstrate economic principles for themselves. In the process, students become informed critics of the applications and limitations of economic theory. For instance, a student skeptical of the claim that markets reach equilibrium becomes convinced when he or she observes the effect of the invisible hand in the laboratory. Students will extrapolate from the laboratory to other market situations, coming to recognize the wide-ranging applications of economic principles. What's more, they will consider how the textbook description of a market compares to the many real-world versions. Students thus draw conclusions about how theory fits particular circumstances. While learning some of the limits of stylized economic models, students also come to appreciate the ability of the models to predict economic behavior.

A good experiment provides frequent opportunities for students to make decisions, so that the activity holds their interest. Students make sufficiently complicated decisions to prevent tedium, but not so complicated as to cause frustration. Preparing for such an experiment requires commitment on the part of the instructor, and running it uses valuable class time. The payback comes when students become excited participants and enthusiastic analysts of their results. They tend to remember the conclusions they themselves draw from experiments, making the experience and results a valuable reference tool during the course. Even one experiment early on can provide the basis for examples that later help introduce complicated concepts.

The past two decades have seen dramatic developments in the design of classroom experiments covering numerous economic concepts at various levels of instruction. Yet despite the wide variety of new experiments, instructors still sometimes find they need to spend significant time and effort modifying an experiment to make it meet their goals. Sometimes that modification involves extending the experiment by adding preparation or debriefing assignments. In other cases, the instructor changes the experiment itself in order to overcome a particular hurdle. For example, few experiments accommodate participation by all of the students in a large enrollment course. Similarly, few experimental designs take into consideration the special needs of a student with a disability such as sight impairment.

This chapter describes how three economics instructors adapted existing experiments to meet their course goals. Kathy Paulson Gjerde extended the Bergstrom and Miller (2000) minimum wage experiment to include a student preparation assignment and follow-up exam questions. José Vazquez-Cognet modified the basic double oral auction experiment so that all 500 of his students could participate. Judith Smrha modified a trading experiment to make it work for a class that included a sight-impaired student.

I. FACTORS TO CONSIDER IN CONDUCTING EXPERIMENTS

Conducting a classroom experiment requires attention to many different factors. This chapter focuses on preparing students for an experiment, setting up the experiment, creating an effective learning environment for the experiment, and following up to check student learning.

First, conducting a meaningful classroom experiment involves significant planning, including considering the following questions: (1) What are your learning objectives for the experiment?; (2) What background information will your students need to have before they participate in the experiment; and, (3) What will you do to insure that they have this background information for their use with the experiment?

Second, the instructor prepares the materials, physical space and support personnel, keeping in mind the following questions: (1) What materials will you need to run the experiment?; and, (2) What logistical issues will you face in conducting the experiment, such as reserving a computer lab, rearranging furniture in a standard classroom, distributing handouts, collecting data, and hiring a student assistant?

Third, effective experiment design is influenced by the students themselves. For instance, students vary in terms of their exposure and openness to experiential learning. In addition, they differ in their functional knowledge as well as in their mastery of more general skills, such as communication, critical thinking, and teamwork. Thus, understanding class composition is critical for effectively adapting an experiment. Questions to consider in this context include: (1) What are the prerequisites for your class?; (2) How much knowledge of economics do your students have?; (3) How comfortable are your students working in teams?; (4) How much exposure have your students had to active learning techniques?; (5) In how many experiments have your students previously participated?; (6) What was the nature and content of the experiments in which your students previously participated?; and, (7) Are there students with physical or learning disabilities in your class?

Finally, running the experiment is not the end of the story. In order to ensure that the learning objectives are achieved, it is important to follow up at multiple points in the course. Questions to consider when designing appropriate follow-up activities include: (1) What data will you collect during the experiment?; (2) How will you collect the data from the experiment?; (3) How will you make the experiment data available to the students?; (4) What questions will you ask to help students analyze the results of the experiment and achieve your instructional objectives?; (5) What reporting format (laboratory report, class discussion, a combination of the two) will you use for asking questions about the experiment?; (6) How will you evaluate whether you have met your instructional objectives with the experiment?; (7) What evidence will you collect for the evaluation?; and, (8) When will you collect the evidence for the evaluation?

What follows are the descriptions of three experiments and their adaption for use in economics courses. Each one illustrates how an economics instructor addresses some of the questions posed in the above lists.

II. THE MINIMUM WAGE EXPERIMENT
Kathy A. Paulson Gjerde

The successful use of an experiment in the classroom begins with appropriate set-up. Research findings suggest that one of the key factors to consider in creating an effective environment is context. In particular, it has been found that students are typically more highly motivated and therefore learn more when instructors utilize contextual strategies (Predmore 2005). Thus, it is important for students to clearly understand the real-world relevance of what they are doing in the classroom. It also helps if students relate to the activities on a personal level. Establishing this connection prior to the experiment draws students into the classroom experience and encourages them to seek answers to their questions.

Preparatory activities not only motivate students, they also assist the instructor in identifying students' preexisting knowledge and misconceptions. Prior research suggests that the extent to which the instructor is able to identify and address preexisting knowledge has a direct impact on student learning outcomes (Bransford, Brown, and Cocking 2000). For instance, a study of the use of preparatory exercises in science courses suggests that such warm-up activities are an effective means of capturing preexisting knowledge, reinforcing class content, and increasing active learning. In order to be effective, however, the preparatory activities should incorporate scenarios with which students are familiar and that require students to speculate or ask "why" (Marrs, Blake, and Gavrin 2003). Using similar follow-up exercises has the potential to enhance learning even more.

When Kathy Paulson Gjerde used Bergstrom and Miller's minimum wage experiment, her objectives were to illustrate the effects of a price control and to expose her students to the concepts of voluntary and involuntary unemployment. What follows is a description of the experiment and the preparation and follow-up activities she used with her 29 principles of microeconomics students.

The Experiment

In this market, the good that is bought and sold is labor, and the relevant price is the wage rate. The instructor divides students into two groups: workers and firms. They use a double oral auction to arrange transactions among themselves. That is, they freely move about the classroom calling out offers to work or offers to hire, at wages they specify. A worker may be hired by at most one firm in a given round of the experiment, and need not stay with the same employer in subsequent rounds.

For the students representing workers, the instructor assigns some a low opportunity cost of working (reservation wage of $5), and the others a high opportunity cost (reservation wage of $12). A worker's opportunity cost is private information. Each round a worker can either take a job or remain unemployed. If hired, the worker earns the wage he negotiated with his employer. An unemployed worker earns a payoff equal to his reservation wage. The worker's objective is to maximize his earnings.

In the first phase of the experiment, each firm can hire zero, one, or two workers per round. The value of a firm's output in a round is $0 if it hires no workers, $20 if it hires one worker, and $30 if it hires two workers. These values are private information. A firm's profit is equal to the total value of its output minus the total wages paid. The firm's objective is to maximize its profits.

The instructor runs several rounds of the experiment under this set of conditions. After convergence to the equilibrium occurs, the instructor introduces a legal minimum wage for the subsequent rounds. The instructor sets the minimum wage to bind, resulting in an increase in both the wage and the amount of involuntary unemployment, compared to the initial equilibrium. Again, the instructor runs several rounds of the experiment. After convergence to the new equilibrium occurs, the instructor starts the next round by announcing a different set of hiring conditions for the firms. The number of workers each firm can hire per round increases to four, with the value of a firm's output being $0, $30, $55, $75 or $95 if it hires zero, one, two, three or four workers, respectively. Workers know that a change in firm values has occurred, but the values remain private information. The minimum wage law is still in effect, but due to the increase in the demand for labor, the minimum wage no longer binds.

Prior to running the experiment, clearly defining the experiment grading policy helps encourage student effort. One option is to simply give students points for participating in the experiment. A second option is to award extra credit points to the two firms and the two workers with the greatest cumulative earnings over all phases and rounds. Alternatively, the instructor can grade each student based on the difference between the gain that a student earns in the experiment and the predicted gain for this student based on her assigned role. This grading option works best with the first and third phases of the experiment, in which there is no binding minimum wage, but can be used in the second phase as well. Kathy Paulson Gjerde has found that students generally respond favorably to this grading scheme when she runs multiple rounds for each phase of the experiment and averages performance across all phases and rounds. In this case, one or two rounds in which the student's gain is less than predicted are more palatable because the performance within a single round does not have a substantial impact on the overall experiment grade. To soften the grading scheme, performance windows can also be used (e.g., if gain is within $2 of expected gain, the student receives all points).

Preparing Students

Prior to conducting the experiment, the instructor takes several steps to ensure that students come adequately prepared. First, the instructor helps students reach a solid understanding of how a free market works. Kathy Paulson Gjerde used a combination of traditional classroom instruction, a basic double-oral-auction market experiment run via the online instructional company Aplia and followed by the Aplia experiment post-test, plus an in-class exam covering the concepts of supply and demand. Then in the class meeting before running the minimum wage experiment, she distributed a recent newspaper article that focused on the minimum wage in the United States. She used the *Wall Street Journal* article, "Economy Not Likely to Flinch as Many Get Raises" (Maher 2007). A news article makes the experiment more relevant to students by tying it to recent events. Thus, the more recent the article, the better. She led a class discussion based on this article, asking the following questions about students' perceptions of the minimum wage and the personal impact it could have on them.

Discussion Questions

1. List all the paid job(s) you have had to date. Indicate the wage rate for each job.
2. Based on your past work experience, would you have benefited from an increase in the minimum wage? Would your friends and/or family members have benefited from an increase in the minimum wage?
3. In general, are you in favor of having a minimum wage? Why or why not? If so, at what dollar amount do you think the minimum wage should be set? Explain.

Finally, her students did warm-up exercises similar to those Bergstrom and Miller suggest. These exercises familiarize students with the specific mechanics of the minimum wage experiment, including the relevant calculations.

Outcomes and Interesting Developments

Because students feel comfortable with the concept of a free market before the experiment begins, they focus their attention not on the mechanics of how a market works, but on the potentially significant role the government can play in altering the market outcome. In addition, the newspaper article provides students with evidence that the minimum wage is much more than a clever classroom experiment. In fact, it is a real issue in the news that impacts multiple groups of people, including the students. After reading the article, but before participating in the experiment, students tend to think of an increase in the minimum wage as a very favorable policy, i.e., government is "doing its job" by ensuring a "reasonable standard of living" for its citizens, particularly as it relates to their current part-time earnings potential. These students' opinions quickly change, however, when they find themselves standing in the experiment's unemployment line the next class period, unable to find a job. It is precisely this contrast between the pre-experiment discussion and the experiment outcome that helps students remember what they learned from the activity.

The Follow Up

So that students can complete the Bergstrom and Miller laboratory report assignment, the instructor gives students the following information: the distribution of types of firms and workers, the number of workers unemployed (by type) in the last round of each phase, and the wages paid to workers by each firm in the last round of each phase. This was the first time Kathy Paulson Gjerde used the Bergstrom and Miller laboratory report as a graded assignment that students completed on their own. She made it due in class the day of the debriefing, and then used the debriefing discussion to clarify and reinforce the primary learning objectives of the activity.

Several weeks later, her students completed an in-class exam containing questions related to the experiment. However, in order to emphasize the relationship between this price control experiment and other market applications and extensions, the mid-term exam had a broader focus than the experiment alone. Finally, her last experiment follow-up occurred at the end of the semester in the form of a final exam that included several experiment-related questions. See Appendix 5A for these questions.

Further Comments

Using this strategy in a principles of microeconomics class seemed to be effective. In particular, students came to the debriefing much more motivated to learn than they had in past experiments. However, in terms of retention of material, student performance on the experiment-related mid-term exam questions was not encouraging. In fact, results suggested that only about half of the students seemed to grasp (and retain) the underlying concepts of the experiment. Although initially disappointed, Kathy Paulson Gjerde observed that students did better on final exam questions relating to the experiment, particularly relative to the scores earned by students in semesters without this extensive follow-up approach. Thus, the frequency of follow-up appeared to play a significant role in student learning.

An interesting side note is that her students reacted more positively to and seemed to learn more from the in-class minimum wage experiment than had their counterparts in previous semesters who participated in an online version of a similar experiment. Somehow seeing the unemployment line physically form made an impression on them. In contrast, unemployment in the virtual world was just a source of frustration. In that setting, students tended to blame their failure to get a job on their inability to type quickly. The students who participated in the in-class version developed a much better understanding of how the dynamics of the labor market caused their unemployment.

III. MODIFYING THE DOUBLE ORAL AUCTION EXPERIMENT FOR LARGE ENROLLMENT COURSES

José J. Vazquez-Cognet

Materials and logistical issues for conducting experiments pose particular problems in large classes, typically taught in auditorium-style classrooms with vast sections of immobile seats separated by aisles. Suggestions for overcoming these problems generally involve running the experiment in small discussion sections, or having a subset of the class participate while the rest observe (Holt 1996). One drawback to the latter approach is that the incentive to pay attention for the observers is not commensurate with that of the participants. Therefore, it is difficult to maintain the interest of the entire class using this mainly passive experimental design.

Instructors' hesitancy in running experiments in large classes is unfortunate for two reasons. First, many university students take their first economics courses in classrooms with at least 100 students. When experiments are only used in courses with lower enrollments, a large proportion of economics students are not being exposed to this alternative method of teaching. Moreover, because large classes can be particularly prone to student passivity, one could argue that students in these classes are the ones who most need active-learning activities, such as experiments, which engage students in more active and innovative ways (Buckles and Hoyt 2005). Second, large enrollment classes create a set of dynamics impossible to replicate in their much smaller counterparts. For instance, in an auction-style experiment where students participate in a hypothetical supply-and-demand market, convergence to equilibrium in a large class could occur at a much different rate than that of a small class. In fact, it could be argued that large classes should assimilate the "many buyers and sellers" assumptions of a competitive market better than a small class. In addition, data collected from an experiment in a large class should be more robust given the larger number of observations.

As described below, José Vazquez-Cognet redesigned and modified the double oral auction experiment so that every one of his 500 students could participate. In doing so, he had to deal with many material and logistical issues.

The Experiment

Perhaps the most popular classroom economics experiment has been the double-oral-auction experiment, first developed in the late 1940s (Chamberlin 1948). In this experiment, students engage in a hypothetical market for widgets, with a set of students assigned the roles of buyers and another the roles of sellers. Buyer values (i.e., their reservation prices) and seller costs are distributed to each student at the beginning of the class. Buyers and sellers make price bids/offers orally in hopes of striking a deal. The goal of each student is to try to make the most earnings during the experiment. Sellers and buyers make earnings according to their costs and values, respectively. If the seller can arrange to sell a widget at a price above his/her cost, then the seller earns a profit equal to the difference between the price and the cost. Similarly, a buyer earns a profit by arranging a purchase at a price that is below the reservation price assigned to him/her.

There have been numerous adaptations of this general experiment structure to teach many different economic concepts. Nevertheless, for the most part, the experiment has been used in classes with fewer than 100 students. However, the logistical challenges are manageable in the context of this experiment, while still allowing everyone to participate in one market.

Limited Space for Mobility

The typical seating arrangement in large classes limits the common space for interaction among students. Therefore, experiments requiring students to interact in a pre-assigned area of the room are generally hard to implement in a large class. In particular, it is difficult to create the necessary space for the trading pit commonly used in double-oral-auction experiments. Even when space for a trading pit does exist, long seat rows make accessing it difficult for students seated in the middle of the rows.

Some minor adjustments can overcome the space and mobility problem. First, even if students do not move outside of the confines of their seat area, they do have some mobility. For instance, a student seated at the center of a row could stand up and easily conduct transactions with at least two students in each of four directions: front, back, right, and left. That radius results in eight possible trading partners. Thus, a large classroom can become numerous overlapping trading pits accessible to students from their seats.

Difficulty in Distributing and Collecting Information

Distributing and collecting information presents two separate sets of challenges for the instructor. With 50 students in a classroom, it is possible for the instructor to distribute separate pages of instructions, role assignments, and record-keeping sheets at the beginning of the class period and introduce the major intricacies of the experiment to the class, all in about 15 minutes. With 500 students in a classroom, this is a whole different story. Parker (1995) states that one of the criteria for a conducting a classroom experiment is for students to be able to learn the roles of participants quickly. José Vazquez-Cognet met this criterion by limiting the hard copy material (instructions, worksheets, etc.) to one page. This limit considerably reduces idling time at the beginning of the experiment. He also advises his students to arrive a little early and warns them that the doors will close at the official starting time of class. Because latecomers would miss out on bonus points they could have earned from participating, students arrive on time.

Data collection presents similar challenges. There are two main reasons why data collection is an important part of an experimental activity. First, many experimental designs require the instructor to collect results in real time (Holt 1996) for each round and present this information to students so they can use it in future rounds. Second, the results are usually gathered at the end of the activity and offered to students for future assignments and discussions. This post-experiment analysis serves to reinforce the concepts presented by allowing students to further assimilate the classroom experience (Bergstrom and Miller 2000; Holt 1996; Hazlett 2006). Real-time data collection typically requires students to report their transactions either verbally or by turning in some document. While precise data collection would be almost impossible in a classroom with more than 100 students without some sort of technical aid such as clickers, it is possible to collect approximate data by calling for a show of hands from students.

Difficulty in Monitoring the Activity

The last logistical challenge associated with running experiments in a large class has to do with monitoring students during the experiment. Obviously, one of the requirements for running a classroom experiment successfully is to prevent students from breaking the rules. Rampant cheating during the experiment frustrates students who behave legally and diminishes the pedagogical benefits for students who behave illegally. The instructor can make the penalty for breaking the rules quite high by tying an incentive such as extra credit points to experimental performance. When extra credit points are directly connected to performance during the game, students often are more concerned with the costs of cheating (i.e., losing the extra credit) than with benefits of the illegal activity. This policing works even in the presence of a low probability of enforcement, which the instructor can produce inexpensively by having assistants walking around the room talking to students. Although it may be impossible to eliminate illegal activity entirely, the use of random checks and disincentives seems to reduce it considerably.

Running the Double Oral Auction Experiment in a Large Class

As soon as students are seated, the instructor distributes the instructions and student record-keeping worksheets. These two documents are contained on one single-spaced sheet with instructions on one side and a record-keeping worksheet on the other. Appendix 5B contains the instructions and two example record-keeping worksheets, one for a seller and one for a buyer. Note that the record-keeping sheet assigns the role of seller or buyer, and assigns a cost (if a seller) or consumption value (if a buyer). Before coming to class, the instructor sorts these sheets so that each area of the room will have roughly the same composition of seller costs and consumption values.

The instructor begins class by reading and discussing the instructions. After explaining the rules and answering student questions, the instructor begins the first round. Students have one minute to make trades in each round. They can price in increments as fine as $0.50. After each round, the instructor counts the number of transactions at different price ranges by calling for a show of hands. For instance, to find out how many students bought and sold at a price of $2.00 or $2.50, the instructor states, "If you are a seller AND ONLY A SELLER and you sold at a price of either $2.00 or $2.50, raise your hand." The instructor and assistant(s) count the hands and write, on an overhead slide, that number next to that price range. See Appendix 5C for a copy of the slide. The reason for using a price range when asking for a show of hands is to limit the number of questions the instructor needs to ask. After counting and recording trades at the rest of the price ranges, the instructor can either engage students in a little discussion or simply leave them to use this information in subsequent rounds.

After the second round, low-value buyers and high-cost sellers typically complain about the unfairness of the process, because they have not been able to make any trades. Therefore, at this point the instructor introduces a government-type mechanism, such as a price ceiling or floor, in order to help those students who have either low values or high costs. As expected, this modification is initially well-received by these low-value buyers or high-cost sellers. Yet, they quickly realize their misjudgment when they are still generally unable to find trading partners. As the model of supply and demand predicts, these price controls make the group as a whole worse off by reducing the total number of transactions. As has been pointed out before, this result is one of the most revealing parts of this experiment, and it works in a large class just as well as in a small class.

The instructor then switches the roles in order to give the unfortunate extra-marginal students a chance to make trades. An efficient way to accomplish this goal is to convert low-value buyers to low-cost sellers and high-cost sellers to high-value buyers, using the following instructions: "If you were a buyer, cross out the word 'buyer's value' and replace it with the word 'seller's costs.' Now Subtract 3 from whatever costs you have. You are all now Sellers and those are your Seller Costs." Similarly, the instructor says to sellers: "If you were a seller, cross out the word 'seller's costs' and replace it with the word 'buyer's value.' Add 3 to whatever values you have. You are now a buyer and those are your buyer's values." The experiment is run for a few more rounds and then the instructor debriefs.

Outcomes and Interesting Developments

The rule that students stay in the general area of their seat and do not go out into the aisles does not seem to present a problem for the dynamics of the experiment. Students are quite resourceful and expand their range of trades considerably. For instance, students often make trades with people sitting two or three rows above or below their own. In fact, some people actually stand on their seats in order to get better deals! As a result, each sub-market turns out to be much larger than one might think.

The method of collecting real-time data by calling for a show of hands works well in the large classroom. Even though collecting information by price ranges is less precise than if students reported their exact prices, it is comprehensive enough to encourage students to alter their behavior in subsequent rounds. Furthermore, this process of counting hands even has an advantage over the traditional method of having students come up to a blackboard or computer to report the transaction, because the show of hands drives home where the equilibrium is. It is dramatic for students to see how many hands go up when the instructor calls out the range that includes the equilibrium price, especially in a class with hundreds of students. For instance, when there are twelve different roles, with seller costs ranging from \$2.00 to \$7.00 and buyer values ranging from \$5.00 to \$10.00 (in increments of \$1.00), the equilibrium price would be \$6.00. When this experiment was used in a class of 500 students, 60 percent of all the transactions occurred in the $6.00–$6.50 range in the first round, and 95 percent of all transactions occurred in that range in the second round. Similarly rapid convergence occurred in classes with enrollments of 180 and 200 students.

This information is also more than adequate for the debriefing part of the activity. Although many students are eager to talk about the results of the experiment, both during and afterwards, it is clear that in a large class the incentive to speak diminishes dramatically with the number of students. For this reason, it helps if the instructor prepares a series of discussion questions, and hands them out at the end of the experiment. These questions appear in Appendix 5D. Students work on the questions in groups of two for 10 minutes, and then the instructor leads a discussion based on the questions. The whole activity, from the instructions through the debriefing, takes about 40–45 minutes, regardless of the number of students participating.

Finally, cheating has not been a major problem during any of the runs of the experiment. Using one assistant for every 100 students to perform random checks during the experiment seems to provide sufficient incentive to play fair. This loose monitoring, along with the disincentive of losing bonus points if caught, seems to work well in reducing illegal behavior.

José Vazquez-Cognet's experience suggests that the main issues associated with using the double oral auction experiment in large classes can be overcome relatively easily. Moreover, he found that incorporating this learning tool in a large-class setting even offers some beneficial dynamics not present in a small class or a subdivision of a large class. First, consider the issue of convergence to equilibrium. Given the large number of students participating, the probability of almost complete convergence to equilibrium is very high. In fact, convergence happens rather quickly, allowing the instructor to introduce new conditions, such as price controls, early in the class period and still complete the entire activity, including follow-up discussion, in a 45-minute class.

Second, a large classroom offers a more dramatic picture of a real market than a small trading pit in the middle of the classroom. Students are usually in a state of shock when the instructor reveals how consistent the results are, after they have just experienced the noisy randomness of 500 people trading in a closed space. Nothing can drive the point of the invisible hand better than this example. This point has been noted quite frequently by students in their course evaluations at the end of the semester. Many of them cite this activity as the single most important example of the supply-and-demand model during the semester. In the words of one student, "I have no problem believing the market can work well after seeing some consistency out of the mess we created in the classroom the day of the experiment."

IV. ADAPTING A MEDIUM-OF-EXCHANGE EXPERIMENT FOR SIGHT-IMPAIRED STUDENTS

Judith A. Smrha

While it is relatively straightforward to deal with some class composition issues, some differences present more challenges. For example, many instructors are observing that increasing numbers of students are being diagnosed with a variety of learning disabilities during their K–12 years. As a result, college instructors have more students asking us to help them navigate the expectations within our courses in light of the difficulties they have processing information presented orally or in writing. In those cases, good pedagogy suggests we should present information in multiple formats to make it accessible. In fact, accommodations or modifications implemented for the benefit of a student facing some specific disability or learning challenge might also enable more effective learning for other students.

Given the graphical nature of the way in which we typically present economic theory, many of us have become quite dependent on using visual tools for students. This use addresses their need to have information communicated in ways beyond text-based or verbal communication. But what do you do if one of your students is completely blind? Is it possible to adapt a classroom experiment so both the visual learners and the nonsighted students find the experience accessible and informative? Judy Smrha modified a money-as-a-medium-exchange experiment and used it with the 19 students in her principles of macroeconomics course, one of whom was blind.

The Experiment

Hazlett (2003) describes a classroom trading experiment she adapted from the Duffy and Ochs (1999) research experiment based on the Kiyotaki and Wright (1989) search model of money. Traders in Hazlett's experiment meet randomly, in pairs, and face a double coincidence of wants problem. Over a series of trading rounds, the consumption good with the lowest storage cost spontaneously emerges as a generally accepted medium of exchange, i.e., an item that many students are willing to accept not for consumption, but because they hope to trade it later for their consumption good. Participating in the experiment allows students to experience the social conditions that give rise to money, namely specialized production and decentralized trade. The experiment also demonstrates how a particular characteristic, such as low storage cost, makes a commodity a good candidate for becoming money.

In the experiment, there are roughly equal numbers of three types of players, each of whom wishes to consume one of three types of goods. The instructor gives students nametags to indicate their assigned types:

- Player Type 1: consumes only good Type 1 and produces one unit of good Type 2 every time she consumes a unit of good Type 1.
- Player Type 2: consumes only good Type 2 and produces one unit of good Type 3 every time she consumes a unit of good Type 2.
- Player Type 3: consumes only good Type 3 and produces one unit of good Type 1 every time she consumes a unit of good Type 3.

At the start of each trading round, students are randomly paired.[1] They come into the first round holding their own production good. Each round, they must decide whether to offer to trade the good they are holding for the good the other person is holding. Trade occurs if both people are willing. No one can hold more than one good at any time.

Players receive 20 points each time they consume their desired good. These points represent the satisfaction they get from consumption. Because storing a good between rounds is costly, players lose points each round that depends on the good. The costs per round of storing goods are: one point for Good 1; four points for Good 2; nine points for Good 3. Every student stores a good between rounds. For instance, a student who does not trade will store the good he continues to hold. A student who trades for an item that is not his consumption good will store that item. Finally, a student who receives in trade his consumption good, and therefore automatically produces, will store his production good. A player's objective in the experiment is to maximize the sum of her points over all the rounds of the experiment. The instructor does not tell students how many rounds the experiment will last.

The Modified Set-Up

To make recognition of the consumption goods visually unique and readily identifiable to a nonsighted person, Judy Smrha's modification uses colored shapes (red squares, yellow rectangles, and green cylinders) for the goods. She provides wooden blocks with these colors and shapes so students can hold and trade them physically. After "consuming" an item obtained in trade, students return it to the instructor and receive the appropriate "produced" item in exchange. In contrast, Hazlett does not have students trading physical objects, but has the trades occurring implicitly, as is typically done in a double-oral-auction experiment. In Judy Smrha's modification, the student nametag shows the object representing that player's type.[2] Seeing a physical object representing each good/person type is an easy way for most students to track what is going on, and the distinct shapes enable the nonsighted student to identify each item by touch. All other aspects of the framework remain as described in Hazlett (2003). The instructions and record-keeping sheet for the experiment, with Judy Smrha's modifications, appear in Appendix 5E.[3]

Outcomes and Interesting Developments

Thinking in terms of accommodations or modifications, it is important to enable students to quickly and accurately grasp the parameters and incentives designed to influence their decision-making. They must understand what they are supposed to be doing and make decisions that fit the rules and constraints built into the experiment. While the modification described above is designed to accommodate the needs of a nonsighted student, the other students in the class may also gain from the modification. In particular, it allows them to quickly and accurately comprehend the information they need to make the primary decision of the experiment: Do I want to offer to trade for the item that my current partner has? Ironically, it is the visual nature of the modification that provides this benefit for the sighted students – the fact that there is a tangible object held by each student that is easily identifiable by its shape and color, rather than the hypothetical possession of, for instance, "Good 2" in Hazlett's design. Making the concept of the good more concrete by giving it a physical existence can be powerful. Using the visual cues inherent in tangible objects speeds up the students' ability to comprehend information and allows them to focus the majority of their attention on the logical or mathematical calculations necessary to achieve their objective.

V. CONCLUSION

We are convinced that experiments work best when they encourage all students to actively participate at the decision-making stage and in the debriefing. This chapter describes innovations that make participating in an experiment and analyzing the results accessible to all of the students in a class. We describe modifications to existing experiments, either by adding preparation and debriefing assignments that stimulate student interest, or by changing the experimental design to overcome barriers imposed by large class size or the sight impairment of a student. We offer this description of our efforts in hopes of encouraging other instructors to think of ways to make experiments work for their students.

NOTES

1. The method for pairing students developed by Hazlett involves the use of numbered stations around the room and an Excel file that randomly assigns two students to each station each round. This is the method Judy Smrha used to implement the experiment.
2. Some instructors might want to reduce the level of complexity in the way items are labeled, and stick with either "squares, rectangles and cylinders," or

alternatively (if the class had all sighted students, none of whom are color-blind), "red, yellow and green."

3. Note that the name of the experiment is simply "The Trading Experiment." Avoiding any reference to money in the experiment's title and instructions allows students to experience money arising endogenously rather than being imposed (or even suggested) from outside.

REFERENCES

Bergstrom, T., and J. Miller (2000), *Experiments with Economic Principles* (2nd ed.), Boston: Irwin McGraw-Hill.

Bransford, J.D., A.L. Brown, and R.R. Cocking (eds) (2000), *How People Learn: Brain, Mind, Experience and School*, Washington D.C.: National Academy Press.

Buckles, S., and G. Hoyt (2006), "Active learning in the large lecture economics class," in W.E. Becker, M. Watts, and S.R. Becker (eds), *Teaching Economics: More Alternatives to Chalk and Talk*, Cheltenham, UK and Northampton, MA, USA: Edward Elgar, 75–88.

Chamberlin, E.H. (1948), "An experimental imperfect market," *Journal of Political Economy*, **56**, 95–108.

Duffy, J., and J. Ochs (1999), "Emergence of money as a medium of exchange: An experimental study," *American Economic Review*, **89** (4), 847–77.

Hazlett, D. (2003), "A search-theoretic classroom experiment with money," *International Review of Economics Education*, **2** (1), 80–90.

Hazlett, D. (2006), "Using classroom experiments to teach economics," in W.E. Becker, M. Watts, and S.R. Becker (eds), *Teaching Economics: More Alternatives to Chalk and Talk*, Cheltenham, UK and Northampton, MA, USA: Edward Elgar, 21–37.

Holt, C.A. (1996), "Classroom games: Trading in a pit market," *Journal of Economic Perspectives*, **10** (1), 193–203.

Kiyotaki, N., and R. Wright (1989), "On money as a medium of exchange," *Journal of Political Economy*, **97** (4), 927–54.

Maher, K. (2007), "Economy not likely to flinch as many get raises," *The Wall Street Journal*, July 21, A2.

Marrs, K.A., R.E. Blake, and A.D. Gavrin (2003), "Web-based warm-up exercises in just-in-time teaching," *Journal of College Science Teaching*, **33** (1), 42–47.

Parker, J. (1995), *Economics 210 Instructor's Laboratory Manual*, Reed College working manuscript.

Predmore, S.R. (2005), "Putting it into context," *Techniques*, January, 22–25.

APPENDIX 5A
Exam Questions for the Minimum Wage Experiment

Minimum Wage Experiment: Sample Exam Questions

Multiple Choice:

Answer the following 2 questions based on the table below. Assume the wage rate is $3 per worker.

Number of Workers	Total Value of Output
0	0
1	$2
2	$12
3	$20
4	$26
5	$30
6	$32

1. The marginal value product of the 2nd worker is:
   a. $2 b. $6 c. $10 d. $12

2. To maximize profit, how many workers should the firm hire?
   a. 2 b. 3 c. 4 d. 5

Problems:

1. In class, we conducted an experiment to explore the effects of a minimum wage in a labor market. Suppose the experiment is run again under the following conditions.

   WORKERS: There are 45 workers with a reservation wage of $4 and 45 workers with a reservation wage of $10.

   FIRMS: There are 30 firms. Each firm can hire 0, 1, or 2 workers. A single firm's total value of output at different hiring levels is indicated in the table below.

Number of Workers	Total Value of Output
0	$0
1	$15
2	$22

a. Draw the supply and demand curves for the labor market described above.
b. What is the equilibrium wage in this market and the equilibrium level of employment?
c. What is the number of voluntarily unemployed workers in equilibrium? What is the number of involuntarily unemployed workers in equilibrium?
d. Now suppose a minimum wage of $9 is imposed on this labor market. What is the prevailing wage in this market after the minimum wage is put into place? What is the level of employment?
e. After the minimum wage is put into place, what is the number of voluntarily unemployed workers? What is the number of involuntarily unemployed workers?
f. According to a recent *Wall Street Journal* article:

> The federal minimum wage went up on July 1 and hardly anyone noticed. The insignificance of the latest wage hike is surprising in view of the intensity of the political debates that preceded it. Liberal Democrats had proclaimed that two million workers would benefit directly from a federal wage hike and millions more would benefit from bumping up the entire wage scale. Republicans warned that a legislated wage hike would cause a labor-market apocalypse, destroying the very entry-level jobs that low-income workers so desperately need to get a toehold on economic security.

Explain under what conditions an increase in the minimum wage may actually be a non-event in the labor market.

APPENDIX 5B
Double Oral Auction Instructions and Example Record-Keeping Sheets

Class Game: TRADING IN A PIT MARKET

Traders' Instructions
We are going to set up a market in which some students will play the role of buyers and some students will play the role of sellers. The goods to be traded are WIDGETS. Your role in this market is described in your *Student Record Sheet*. Please do not show your record sheet to others.

Trading: Staying in the general area of their seats (you can stand up if you want) buyers and sellers will negotiate during a one-minute trading period. **Prices must be multiples of 50 cents.** When a buyer and a seller agree on a price, they will record in each of their respective record sheets: 1) the negotiated price, 2) the profits made, and 3) the name of the person they traded with. ANY TRANSACTION THAT DOESN'T INCLUDE THE NAME OF THE PERSON YOU TRADED WITH WILL BE INVALIDATED. There will be several market periods.

Sellers: You can each sell a single widget during a trading period. The number on your *Student Record Sheet* is the dollar cost that you incur to make 1 widget. You will be required to sell at a price that is no lower than that cost. Your earnings on the sale are calculated as the difference between the price that you negotiate and the cost number on your *Student Record Sheet*. If you do not make a sale, you do not earn anything or incur any cost in that period. Suppose that your cost is a \$2.00 and you negotiate a sale price of \$3.50. Then you would earn: \$3.50 − \$2 = \$1.50. So, if your seller cost is \$2.00, you would not be allowed to sell at a price below \$2.00. If you mistakenly agree to a price that is below your cost, then the trade will be invalidated.

STUDENT RECORD SHEET: SELLER

TYPE A: SELLER YOU ARE A SELLER Name: ______________________

SELLER COST = \$2.00 TA: ______________________

In this experiment, you are a widget seller. Your seller price is \$2.00. THIS IS THE COST YOU INCUR TO MAKE ONE WIDGET AND ALSO THE MINIMUM PRICE YOU WOULD ACCEPT TO SELL ONE WIDGET. So, if you sell a widget for a price of \$P, your profit is \$P − \$2.00. If you don't sell any widgets, your profit is \$0. **You are not allowed to make trades that result in negative profits!!!**
Every time you sell a widget please record the price you receive, the name of the person you traded with, and the profits you made. If you do not sell any widgets, simply mark an X under both price and profits.

Round # 1

______	−	\$2.00	=	______
(Price)		(Cost)		(Profits)

Buyer's Name ______________________________________

Total Profits for the Whole Game = ______________________

Buyers: You can each buy a single widget during a trading period. The number on your *Student Record Sheet* is the dollar value that you receive if you make a purchase. You will be required to buy at a price that is no higher than that value. Your earnings on the purchase are calculated as the difference between the value number on your *Student Record Sheet* and the price that you negotiate. If you do not make a purchase, you do not earn anything in the period. Suppose that your value is $9.00 and you negotiate a purchase price of $4.00. Then you would earn: $9 − $4 = $5. So, if your buyer value is $9.00, you would not be allowed to buy at a price above $9.00. If you mistakenly agree to a price that is above your value, then the trade will be invalidated.

STUDENT RECORD SHEET: BUYER

TYPE A: BUYER *YOU ARE A BUYER* *Name:* ______________________
BUYER VALUE = $10.00 *TA:* ______________________

In this experiment, you are a widget buyer. Your buyer value is $10.00. THIS IS THE MAXIMUM YOU ARE WILLING TO PAY FOR A WIDGET. So, if you buy a widget for a price of $P, your profit is $10 − $P. If you don't buy any widgets, your profit is $0. **You are not allowed to make trades that result in negative profits!!!**
Every time you buy a widget please record the price you paid, the name of the person you traded with, and the profits you made. If you do not buy any widgets, simply mark an X under both price and profits.

Round # 1

$10.00 – ______ = ______
(Value) (Price) (Profits)

Seller's Name ____

Total Profits for the Whole Game = ______________________

Recording Earnings: Some sellers with high costs and some buyers with low values may not be able to negotiate a trade, but do not be discouraged since I may intervene in future rounds to make things more equal. Remember that earnings are zero for any widget not bought or sold (sellers incur no cost and buyers receive no value). At the end of the game your total earnings equal the sum of earnings for widgets traded in all periods. Please do not talk with each other until the trading period begins. Are there any questions?

Final Observations: Remember, although you're not allowed to move from the general area of your seat, you can move. As a matter of fact, in order to obtain the best possible price it is a good strategy to move and try to trade with different people on each period.

Everyone ready? BEGIN CALLING OUT PRICES AT WHICH YOU ARE WILLING TO BUY OR SELL. You have one minute remaining.

APPENDIX 5C
Price Table for the Double Oral Auction Experiment

Questions for **Sellers** Only

How many of you sold a widget for:

Price	Number of transactions					
	Round					
	1	2	3	4	5	6
\$2.00 or \$2.50						
\$3.00 or \$3.50						
\$4.00 or \$4.50						
\$5.00 or \$5.50						
\$6.00 or \$6.50						
\$7.00 or \$7.50						
\$8.00 or \$8.50						

APPENDIX 5D
Discussion Questions for the Double Oral Auction Debrief

Class Game: TRADING IN A PIT MARKET

Discussion Points

1. What happened during the game?
2. Who do you think have more control over the price, sellers or buyers?

To answer these questions you need to use the tables and figures from the Excel Worksheet.

3. At a price of \$5, who would be willing to trade more units, buyers or sellers?
4. Would the excess of buyers tend to raise or lower the price from the initial level of \$5?
5. How high would the price go before the excess of buyers is eliminated?
6. What happened when I tried to help out buyers with low values by fixing the price at \$5.00? Did it help out those buyers with low values? Why or why not?
7. What would have happened if I had tried to help out sellers with high costs by fixing the price at \$9.00?
8. Were you paying attention to the trend of prices reported after each round to change your strategy in future rounds? Why?

9. Was your strategy in later rounds different from earlier rounds?
10. What do think? Did you like the game? Do you think it helps you understand something about the Supply and Demand model? Do you think it was realistic? Why or why not?

APPENDIX 5E
Instructions and Record-Keeping Sheet for the Trading Experiment
Instructions for the Trading Experiment

1. You are about to participate in an experiment that will last several trading periods. Participants are divided into three types, called Red Square, Yellow Rectangle and Green Cylinder. For each type of group, there is a matching type of good: red squares, yellow rectangles, and green cylinders. Each type of person consumes their type of good. In addition, whenever a Red Square person consumes a red square, he or she automatically produces a yellow rectangle. Similarly, Yellow Rectangle people consume yellow rectangles and produce green cylinders. Green Cylinder people consume green cylinders and produce red squares. Your ID tag indicates which type of person you are. There are roughly equal numbers of each type of person.

2. Because you do not produce the good that you wish to consume, you will have to trade with someone else to get your good. Each period you will be randomly matched with someone else in the experiment. You and the person you are matched with will each be holding one unit of a good. You may trade the good you are holding for the good that person is holding, provided both of you are willing to trade. All trades are one for one, so you may not trade any fractions of a good. Note that there are three possible outcomes of a meeting:
   a. You trade for the good you consume. Then you automatically consume your good and produce the good that your type produces. Then you store your production good until the next period.
   b. You trade so that you receive some good which is not your consumption good. Then you store that good until the next period.
   c. You do not trade. Then you store the good you are currently holding until the next period.

3. At the beginning of the next period, you will again be randomly matched with another participant. You will then decide whether you want to offer to trade the good that you have, in exchange for the good that the other person has.

4. Your objective is to get as many points as possible over the course of the experiment. Points represent the satisfaction you get from consuming your good minus the costs of storing goods. Each time you consume your good, you earn twenty points. At the end of every period, you pay a cost in points for whatever good you are storing. The cost of storing goods are: one point for storing red squares, four points for storing yellow rectangles, and nine points for storing green cylinders.

5. Each player begins the experiment with 40 points, plus one unit of the good that he or she produces.

6. Let's consider how you earn points. Suppose that you just received in trade your consumption good. Then, you earn the net payoff shown in the table below.

Type	**Points for consuming**	**Storage cost of good produced**	**Net points earned**
RS	Gets 20 for consuming red square	Pays 4 to store yellow rectangle	16
YR	Gets 20 for consuming yellow rectangle	Pays 9 to store green cylinder	11
GC	Gets 20 for consuming green cylinder	Pays 1 to store red square	19

7. Recall that at the end of every period you must pay a storage cost for whatever good you store, whether you consumed that period or not. Please keep track of your points on your record-keeping sheet.

Record-Keeping Sheet for the Trading Experiment

Your Type: ____________ Your name: ___________________________

Type of Person	**Consumes**	**Produces**
Red Square (RS)	red squares	yellow rectangles
Yellow Rectangle (YR)	yellow rectangles	green cylinders
Green Cylinder (GC)	green cylinders	red squares

Good	Storage cost in points
RS	1
YR	4
GC	9

You start Period 1 with one unit of the good that you produce, and 40 points.

Period	Good with which you started	Type of person with whom you were matched	Good that person is holding	Did you trade? Y or N	Did you consume? If yes, mark 20 points	Storage cost at end of period	Total points
1							
2							
3							
4							
5							
6							
7							
8							
9							
10							
11							
12							
13							
14							
15							
16							

CHAPTER 6

Classroom Discussion

Michael K. Salemi
Kirsten Madden
Roisin O'Sullivan
Prathibha Joshi

An inquiry-based or structured discussion (SD) is an instructional strategy where students meet in class to respond to questions about a text that the instructor has prepared and distributed in advance. Discussion questions are of three types. Interpretive questions ask participants to interpret the author's meaning. Factual questions ask about relevant and important facts in the reading. Evaluative questions ask for participant opinions about the reading.

In SD, the classroom instructor organizes questions into clusters that target important concepts in the reading and important learning objectives in the course. The typical question cluster begins with an interpretive question that prompts participants to investigate an important theme in the reading, continues with supporting questions that help participants consider aspects of the theme, and concludes with a question that invites participants to wrap up inquiry before moving on to another activity or to judge the importance of the text author's ideas.

During a structured discussion, participants are responsible for the quality of responses to posed questions. The instructor functions more like a facilitator and less like an expert. The instructor probes the responses of participants by asking follow-up questions and asks respondents how their contributions relate to contributions made earlier in the discussion. The instructor does not correct mistaken contributions or provide an ideal response to any question. Instead, the instructor gently but firmly raises awareness of flaws in responses and invites all participants to help repair those flaws. The instructor, in sum, oversees a process whereby participants refine their answers to the posed questions.

A structured discussion is very different from strategies most instructors have in mind when they use the term "discussion." Structured discussion is described in detail by Hansen and Salemi (1998) and Salemi and Hansen (2005). Salemi (2005) compares SD and unstructured discussion (UD).

In this chapter, three TIP participants who completed the TIP instructional module on structured discussion explain how they implemented and extended SD and document the reactions of their students.[1] Kirsten Madden reports on her implementation of SD in a principles of macroeconomics course at Millersville University. She finds that while students typically preferred other instructional activities, they appeared to better retain and more deeply understand concepts they learned through SD. Roisin O'Sullivan compares the performance of three separate ways of allowing students to engage in a reading in an Intermediate Macroeconomic Theory course at Smith College. She finds that students participated more actively in structured than in unstructured discussions and perceived that they learned more when they did so. Prathibha Joshi explains how she implemented SD at Gordon College, an open-enrollment college, and how her students judged the relative merits of SD in comparison to several other learning strategies.

I. COMPARISON OF STRUCTURED DISCUSSION OF ADAM SMITH WITH OTHER ACTIVE LEARNING STRATEGIES
Kirsten Madden

During spring semester of 2007, I led five structured discussions in an upper level History of Economic Thought course at Millersville University. In May, the students completed an opinion survey concerning SD and other learning techniques used in the course. Although SD causes some confusion and leaves some questions unresolved, Madden (2010) concludes that SD has a positive impact on student interest, learning, and retention. In my contribution to this chapter, I investigate whether principles students also benefit from structured discussion.

I led structured discussion of Adam Smith's *The Wealth of Nations* on the third day of class in fall 2009 in two sections of macroeconomics principles at Millersville University. Over the next few weeks, I employed a variety of other learning techniques. At the midpoint of the semester, students completed an opinion survey similar to that completed by students in the History of Economic Thought class. My principles students did not like SD as well as several other strategies I employed and did not rate SD as highly as did my history of thought students. However, I found that SD better promoted retention and depth of understanding for principles students than the techniques they enjoyed more.

On the first day of class, I provided my students with written and verbal instructions for SD and warned them that I would spot check their pre-discussion preparation work. I also explained that I would evaluate the quality of their responses to discussion questions by having them submit their responses in essay form after the discussion. Finally, I provided them with a copy of the assigned reading and a "contract for discussion" that explained their responsibilities.

Prior to discussion, students read the first three chapters of *The Wealth of Nations* and prepared written preliminary responses to the cluster of questions displayed in Figure 6.1.

Figure 6.1

Question Cluster for *The Wealth of Nations* (chapters 1–3)

1. Why, according to Adam Smith, is the division of labor limited by the extent of the market?
2. What does Smith mean by "division of labor"? By "extent of the market"?
3. How, according to Smith, does a comparison of a farmer in the Scottish Highlands and a porter in London illustrate that division of labor is limited by the extent of the market?
4. How does Smith's discussion of dogs and humans relate to his argument about division of labor being limited by the extent of the market?
5. How, according to Smith, are the Rhine and the Ganges different from the rivers of southern Africa and Siberia?
6. What, according to Smith, is the connection between the development of water transportation and the extent of markets?
7. What is the practical importance of Smith's principle that the division of labor is limited by the extent of the market?

My principles students also learned through a variety of other techniques including my lectures, my use of physical "props" to illustrate a point during lecture, my use of cause-and-effect diagrams, three experiential learning activities,[2] quizzes and an exam conducted the period before the survey.

Sixty-seven students completed the half-hour survey[3] during the sixth week of classes. The typical respondent was a sophomore who had earned 32 hours of college credit. Of the 67, 39 students were humanities and social science majors, 13 were education majors, 11 were math and science majors and 4 had yet to declare a major. Thirty-seven respondents were male, and

30 were female. About 70 percent of the respondents indicated that they were motivated to do the course work to complete a graduation requirement and about 30 percent reported that their motivation was a desire to learn the subject matter.

After describing and providing examples of each learning technique, the survey asked students to estimate the amount of out-of-class time they spent completing tasks associated with each technique. The survey asked students to evaluate how well the technique contributed to their learning. In particular, it asked them to use a scale of 1 (low) to 10 (high) to judge: (1) the clarity and depth of understanding of the content derived from the technique; (2) their retention of the content targeted by the technique; (3) the level of confusion they experienced during application of the technique; and (4) the extent to which unresolved questions remained after use of the technique. Finally, the survey asked students to recommend future use of the technique using a scale of 1 (most recommended) to 8 (least recommended).

Table 6.1 reports sample averages and standard deviations for the survey responses. On average, students spent 38 minutes preparing for the Adam Smith discussion and 37 minutes reviewing their discussion notes and revising the post-discussion essays that they submitted as a graded homework assignment. Discussion ranked third among the seven techniques in terms of student out-of-class time – requiring less time than quizzes and exams and more time than the other four techniques.

On average, principles students preferred other learning strategies to discussion. When asked to compare discussion to lecture and textbook study, 22 percent responded that discussion was "worse," 48 percent responded "just as good," and only 28 percent responded "better." Discussion had the lowest average score for clarity and depth of understanding and retention of learned concepts. With the exception of exams, it had the highest average score for confusion and the presence of unresolved questions. Students reported that all four of the other non-exam strategies stimulated their interest more than discussion. Only 37 percent indicated that discussion increased their interest in economics relative to their pre-course interest level. It is not a surprise then that, on average, students recommended discussion less enthusiastically than any other learning strategy except examinations.

It is interesting to compare the survey results for my principles course with those for my history of thought course. Like my principles students, my history of thought students spent more out-of-class time completing tasks associated with discussion than they spent on tasks associated with any other technique except examinations. My history of thought students also reported that discussion resulted in more unresolved questions than did other learning techniques.

Table 6.1: Student Opinion Survey Results

Technique	Pre-Class Time[a]	Post-Class Time[a]	Clarity-Depth[b]	Retention[b]	Confusion[b]	Unresolved Questions[b]	Interest[b]	Recommend Technique[c]
Lecture	21 (28)	38 (34)	6.9 (1.9)	6.7 (2.0)	3.5 (1.9)	2.8 (1.8)	5.8 (2.2)	3.4 (2.1)
Instructor "Props"	10 (17)	20 (21)	7.7 (1.7)	7.6 (1.9)	2.6 (2.0)	2.1 (1.7)	7.4 (2.0)	3.0 (2.3)
Cause–Effect Diagrams	25 (20)	30 (23)	6.6 (2.0)	6.5 (2.0)	3.8 (2.0)	3.2 (2.1)	5.8 (2.1)	4.3 (1.9)
Experiential Learning	23 (26)	31 (24)	7.3 (2.0)	6.8 (2.0)	3.2 (1.7)	3.0 (2.0)	6.9 (2.3)	3.3 (2.1)
Discussion	38 (30)	37 (27)	6.2 (2.1)	6.1 (2.0)	4.4 (2.1)	3.5 (2.1)	5.5 (2.2)	5.0 (1.8)
Quizzes	42 (32)	35 (29)	6.2 (2.0)	6.3 (2.0)	4.3 (2.5)	3.5 (2.4)	5.2 (2.4)	4.7 (1.8)
Exam[d]	131 (69)	53 (43)	6.3 (2.2)	6.5 (2.1)	4.5 (2.5)	4.1 (2.8)	5.1 (2.6)	5.9 (1.7)

Note: The table reports the mean and standard deviation (parentheses) of student responses to survey questions described in the text.
[a]The number of minutes spent by students completing tasks associated with the learning technique.
[b]Student assessment of the quality of the learning experience associated with the use of the technique with 1 designating the lowest value experience and 10 the highest. Students assess the clarity and depth associated with learning, their retention of the covered concepts, the level of confusion they experienced, the degree to which conclusion of the technique left students with unanswered questions, and the level of their interest stimulated by the technique.
[c]Student ranking of the seven learning techniques used in the course with 1 designating the most preferred technique and 7 the least preferred.
[d]Students responded to the survey before they received the results of their exam.

In other dimensions, the survey results diverge. On average, history of thought students gave discussion the highest score for clarity and depth of understanding, retention of concepts, and stimulation of interest. They also recommended future use of discussion more highly than every other learning technique used in the course. Only 5 percent of principles students, but 56 percent of history of thought students described discussion as a "particularly good technique."

The comments that principles students volunteered on their surveys provide additional insights. One student wrote: "Adam Smith, I get the concept, but it was confusing and hard to understand." A second student listed discussion as particularly bad "because it did not clear up many questions I had." A third student disliked discussion of new material because "(I) can't discuss accurately if I don't understand fully myself."

When invited to explain their recommendations for the future use of the various learning techniques, several students raised similar points. One wrote "You can really remember the seat auction with no problem." Another explains that "experiments stick in memory easier." A third, who favored instructor use of "props" writes, "Even though lectures have to happen, they are boring and it's hard to retain all the info presented. Having physical props helps to apply the issues discussed." A fourth suggests that the use of "props" provides "something to visualize when taking the exam." Many students did not like discussion because they prefer direct answers. Some students were concerned that during discussion the "entire class could've been persuaded to believe false information was true." They complained that they could not know "if what we were saying was correct without the prof. moderating discussion w/ input."

The reader should keep in mind that my principles students reported their views after experiencing only one discussion on difficult reading material during the first week of the semester. In contrast, my history of thought students participated in several discussions before reporting their views. Even though principles students report disliking the technique relative to others, it would be surprising to learn that they were immune to the educational benefits of discussion reported by my history of thought students. Additional evidence suggests that they were not and that discussion better promoted retention and depth of understanding than instructional strategies that the students rated more highly.

A second part of the survey asked students to "list the main economic idea" learned in association with each of the employed instructional techniques. The survey provided 134 responses associated with the use of props in two different classes, 134 observations associated with two uses of cause-and-effect diagrams, 201 observations on three experiential learning activities, and 67 observations on discussion.

I assigned student descriptions of what they learned to one of three hierarchical categories: accurate explanation using a relevant concept, accurate statement using a relevant concept, or other. I assigned a student description to the "accurate explanation" category if the response included either a correct explanation of the concept or a correct explanation of how the concept relates to another relevant concept. For example, I assigned the following description of what one student learned from the *Wealth of Nations* discussion to the "accurate explanation" category: "division of labor increase production → limited by market reach affected by geography." Such accurate explanations are evidence of more complex learning from a technique than simply listing a concept.

I assigned a student description to the "concept accurate" category if the responses correctly identified the economic concept associated with the learning activity, provided that the student used words different from those used in the survey cue to describe the learning technique. For example, if a student responded that they learned about "auctions" from the classroom-seat auction, I assigned their response to the "other" category. If they responded that they learned about markets, I assigned the response to the "accurate concept" category. Two examples of student responses to the discussion prompt that I assigned to the "accurate concept" category are "division of labor" and "humans have the want/ability to trade."

I assigned responses to the "other" category when they incorrectly identified a target concept of the exercise, were too general to suggest substantive learning, reported non-economic concepts or indicated a lack of recall. By way of example for the Smith discussion prompt, I assigned the response "goals of macro" into the "other" category because it does not reflect any learning derived from the Smith discussion. Similarly, I assigned "How different examples supported Smith's views" to the other category because it was too general. And I assigned "Different people's perspectives" and "I learned how to think more deeply into the reading" to the other category because neither describes an economic concept.

In summary, I assigned a student's response to the "accurate explanation" category when it indicated that the student had higher-than-recall mastery of concepts. I assigned a response to the "accurate concept" category when it indicated that the student had recall mastery of the concept. And, I assigned the response to the "other" category when the response indicated no mastery of an economic concept.

Table 6.2 describes the distribution of survey responses into three depth-of-learning categories by learning technique. The table reveals interesting differences in the learning reported for each technique. Use of props was the technique that received the highest average student recommendation for

Table 6.2: Percentage of Student Responses about Concepts Learned Assigned to Three Depth-of-Learning Categories for Each of Four Learning Techniques

Learning Technique	**Number of Observations**	**Accurate Explanation**	**Accurate Concept**	**Other**
Instructor Props	144	27.6	3.7	67.2
Cause–Effect Diagrams	144	29.1	20.1	50.0
Experiential Learning	201	38.1	17.9	39.6
Discussion	67	34.3	17.9	46.3

Note: The survey prompts students to write "missed class" if they did not attend the class period in which a learning technique was used. The observations for "missed class" are not reported in this table with the result that row sums are less than 100.

future use. However, 67.2 percent of responses to the survey invitation to identify the economic idea learned with the aid of props contained no reference to a valid economic concept. Discussion received the lowest average student ranking after exams for clarity and depth of understanding, but 17.9 percent of responses to the survey's request for students to identify economic ideas indicate that the responding student recalled a relevant concept. Moreover, 34.3 percent of student responses to the invitation indicate higher-than-recall mastery of a relevant concept – second only to experiential learning. The near-equal performance of discussion and experiential learning is noteworthy because students experienced only one discussion in week one but three experiential activities (seat auction, ultimatum game, and supply of naked bodies) in weeks two through four.

In summary, the survey reveals an interesting contradiction. Of the seven instructional techniques, students assign to the use of props the highest scores for clarity and depth of understanding and retention and the lowest scores for confusion. In contrast, they assign to discussion low scores for clarity and retention and a high score for confusion. But the results are reversed when considering student reports of what they learned. Principles students may like it when the instructor uses props, but the evidence suggests that they do not remember the target concept. Students may dislike some features of discussion, but the evidence suggests that they learn the target concept better than they do with all other techniques save experiential learning strategies.

Through their survey comments, my principles students recognized some of the same benefits of discussion as my history of thought students. One appreciated that discussion "helped to see different people's standpoints on ideas." Another wrote: "I was confused and got to hear other people's problems I hadn't thought about." Still another appreciated that members of the class "can see what everyone else is thinking" and that discussion "allowed ideas to be thrown around, clarification to be made, and allowed us to articulate ideas in our heads by verbalizing." One female student liked having to respond to the basic discussion question because doing so "had me think outside the box and bring ideas outside economics in." This latter quote appears in nearly identical form in a 2007 history of thought student survey. The discussion encouraged one principles student to "sit down longer and focus more and re-read to understand. This helped me to get a better grade & understanding on Adam Smith." Another simply sums up that the "Adam Smith thing was very interesting."

A number of reasons can explain why the survey results differed between my principles and history of thought students. First, the history of thought students completed five structured discussions whereas the principles students completed only one. Second, the history of thought class met at 11:00 am and the two principles classes met at 8:00 am and 9:00 am. Third, the *Wealth of Nations* is a more advanced reading than others in the principles course, but is similar in difficulty to the other readings in the history of thought course. Because the reading requirements were known in advance, the history of thought course may select students with advanced reading skills. Finally, I did not use experiential learning strategies in the history of thought course.

Mixed results may be the best we can hope for when a captive audience of teenagers participate in discussion for the first time at 8:00 am and 9:00 am. Direct evidence of what students learn indicates that discussion promotes learning better than other more popular strategies. And three-fourths of my principles students did agree that discussion was "as good" or a "better" use of their time than traditional learning methods.

II. STUDENT PARTICIPATION DURING UNSTRUCTURED DISCUSSION, STRUCTURED DISCUSSION, AND LECTURE

Roisin O'Sullivan

Does the potential for higher-order learning through inquiry-based discussion stem primarily from the opportunities it creates for student participation or is the way in which the technique formats the discussion also important? To investigate this question, I compare the in-class experiences for sub-groups of students from the intermediate macroeconomic theory classes taught at Smith College during the spring and fall semesters, 2008. In each semester, I used three different techniques for discussing Mankiw's article, "The Macroeconomist as Scientist and Engineer," from the *Journal of Economic Perspectives* (Mankiw 2006). In one section, the discussion focused around interpretive question clusters, following the inquiry-based structured discussion technique (SD) suggested by Hansen and Salemi (1998). In a second section, the discussion was somewhat unstructured (UD), where the students were provided with three general questions to guide their reading. The final section consisted of a lecture where the material was presented in a formal manner to the students using PowerPoint.

Comparing the experiences of each sub-group of students, the study finds that, in addition to differences between those receiving one of the discussion treatments versus the PowerPoint lecture treatment, there were interesting differences attributable to the discussion format. The SD technique not only resulted in a greater degree of participation by students, it influenced the nature of the participation. In SD, the instructor functions as a facilitator rather than as a content expert with the result that students responded directly to each other more frequently and to the instructor less frequently. This study suggests that inquiry-based discussion has benefits beyond those associated with a less-structured discussion format.

Implementation

The intermediate macroeconomic theory course at Smith College includes both lecture meetings and three smaller section meetings each week. The smaller weekly meetings provided an opportunity to examine the impact of different section formats on the learning of students who had been exposed to the same material in lectures. The number of students exposed to each treatment was increased by implementing the experiment in both spring and fall semester classes where enrollment was 42 and 50 students, respectively.

The choice of article for the project was guided by the criteria that the reading should contain a sufficient number of ideas to warrant discussion, be self-contained and well-written, and be interesting to both the instructor and the students. Mankiw's article pulls together the main developments in macroeconomics since the Great Depression and looks at these developments from both a theoretical and a policy perspective. Therefore, it focuses on ideas that are at the absolute core of any course on intermediate macroeconomic theory. Given some background in macroeconomics that all intermediate-level students should have, the article is self-contained and is certainly well-written, and, given the centrality of the themes covered to a course in macroeconomics, the article should be of major interest to both the students and the instructor.

Each of the three formats shared certain elements. For example, the instructor knew students individually and regularly called on them by name. In most of the sessions, students sat in a circular or semi-circular arrangement and all students were informed in advance that there would be a short quiz at the end of the session. The major differences between the sessions were that different preparation materials were distributed in advance and, for the SD format, learning objectives were specified. It should be borne in mind that the students were familiar with the UD format, as it was used weekly throughout the semester. The format of each session is described in more detail below.

Inquiry-based structured discussion format

Preparation for the SD format involved specifying learning objectives for the session and developing a set of three question clusters based on the reading (Figure 6.2). Students were also provided with a contract for effective discussion in advance.[4] Following the method of Hansen and Salemi (1998), each question cluster began with an interpretative basic question that was supported by factual and evaluative questions. Each cluster ended with an evaluative question, where students were asked to form a judgment based on evidence from the reading. As the discussion progressed, the instructor supplemented these pre-circulated questions with follow-up questions.

Figure 6.2
Question Clusters for Article
Mankiw, N. Gregory, "The Macroeconomist as Scientist and Engineer," *Journal of Economic Perspectives*, **20** (4), Fall 2006, 29–46

1. According to Mankiw, what potential contributions can macroeconomists make?
   a) How does Mankiw distinguish between a macroeconomist fulfilling the role of scientist versus that of engineer?
   b) According to the author, what contributions were made by "Keynesian Revolution" economists to clarify and elaborate on Keynes' *General Theory*?
   c) According to Mankiw, was the Keynesian revolution a scientific/engineering success?
   d) Do you think the distinction between "scientist" and "engineer" is an appropriate one for macroeconomists? Why?
   e) Can you think of an example of a macroeconomic engineer in today's economy? Explain why you think they fit the bill.
2. Why, according to the author, did the Keynesian consensus breakdown after a couple of decades?
   a) What were the main elements of the three waves of New Classical economics?
   b) What were the key elements of the three waves of New-Keynesian research?
   c) What was the main goal of the New Classical economists? Do you think they achieved that goal? Why?
   d) Do you think the New Keynesian developments were successful i) as a matter of science ii) as a matter of engineering? Support your answer with evidence from the reading.
3. According to Mankiw, how have elements of both the New Classical and the New Keynesian research paths contributed to the new neo-classical consensus that emerged in the 1990s?
   a) What are the main elements of the new neoclassical synthesis and which school of thought (early Keynesian, New Keynesian, New Classical) do they most reflect?
   b) What evidence does the author present on how theoretical developments since the 1970s have/have not altered how monetary and fiscal policy is conducted in practice?
   c) How would you grade the development of macroeconomics since the 1970s? Justify your grade using material from the reading.

Unstructured discussion (UD) format

Preparation for the UD section comprised the circulation of three very general questions about the reading that were developed without taking account of question type or role (Figure 6.3).

The instructor played a leadership role, providing context and motivation for the discussion. There were some follow-up questions to each of the questions in Figure 6.3, but these tended to be factual in nature, prompting relatively short and "dead-end" responses. The instructor wrote a very brief summary of the student responses on the board, including a timeline of the developments from the Keynesian revolution onwards.

Lecture format

During the lecture sessions, the instructor dominated, presenting the material from the reading using a PowerPoint presentation. At the beginning of the session, students were encouraged to intervene with questions or comments at any time during the presentation. A handout of the PowerPoint slides was distributed at the beginning of the session but no preparation materials other than the article to be read were distributed in advance. As expected, these sessions (both in the spring and fall semesters) were far less interactive than either of the other two formats.

Figure 6.3
General Questions for Unstructured Discussion for Article
Mankiw, N. Gregory, "The Macroeconomist as Scientist and Engineer,"
Journal of Economic Perspectives, **20** (4), Fall 2006, 29–46

1. What is a macroeconomic scientist? What is a macroeconomic engineer?
2. What were the major developments in macroeconomics discussed in the article?
3. What are the main elements of the new neo-classical synthesis?

Student Participation during the Sessions

Table 6.3 documents the extent and nature of student participation for each of the session formats for the spring and fall semesters, 2008.[5] Clearly, the format of the session influenced the behavior of both the students and the instructor. Unsurprisingly, the lecture format resulted in the lowest level of student participation with only twelve interventions over the two semesters. The infrequency of interventions reflected both the behavior of the instructor, who asked far fewer questions of the students compared with the other formats, and the more passive behavior of students.

The more interesting comparison is between the two discussion formats – SD and UD. In both semesters, students intervened almost twice as frequently in the SD sessions than in the UD sessions.[6] The nature of the interventions was also different, with a greater degree of student-to-student interaction in the SD sessions. An intervention is classified as student-to-student when a student intervention is followed immediately by a contribution by another student without the intervention of the instructor, either building on the answer of the first student or reacting directly to what that student said. On a few occasions during the SD sessions, there was a string of several student interventions, something that didn't happen during the sessions using the other formats.

Instructor behavior also differed across the SD and UD sessions. In the UD sessions, the instructor acted as a leader, providing a summary of what the discussion would be about and motivation for why the topic was important at the beginning of the session, answering student questions directly and drawing together issues on the board. The instructor was in

Table 6.3: Student Participation in Discussion Sections

	Structured Discussion	Unstructured Discussion	Lecture
Number of students in the Section	30 (13, 17)	31 (19, 12)	31 (10, 21)
Number of Student Interventions	**152 (77, 75)**	**83 (43, 40)**	**12 (8, 4)**
Comprising			
Student responses to instructor questions	126 (61, 65)	74 (37, 37)	9 (6, 3)
Student to student interaction	20 (13, 7)	1 (1, 0)	0 (0, 0)
Student questions to instructor	6 (3, 3)	8 (5, 3)	3 (2, 1)

Note: Figures in parenthesis refer to the spring and fall semesters, respectively.

"sheep-dog" mode for much of these sessions, shepherding the students towards the reading's main issues and working to ensure the quality of the information stream was accurate.[7] More factual questions were asked by the instructor compared with the SD sessions and the instructor provided information when students failed to identify a salient point. When students asked questions directly of the instructor, the instructor provided an answer.

In contrast, during the SD sessions, the instructor played the role of facilitator rather than leader. At the beginning of these sessions, the instructor made it clear to students that they were responsible for coming up with answers or identifying different viewpoints on a certain topic: The instructor would not provide answers but would direct the discussion or act as a "traffic cop" rather than a "sheep dog." When students did ask questions directly of the instructor, the instructor either referred to a point made earlier by another student, helping the questioner answer her own question, or asked other students to weigh in on the issue. On several occasions in both the SD sessions (seven and five times in the spring and fall sessions, respectively), the instructor referenced points made by students earlier in the discussion. In both these sessions, student interventions accounted for a far greater percentage of the "air time" compared with the other two formats and there was participation across a wider range of students.[8] Overall, the evidence indicates that students took greater responsibility for the outcome of discussion under the SD format.

Students' Reactions to the Discussion Formats

A day after the discussion sessions, the instructor distributed a feedback form to students that asked them to compare the new section formats to the UD structure usually employed. Completion of the form was voluntary and students had the option to keep their responses anonymous.

Table 6.4 contains the questions asked on the brief survey and summarizes student responses. The first question revealed that 20 of 27 respondents exposed to the SD format either preferred it or liked it as well as the usual UD format while only 12 of 27 respondents who received the lecture treatment felt that way. All respondents but three reported that they spent as long or longer preparing for the Mankiw discussion[9] and only students expecting the lecture format responded that they spent less time preparing.

The students also were invited to share any general comments about their discussion experience with the alternative formats. In response to the PowerPoint lecture format instead of the usual unstructured discussion, students said:

> "I find regular discussions more helpful because I am learning more actively."
>
> "In lectures, I need to go over my notes to understand the material. During our usual discussions, talking about the material helps me understand/remember more."
>
> "The lecture format was okay, but I prefer the discussion format because it is easier to absorb new information."
>
> "I prefer classes that are more discussion-based because the interaction in class helps me to learn more effectively. Being involved in the discussion usually allows me to master the material better."
>
> "Just to clarify, I think the reason I did not like the Mankiw discussion as much as our normal discussions was because we covered so much material and there was a lot less time for participation. It was also less interactive."
>
> "I feel like the power point teaching method is inhibiting. I don't think you need it, especially not during a discussion, although it also wouldn't be good for our lectures. I think the way we usually did discussions worked well."

These responses are consistent with the education literature that states discussion promotes more active learning. It also indicates clearly that students value the opportunity to participate in class and are less likely to participate when the format of the class is not structured deliberately to encourage that participation.

In response to the SD format instead of the usual unstructured discussion, students volunteered the following comments:

> "I really liked this new kind of discussion set up. I felt like the prompting questions effectively engaged students and gave us more opportunity to speak. Also, having question clusters enabled me to read with more

Table 6.4: Student Responses to the Different Discussion Formats

	Lecture	Structured Discussion
Total Number of Responses	**27 (8, 19)**	**27 (12, 15)**
1. Compared with the usual discussion format (UD), what did you think of the format you experienced for the Mankiw discussion?		
I **much preferred** the Mankiw discussion format.	1 (1, 0)	4 (2, 2)
I **preferred** the Mankiw discussion format – **but not by a big margin**.	5 (1, 4)	6 (4, 2)
I **liked** the usual format and the Mankiw discussion format **equally**.	6 (1, 5)	10 (4, 6)
I liked the Mankiw discussion format **less** – **but not by a big margin**.	8 (2, 6)	5 (2, 3)
I like the Mankiw discussion format a **lot less**.	7 (3, 4)	2 (0, 2)
2. How did the amount of time you spent preparing for the Mankiw discussion compare with your usual preparation time for discussion?		
I spent a **lot longer** preparing for the Mankiw discussion.	5 (1, 4)	15 (5, 10)
I spent a **bit longer** preparing for the Mankiw discussion.	16 (6, 10)	9 (7, 2)
I spent about **the same** amount of time preparing for the Mankiw discussion.	3 (1, 2)	3 (0, 3)
I spent a **bit less time** preparing for the Mankiw discussion.	3 (0, 3)	0 (0, 0)
I spent a **lot less time** preparing for the Mankiw discussion.	0 (0, 0)	0 (0, 0)
3. Did the anticipated format of the Mankiw discussion (rather than the length of the reading) influence your decision about the matter of time you spent preparing?		
Yes, I spent a longer time preparing because of the discussion section format.	11 (2, 9)	17 (8, 9)
Yes, I spent a shorter time preparing because of the discussion section format.	1 (0, 1)	0 (0, 0)
No, the format of the discussion session did not influence my preparation time.	15 (6, 9)	10 (4, 6)

Note: Figures in parenthesis refer to the spring and fall semesters, respectively from written additional comments that students were factoring in the length of the reading as well as the discussion format when answering the question.

direction. I felt like I had a better idea of what we would be discussing and was more prepared to answer questions in class. I would also like to note that my response to number 3 is attributed to the fact that the article was much longer than other articles and we had more questions to consider. Because there were more questions, I feel like I did more preparation outside of class and was better prepared for the discussion."

"Although open discussion isn't usually my favorite format, I found today's discussion useful. Advantages of this format: 1. Clear structure lets students know what to expect and how to prepare. 2. Student learning was more collaborative. Disadvantages of this format: 1. Preparation level would probably fall off quickly as the semester went on 2. A lot of regurgitation of the text took place."

"I really liked the student-led discussion style with you just as facilitator. I think it was great that we sat in a circle and I wished we would have done a similar activity for the other discussions. Perhaps you should use a seminar room with one big table for the discussion groups next year?"

"The fear of a quiz did induce me to study a little more. Also, though, I did prefer the discussion-style session and you did an extraordinary job facilitating in one or two situations, it would have been nice if you said – here is the answer. Example, I said one thing (I forget what) someone else said the opposite, we evaluated each side (good so far) but after doing so there was no conclusion. An eventual conclusion would be nice."

Again, these comments show that students are motivated by opportunities to participate actively in class and to take more responsibility for their own learning when given sufficient structure.[10] The comments also point to the importance of the preparation materials and the expectations set for students before the discussion. It is interesting to note, however, the observation made in the final student comment above about the lack of an instructor-provided conclusion. While students welcome the additional responsibility this format gives them, there is still a tendency to look to the instructor to tie everything up neatly for the students. Perhaps repeated exposure to the SD technique would change that.

This study investigated whether the format of discussion sessions impacts the extent and nature of student participation by using three different formats for sub-groups of students from an intermediate macroeconomic theory course. The evidence reveals that the format of the discussion does matter. In a structured discussion, students engage more fully than they do in lecture and in unstructured discussion.

Students participated more actively when expectations were made explicit about their role and responsibilities. The nature of students' participation was also influenced by the format of the discussion. When the role of the instructor was clearly defined as that of facilitator, students were more inclined to respond directly to each other's contributions. They intervened more often in class when the SD format was utilized although the level of intervention for the UD format was also significantly higher than during the PowerPoint lecture sessions. Students responded positively to the more interactive session formats and their comments indicate that they perceived they learned more when they were more active participants in the process.

III. EVALUATING DISCUSSION AS A LEARNING TECHNIQUE IN A PRINCIPLES OF MACROECONOMICS CLASS

Prathibha Joshi

How effective is structured discussion (SD) technique in an open enrollment institution? My experience in teaching principles of macroeconomics in the spring, summer and fall semesters of 2009 at Gordon College in Barnesville, Georgia is instructive.

Gordon College is a two-year residential college. It admits students regardless of SAT and ACT results, requires on-site computerized placement testing of any applicant with deficient preparatory classes or low standardized test scores (SAT Verbal below 430, SAT Math below 400, ACT English or ACT Math below 17), and provides learning support to enable students to repair deficiencies before enrolling in regular college classes. Most graduates earn an Associate's degree. Many then go on to complete four-year degrees elsewhere; Gordon Core Curriculum courses are transferable to all other University of Georgia System institutions without loss of credit. The college currently has four-year programs in Early Childhood Education, Nursing, and Biology that award a Bachelor of Science degree.

Gordon offers two economics classes, both at the introductory level: macroeconomics and microeconomics. Students in these courses are usually business majors; the majority are traditional students in their late teens and early twenties, with only a few older students. Some summer session enrollees are transient students who attend other institutions and enroll at Gordon during summer break to earn credits towards their degrees.

In 2009, 20 to 24 students enrolled in each of the spring and fall sections of principles of macroeconomics and 13 enrolled in the summer section. These class sizes are typical of Gordon. Students quickly became acquainted and addressed each other by name. The two spring classes met at 11:00 am and 2:00 pm, the summer class at 10:00 am, and the fall class at 2:00 pm, all during the hours when students seem most alert and most willing to pay attention. Class periods lasted 75 minutes.

For the most part, I taught the class through lectures, writing key concepts and problems on the whiteboard for emphasis and easy reference. Each student made a required individual PowerPoint oral presentation to the class once during the semester. Regular in-class problem-solving exercises demanded both individual and collaborative effort. Students also had three in-class exams throughout the semester. The SD exercise was scheduled for a full class period once in each class, in the middle of the semester after students had some exposure to economic concepts and their applications.

Discussion Technique Description

The discussion exercise used in the 2009 classes is modeled on the *Wealth of Nations* example in Salemi and Hansen (2005, Chapter 6). To allow students ample time to prepare, I distributed Chapters 1–3 and the discussion questions two to three weeks in advance. At that time, I warned the students that the English language had changed a great deal since the 1776 publication of Adam Smith's book. I suggested ways to make sense of strange words, phrases, and sentence structures. I also explained the SD procedure in full detail so the students would know what to expect during the discussion itself.

I posed five discussion questions (Figure 6.4). The first was an interpretive question, the next three were factual questions, and the final question was evaluative.

Figure 6.4
Structured Discussion Questions for *The Wealth of Nations*

Interpretive	What, according to Smith, is the connection between trade, specialization, and division of labor?
Factual	Explain, according to Smith, the meaning of division of labor and extent of market.
Factual	What evidence does Smith provide on the relationship between division of labor and extent of market?
Factual	Illustrate further by providing geographical examples provided by Smith.
Evaluative	What is the relevance of Smith's argument connecting the principles of specialization, division of labor, and the extent of market in today's global economy?

In response to the interpretive question, "What, according to Smith, is the connection between trade, specialization, and division of labor?," students in every class explained the ways in which Smith's pin factory exemplified the concepts of division of labor and specialization. Students also discussed the impact of waterways on trade and specialization. In most classes, discussion contrasted the generalist approach to labor in rural areas and labor specialization in urban areas and towns (e.g., manufacturing work and porters). Students were told to refer only to the selected readings from *Wealth of Nations*. It seemed to me that this forced them to, first, try and figure out what Smith meant for themselves and, second, reexamine their comprehension of Smith's ideas during a discussion with other students with different viewpoints.

The three factual questions required that the students express a clear understanding of Smith's arguments, definitions, and evidence. Unlike the interpretive and evaluative questions, these questions had clear answers. Keeping these questions in mind may have focused the students' attention on key concepts as they studied the Smith selections. During the class discussion, hearing other students answer these factual questions helped students who had failed to do the reading or had trouble understanding the selections to begin to comprehend the concepts.

The evaluative question prompted students to use their own experiences as further evidence for their arguments and to apply their knowledge of Smith to today's global businesses and international trade. This served as a conclusion to the discussion.

Discussion Technique Evaluation[11]

Near the end of the semester, I asked the students to complete a voluntary survey to judge the comparative effectiveness of the learning techniques used in the course: discussion (the Adam Smith SD exercise), lecture, presentation, report on an *Economist* article, in-class activities, quiz, and exams. Surveys varied by session because certain techniques were only used in a single session (the *Economist* article report in the spring and a quiz in the fall). Sixty out of 91 students chose to turn in survey responses.

The survey asked students to evaluate each learning technique on a 1–10 scale corresponding to the "level of interest stimulated in the content material through use of the technique" (Table 6.5). It prompted respondents to rank on a 1–10 scale how strongly they would recommend the different techniques for use in future classes or with other topics (Table 6.6). Finally, it asked two open-ended questions: "Which technique did you like the best and why?" and "Which technique did you learn from the most and why?"

Student responses to the survey questions are important because instructional techniques that stimulate interest lead students to greater engagement and more learning. Combining student views as revealed by the survey and instructor observations yields a clearer picture of the usefulness of the SD technique.

In Table 6.5, evaluation responses are reported separately for the spring, summer, and fall terms, with responses from the two spring classes combined. Evaluations are categorized as low interest (1–3), medium interest (4–7), and high interest (8–10). The percentage of response in each category is shown. In the following discussion, the evaluations and selected answers to the open-ended questions are discussed separately for each term.

Table 6.5: Reported Interest in Learning Techniques by Session

Learning technique	Low Interest	Medium Interest	High Interest
SPRING 2009			
Lecture	3.33%	40%	56.7%
Presentation	3.33	46.7	50
Economist article	6.67	53.33	40
Discussion	6.67	23.33	66.7
In-class activity	0	10	90
Exams	10	63.33	26.66
30 responses from 51 students.			
SUMMER 2009			
Lecture	0%	63.6%	36.36%
Presentation	0	27.3	72.7
Discussion	9.09	36.36	54.54
In-class activity	0	9.09	90.91
Exams	18.18	54.54	27.27
11 responses from 13 students.			
FALL 2009			
Lecture	0%	57.9%	42.1%
Presentation	5.3	26.3	47.36
Quiz	21	47	31.6
Discussion	10.5	57.9	31.6
In-class activity	0	21.05	78.95
Exams	21.05	47.37	31.57
19 responses from 27 students.			

Notes: Students in principles of macroeconomics classes were asked to report the level of interest stimulated by each learning technique on a 1–10 scale. Responses in the range 1–3 are reported as Low, 4–7 as Medium, 8–10 as High. All responses are reported as percentages. Responses from two sections taught in spring 2009 are combined. In fall 2009, only one of two sections used the SD technique, and only that section was surveyed.

In the spring term, 3.33 percent of the student sample indicated a low level of interest in the lecture component of the course, 40 percent medium interest, and 56.7 percent were highly interested. Overall, the in-class activities earned the highest level of interest from 90 percent of the students. The popularity of this technique is not hard to explain. The weekly activity was a small group problem-solving exercise. Even though group work may raise free-rider concerns, students found this technique relatively non-threatening, particularly engaging, and fun. The discussion generated the highest level of interest for the second largest group of students, 66.7 percent. Exams interested the fewest students, with 26.66 percent at the highest level and 10 percent at the lowest.

Here are a few of the spring students' responses to the survey questions:

1. *Which technique did you like the best and why?*
   (a) "Class discussion of Smith article. Some of the lecture in this format would in my opinion help students prepare for exam and understanding of macroeconomics."
   (b) "I really enjoyed the Adam Smith article because it gave some very interesting and historical background to the subject."
   (c) "I like in-class activities. It allows for more practice and helps me better understand."
2. *Which technique did you learn from the most and why?*
   (a) "Smith article – the *Wealth of Nations* laid the foundation for the capitalist society. Since it was econ class I enjoyed it."
   (b) "In-class activities because its hands on and you actually have to try to figure the problems out."
   (c) "I learned the most from both lectures and the in-class activities."

The summer term lasted one month. Class met every weekday. Nearly every student expressed moderate or high interest in all the learning techniques. Almost 91 percent (90.91%) indicated a high level of interest in the in-class activity. This response may be due in part to familiarity, since the technique was used every day. Approximately three fourths (72.7%) were highly interested by the presentation exercise. Discussion, though, was among the techniques that stimulated less interest: 36.36 percent ranked it medium range and 54.54 percent in the high range. Students reported the least interest in exams, with 18.18 percent giving them a low ranking and 27.27 percent ranking them high.

Here are a few of the summer students' responses to the survey questions:

1. *Which technique did you like the best and why?*
   (a) "I love in-class activities because it gives us an opportunity to apply what we learned and to get help (if needed)."

   (b) "In-class exercises and presentations because I enjoy formulas and making myself a better/more confident speaker."
2. *Which technique did you learn from the most and why?*
   (a) "Most real world knowledge was learned from presentation and Smith's article because it connected written facts to current events to increase retainable knowledge."
   (b) "I liked Smith's article it gave a good look at why there would be movement in the market."
   (c) "In-class exercises we got to help each other understand the material."
   (d) "I learned the most from the in-class exercises because we actually put the formulas to use and were able to understand the concept better."

In the fall term, one of the two sections of principles of macroeconomics included structured discussion (SD) as a learning technique while the other acted as a control group. Compared with the spring and summer, students in the fall reported less interest: 57.9 percent ranked the technique in the medium range, and 31.6 percent ranked it high. Students preferred discussion to the quiz and exams as learning experiences.

Here are a few of the fall students' responses to the survey questions:

1. *Which technique did you like the best and why?*
   (a) "Adam Smith, because we get a chance to discuss with our classmates."
   (b) "In-class exercises because I got to talk out each problem."
   (c) "Probably Smith's article because it really helped me learn about trade, division of labor and specialization."
2. *Which technique did you learn from the most and why?*
   (a) "Probably Smith's article because it really helped me learn about trade, division of labor, and specialization."
   (b) "In-class assignments, being able to talk to peers."

Table 6.6 shows how responding students in each session ranked the different techniques to recommend for or against their use for future classes or topics on a 1–10 scale. The rankings are calculated on an average with a lower rank indicating a highly recommended technique and the highest rank meaning it was the least recommended technique. Comparisons among the techniques were done within individual semesters, not across semesters.

In the spring, the discussion exercise was most highly recommended for future use; presentation was least recommended. In the summer, the in-class activity was most recommended and exams were least recommended. The summer class gave discussion the second highest recommendation with an average ranking of 4.0. Although the presentation technique created higher levels of interest among students than did discussion, discussion was more highly recommended for future use. In fall 2009, presentation was the most recommended technique, although students had yet to engage in this activity. Such a result probably stemmed from the students' expectations about the presentation based on information provided to the students through class instructions. Again, exams were least recommended. For this semester, discussion was the fourth highly recommended technique with a ranking of 4.32, indicating that the students were ambivalent about using this technique in comparison to the other techniques that had higher recommendations.

Table 6.6: Rank Recommendation of Learning Techniques

Learning techniques	**Spring 2009 Ranking**	**Summer 2009 Ranking**	**Fall 2009 Ranking**
Lecture	5.5 (3.56)	4.91 (3.65)	4.11 (2.33)
Presentation	5.87** (2.96)	4.82 (2.96)	3.63* (2.79)
Economist article, Quiz	5.8 (2.75)	-----	4.84 (2.38)
Discussion	4.87* (3.94)	4.0 (2.32)	4.32 (3.38)
In-class activity	5.33 (3.92)	3.09* (3.08)	4.11 (2.85)
Exams	5.03 (2.8)	5.91** (3.39)	5.21** (2.59)
Number of responses	30 of 51	11 of 13	19 of 27

Notes: *denotes most recommended technique. **denotes least recommended technique. The rank is based on the average calculation. Standard deviations are shown in parentheses. The spring classes included an *Economist* article as an additional learning technique; the fall class included a quiz.

This study sought to determine whether an SD technique could enhance student learning about course materials. Students reported that the technique stimulated their interest in the topic being discussed. As the students participated more fully in their own learning by sharing their thoughts and their interpretations of Smith's *Wealth of Nations*, they invested more of themselves into their education. They took on the responsibility to master the class topic, evaluate it through critical thinking, and share their perspectives with the other students in the class. Most of these students also did recommend the structured discussion technique for future classes.

IV. CONCLUSIONS

What do we, as instructors, learn from these three studies? Three conclusions are warranted. First, taken together, the studies suggest that structured discussion, while not necessarily popular with students who first encounter it, does promote higher-order mastery of economic concepts. Second, it appears that students may adapt better to structured discussion when it is used several times during a course than when it is used only once or twice. Finally, it may be important to explain the benefits of structured discussion more energetically to first-year students than to third- and fourth-year students. Less-experienced students may be more uncomfortable with the absence of instructor-sanctioned answers to discussion questions. More-experienced students may more readily buy into the challenge of taking responsibility for the creation and revision of responses to interpretive questions.

NOTES

1. The authors thank participants at the Final TIP Conference held in Atlanta on January 5–6, 2010, for their helpful comments and Patrick Inman for his very helpful suggestions on word craft.
2. The three activities were a seat auction, the ultimatum game and the supply of naked bodies. In the seat auction, pioneered by Dirk Mateer (1997), students bid to obtain their preferred class seat for the semester and pay their winning bids into a classroom snack fund. In the ultimatum game (Dickinson 2002), one student proposes a way to split $10 and a second student either accepts or rejects the proposal. If the responder accepts, the two students split the $10 as proposed. If the responder rejects, both receive nothing. In the supply of naked bodies, also designed by Dirk Mateer, students trace out a positively sloped supply schedule without ever actually disrobing.
3. A copy of the 2007 student opinion survey is available online through a link under "sample publications" on my Millersville University faculty webpage: http://www.millersville.edu/economics/faculty/madden_k/ index.php. The 2009 version may be obtained by contacting me via email at kirsten.madden@ millersville.edu.
4. See Figure 14-7 in Hansen and Salemi (1998) for an example.
5. The discussion sessions were recorded with the consent of the students in order to keep track of interventions.
6. The seemingly large number of interventions for a 50-minute period reflects the fact that responses as short as a single phrase or sentence were counted as interventions.
7. The terms "sheep dog" and "traffic cop" used to describe instructor behavior are attributed to Michael Salemi.

8. Whether this outcome would have occurred by simply designating the role of the instructor as that of facilitator without providing the structure of the question clusters is an interesting question for future investigation.
9. No doubt, the expected quiz at the end of each section influenced preparation time for many students.
10. Whether students learned more by being exposed to a particular format is obviously a question of major interest. Results of the post-discussion quiz are somewhat mixed, with students doing better relative to their performance in the course as a whole when they received either the SD or UD treatment versus the lecture treatment. In the spring semester, however, it was the SD students who dominated, whereas in the fall, the UD students performed relatively better. Interestingly in both semesters, it was the smallest non-lecture group that showed the largest performance improvement. This is an area that warrants further investigation and calls for the development of a better way to assess learning outcomes.
11. I thank Kirsten Madden for the survey format used in this study.

REFERENCES

Dickinson, D.L. (2002), "A bargaining experiment to motivate discussion on fairness," *Journal of Economic Education*, **33** (Spring), 136–51.

Hansen, W.L., and M.K. Salemi (1998), "Improving classroom discussion in economics courses," in W.B. Walstad and P. Saunders (eds), *Teaching Undergraduate Economics: A Handbook for Instructors*, New York: Irwin McGraw Hill, 207–26.

Madden, K. (2010), "Engaged learning with the inquiry-based question cluster discussion technique: Student outcomes in a history of economic thought course," *Southern Economic Journal*, forthcoming.

Mankiw, N.G. (2006), "The macroeconomist as scientist and engineer," *Journal of Economic Perspectives*, **20** (4), 29–46.

Mateer, G.D. (1997), "Selling seats through an English auction," *Classroom Expernomics*, (Fall), [http://www.marietta.edu/~delemeeg/expernom/f97.html#mateer] (accessed summer, 2009).

Salemi, M.K. (2005), "Asking the right kind of questions promotes learning during discussion," *Australasian Journal of Economic Education*, **2**, 55–65.

Salemi, M.K., and W.L. Hansen (2005), *Discussing Economics: A Classroom Guide to Preparing Discussion Questions and Leading Discussion*, Cheltenham, UK and Northampton, MA, USA: Edward Elgar.

Smith, A. (1776), *An Inquiry into the Nature and Causes of the Wealth of Nations*, Modern Library edition, 1994, New York: Random House, Inc.

CHAPTER 7

Formative Assessment in Economics Courses

William B. Walstad
Michael Curme
Katherine Silz Carson
Indradeep Ghosh

When most economics instructors consider the term assessment, they typically think about preparing tests, assigning homework, grading papers, or doing some task that involves evaluating achievement. Other instructors may think about assessment in terms of student ratings of teaching administered at the end of a quarter or semester course and used by economics department or college administrators to evaluate teaching in conjunction with other information. Such ex post evaluations would be categorized as *summative assessments* because they occur after economics instruction is given. In the case of tests and graded assignments, they offer a summary judgment of the student achievement at a point in time and, in the case of student evaluations of teaching, they provide summary ratings about courses or instruction.

Assessment of economics instruction, however, extends beyond the traditional bounds of testing and grading or the administration of end-of-course student evaluations. Another form of evaluation practice, referred to in this chapter as *formative assessment*, can be viewed as a continuous process for helping students discover what they know or do not know about an economics topic, letting students express their thoughts and opinions about economics topics or instruction, and assisting faculty members in designing teaching strategies that improve understanding and appreciation of economics. From a formative perspective, assessment should not be thought of solely as a final course product which has to be graded but as an ongoing process that is tied to course goals and objectives.

This form of assessment often has three general and different purposes. The first one is to give students an opportunity to check their economic understanding and overcome learning problems through a *self-assessment*. Such a teaching strategy allows students the opportunity to practice their economic thinking and self-evaluate their economic understanding with a low-stakes assignment (or activity) well before they get evaluated by the instructor with a high-stakes economics test or major written assignment. The low-stakes assignment may be ungraded and rely completely on the voluntary cooperation of students or it can be graded. In the latter case, minimal weight is given to the assignment in the course grading scheme, but the weight is sufficient to encourage students to treat it as a serious request because as economists know full well, even small changes in incentives can produce desired outcomes from students.

Students also benefit from interaction with other students in learning economics. The adoption of formative assessment techniques in the classroom can foster positive interactions with other students in the discussion of economics content and enrich the economics course experience for students. In most cases, student work on an assignment that is designed to be used for self-assessment also can be used for peer assessment. For example, students' written responses to economics questions or problems can be shared with other students in small groups or teams as part of group work. Students can self-assess their written work and at the same time get feedback from other students through this peer assessment that helps them understand the economics content or gain an alternative perspective on an economic issue. This second purpose for formative assessment can be powerful for student learning in an age when students attach high value to social connections, make active use of electronic media to share information, and seek opportunities to collaborate.

A third purpose for using formative assessment, and perhaps the most important one from an instructor's perspective, is to give more information and insights about students' economic thinking and their learning processes. This feedback can then be used by instructors to allocate valuable classroom time to eliminate confusion about an economic concept or to give additional explanation about important ideas. Such feedback is difficult to obtain from summative assessments and cannot be used in a timely manner because the learning opportunity often has passed if students already have their grade. If given the right classroom assessment activity, students are willing to state whether they understand an economic concept presented in a lecture, learned anything from a class discussion, or were able to solve correctly a homework problem. The reason, however, for obtaining this feedback is not to use it to criticize students for their lack of economic understanding or interest in economics, but rather to get the instructor to think about how to help students increase their understanding and appreciation of economics.

While this approach to assessment may seem alien to economics instructors who rely exclusively on tests or written papers to evaluate student achievement, many classroom activities or assignments for formative assessment have been developed and used over the years in higher education in general and particularly in economics (e.g., Angelo and Cross 1993; Walstad 2006). They can be as simple as asking students at the end of an economics lecture to write a short statement (a one-minute essay) on the most important point made in a lecture or to identify the most confusing idea presented. They can involve asking students to work individually to solve homework problems and then having students work together in small teams to prepare a written group-answer to the problems. Students can be asked to write content statements on stimuli (e.g., articles, data, graphs) to interpret and explain what they mean and share that work with other students. In addition, the instructor can use formative assessment techniques to get feedback from students through opinion surveys or reflective essays about what they think they are learning during an economics course.

The above explanation and examples suggest that *in theory* there are many options for economics instructors who want to use classroom or course assessment techniques in their undergraduate economics courses. Skeptical economics instructors who might be interested in such strategies and want to use them in their courses may realistically question whether they actually work *in practice* in the wide range of undergraduate economics courses. The main purpose of this chapter, therefore, is to provide some evidence to support the conclusion that formative assessment techniques can be adapted for undergraduate economics courses and that they do work. This evidence comes in the form of first-hand accounts from the experiences of three economics professors with the development and usage of assessment strategies with their students.

The only common element among the three professors is that each one attended one of the Teaching Innovations Program (TIP) workshops. These workshops introduced them to the wide range of pedagogical strategies described in this chapter and other chapters in this volume. They returned to their own institutions, did some additional readings on assessment through an online instructional module, and developed a plan to integrate some types of assessment practices that were new to them into their economics courses. The completion of the work for the assessment module involved implementing the plan in their economics courses, reflecting on the experiences, and preparing a report on the outcomes.

Aside from all having attended a TIP workshop, everything else was different. They attended TIP workshops in different years (2005, 2006, and 2008), so they had different sets of workshop leaders. They each teach economics at different universities (Miami University, United States Air Force Academy, and Haverford College) where they hold different academic ranks (assistant, associate, and full). For their assessment work, they each taught different economics courses (principles of microeconomics, data analysis and introductory econometrics, money and banking). Regardless of the above differences, their individual accounts reveal that each one was able to implement the assessment strategy or multiple strategies successfully in their courses and each one found it to be a beneficial experience. Taken together they demonstrate the flexibility and applicability of formative assessment for use in undergraduate economics courses.

I. ASSESSMENT PRACTICES USING TEAMS
Michael Curme

As is generally the case when I participate in a teaching-focused workshop, I left the 2005 TIP conference in North Carolina wondering what I was doing in the classroom and what students were learning from my principles courses. I suspect that like most faculty, my focus had been on inputs rather than outputs, figuring that the in-class production process could not fail to create good product (student learning) as long as I was using high quality inputs. I was reminded at the workshop, however, that the production function is not only largely intractable, but different across students. And while exams and quizzes uncover, to a degree, what individual students have retained, it may also be valuable to be more deliberate about the process, to experiment with it, and collect some information along the way that might, through minor changes in the production process, help improve the learning outcomes for a large number of students.

The course I selected for the TIP assessment module was principles of microeconomics, a three-credit-hour course at Miami University. I was scheduled to teach one section of the class in the fall semester 2005 with an enrollment of about 40 students. In addition to a standard economics textbook (Frank and Bernanke 2005), students were required to read roughly a chapter per week from *Naked Economics* (Wheelan 2002). As described below, I adopted three assessment innovations: a pre- and post-quiz on critical course concepts, team discussion of the muddiest point, and personal reflection. While these assessments were used in a single section of this micro principles course, the informal control group was the other sections of this course I had taught in the past without these innovations. I do not claim to have formally measured the efficacy of the assessments described, but I've been teaching long enough to trust my feeling that just going through the exercise was a valuable experience. The innovations, however, were designed with a 40-student limit in mind, and a different approach may be necessary to accomplish similar goals in larger sections.

One other background item should be noted before I describe the assessments. The micro principles course is a "Miami Plan Foundation" course; the Miami Plan is effectively the university's set of general education requirements, and Miami Plan courses must be approved and periodically reviewed/assessed by a non-randomly appointed university-wide council. Courses are evaluated, in part, on the basis of their demonstrated success in promoting four student learning goals: critical thinking, understanding contexts, engaging with other learners, and reflecting and acting. The assessment innovations I adopted were intended, at least in part, to promote the four Miami Plan learning goals, and in particular critical thinking and engaging with other learners. Prior to these innovations, student evaluations of teaching in the micro principles course tended to yield high marks with respect to critical thinking. To a lesser degree, students also evaluated the course highly with respect to understanding contexts and reflecting and acting. The course received its lowest marks on engaging with other learners.

Pre- and Post-Quiz Using Teams

I designed a 10-question multiple choice quiz that covered what are, in my view, the most important principles in the course (e.g., opportunity cost, price controls, tax incidence, monopoly, etc.) These questions were written so as to require higher-order critical thinking skills such as application and analysis as opposed to simply knowledge and comprehension. The goal here was to explicitly demonstrate some degree of value added over the semester by establishing a baseline coming into the course. Each student took the pre-quiz on the first Friday of the semester, and the exact same quiz (the "post-quiz") on the penultimate Friday of the semester. As an incentive, students were told that their highest score on either the pre- or post-quiz would be used to replace their lowest "regular" quiz score for the semester (regular weekly quizzes were administered in the course).

To promote the goal of engaging with other learners, students were divided into ten teams, and each team was assigned one of the ten questions on the quiz. The teams met during the second week of class (after taking the quiz individually) to construct an answer to their assigned question. These answers, along with a written defense, were posted to the course Blackboard site for all students to see. It should be noted that for both the individual and team pre-quiz, students were instructed to attempt to work out the answer on the basis of what they already knew, and explicitly told not to search in the textbook or online for the "correct answer." The teams then repeated this exercise during the last week of the semester (again, after individually completing the post-quiz), again posting a written defense with their answer.

Evaluation

In terms of individual performance, the average pre-quiz score was 3.6 out of 10, a bit higher than what would be expected with pure guessing on the 10 four-response multiple-choice questions. The average post-quiz score was significantly higher, but still a disappointing 6.2 points. In retrospect, I believe that at least two of the questions could have been written more clearly, and this may have contributed to the low overall average. Consistent with the "wisdom of the crowds," the team responses resulted in higher average scores for both the pre- and the post-quiz. For the pre-quiz, teams provided the correct answer to six of the ten questions; on the post-quiz eight of the ten teams gave the correct response. Of the four teams that had offered incorrect responses on the pre-quiz, two revised their answers and chose the correct response on the post-quiz; the other two teams remained steadfast in their commitment to their original incorrect answer (suggesting perhaps the intellectual equivalent of a sunk-cost effect). Somewhat reassuringly, no team that had initially arrived at a correct answer on the pre-quiz changed its answer to an incorrect response on the post-quiz after spending a semester formally studying and learning principles of microeconomics.

Of course, for a variety of reasons it is very difficult to determine exactly what can be learned from this classroom assessment technique (CAT). I suspect, but cannot support with evidence, that for both the individual pre- and post-quizzes students really tried to work out the correct answer to each question. I also suspect that because of the time between the pre-quiz and the post-quiz, each question seemed new again when encountered on the post-quiz, with the possible exception of each student's team question.

My impression was that the students were quite surprised when I reminded them – on the due date – that they had to take the post-quiz. Since there was not a large grade incentive, gaming was probably not a big problem; certainly the scores do not seem inflated. On the other hand, the (lack of) incentives may have resulted in lower effort and therefore lower average scores. Since this would apply to both the pre- and the post-quiz, the pre/post difference is perhaps the most important statistic generated in the exercise – the average score rose, but the post-quiz average was still less than 70 percent. The pre-quiz results were certainly consistent with the expectation that students know very little about microeconomics coming into the course, despite the fact that more than half of them had some form of economics in high school. While the higher post-quiz average suggests that the course added some value, the course grade almost certainly was a better measure of broad content mastery.

I did perceive some indirect benefits related to this CAT. The 10-question pre-quiz immediately introduced students to the most critical concepts in the course, and also set a standard for evaluation rigor that otherwise often catches principles students by surprise on the first exam. On a couple of occasions during the semester, a student would remark during class "Oh, this is like one of those problems we worked out in the beginning of the semester," which then allowed me to again emphasize the importance of the concept being developed. The group dimension of this exercise also served the useful purpose of giving the teams a challenging assignment early on, one that required them to stretch beyond their current knowledge while also capturing a written record of their thought processes. A number of students commented on how interesting it was to compare the written defense of their answer at the end of the semester (often well organized and grounded in a coherent model) to what they submitted the first time through (often incoherent and based on opinion or a single observation).

Ultimately, in my view the greatest benefit I derived from this assessment innovation was related to the construction of the quiz. The exercise required me to clearly identify, in my own mind, the ten most critical concepts in the course. As I narrowed down my choices and worked up the questions, I had to think very clearly about the set of content-specific learning goals for the course and ways that I might best promote student mastery of those critical concepts. One outcome of this exercise was that I changed my entire treatment of the relationship between diminishing returns and marginal cost. I did virtually no lecturing on this, but rather set up an experiment which allowed us, as a class, to derive marginal products. From this point, we then discussed what additional information we would need to obtain estimates of a firm's marginal cost. Then, after specifying a wage rate, and with all of our work spread out over three blackboards in clear view of everyone in the class, we calculated marginal cost and observed and discussed, as a group, the nature of its relationship to marginal product.

Using Teams to Identify the Muddiest Point

Prior to this class, I had experimented with muddiest-point exercises. However, they were done exclusively at the individual level, where I typically had each student identify the most confusing or complicated point from each lecture, and then submit their entry – usually one or two lines – at the end of each class or the beginning of the next.

For this TIP project, students were asked to keep a journal of the muddiest point from each class. Then, at the end of each week, students would communicate with their team, either electronically or in person, and share their muddiest points for the week. Then, together, each team would discuss the individual muddiest points and agree on a single muddiest point for the week.

Perhaps more importantly, each week three or four teams were randomly selected to identify a single muddiest point, and attempt to resolve that point of confusion. The selected teams were then required to write up and submit their report to the course Blackboard site. I expected this assignment to promote the four Miami Plan goals, particularly the goal of engaging with other learners. I also expected this exercise to provide valuable feedback to me about how well I was covering difficult topics, and I expected it to be a useful formative self-assessment tool for students. Teams were encouraged and allowed to use all available resources – e.g., their class notes, the book, my office hours – to work through and resolve their muddiest points.

Evaluation

I had very high hopes for this CAT, but have mixed feelings about its actual effectiveness. I had hoped to promote the goal of engaging with other learners, but this was compromised to a degree by a tendency for some teams to meet "electronically," a practice that I did not explicitly discourage. I did anticipate that students would attempt to communicate in this way, and I continue to feel that meaningful e-engagement is possible. However, comments on student evaluations and informal input during the semester suggested that, on some occasions, the task of identifying and writing up a muddiest point may have been taken up largely by a single student in the group and perhaps under less than ideal circumstances – faced with an approaching deadline, a conscientious student would submit to the group, via e-mail, a single muddiest point seeking comments and suggestions from the rest of the team. If executed in this way, the assignment is far less likely to promote the type of engagement among team members I had intended, and as such is also less likely to achieve the secondary goals of critical thinking and understanding contexts. For at least one team it appears to have been an exercise in intertemporal division-of- labor, with team members simply taking turns individually completing the assignment for the entire team.

Despite some minor disappointment, I adopted this assignment in a modified form in my spring semester (2006) principles of macroeconomics course. At Bill Walstad's urging, I also increased the grading weight of the assignment. While it still comprised a small percentage of the overall grade (less than 10%), Miami students tend to exhibit a very high effort elasticity. Indeed, this small change seemed to make a big (positive) difference. In addition, I think I may have embraced the assignment more in the spring, by both praising, in class, the first round of posts (which also set a high bar for the teams that followed), and by more deliberately integrating some of the issues raised by the posts into classroom discussion.

This exercise also encouraged students to visit my office *prior to* the day before an exam. So, much like weekly quizzes, the CAT seemed to help provide an incentive for students to keep up with the material, and also to explicitly grapple with more difficult concepts. On one occasion in the microeconomics course, one team selected the relationship between demand and marginal revenue as their muddiest point. In their post, they were able to numerically show why, under their implicitly assumed conditions, marginal revenue was less than price. However, their explanation was so convoluted that it confused many of the other students in the class who looked to their post for insight. As a result, the controversy spilled over – somewhat humorously – into class, at which point we collectively deconstructed the team's post and identified the issue of price discrimination as a critical factor in the relationship. The discussion went well beyond where I had expected to go on the matter at that point in the course, but the student response to the exercise was extremely favorable, and it saved me lecture time later.

Creating Personal Reflections with Team Feedback

The last assessment innovation that I adopted was much in the spirit of the Chinese proverb, "What I hear, I forget; what I see, I remember; what I do, I understand," and also consistent with a national trend – and a growing Miami University emphasis – on "discovery" and increased student engagement. While there are alternative approaches available for promoting this goal (e.g., experiments; in-class cooperative learning exercises), my approach was to have students actively reflect – both informally and formally – on the relevance of the principles we were studying to their everyday lives.

This activity became part of our everyday classroom discussion. Students were instructed to think about the material from the previous lecture(s), and then were given an opportunity, usually at the start of each class, to offer their perspective on the relevance of the course principles. The incentive for students was a small participation grade and the prospect of being called upon randomly, along with the ability to prepare for the more formal assignment associated with this innovation. All students were required to document at least one of their observations in writing, via a reflective essay describing the relevance of the course concepts to current events in the news or their own lives. The essays were posted to the course Blackboard site in what was designed to be a virtual poster session.

Before posting their essays to Blackboard, students shared a draft with their team. Given the formative review within this small group that had been working together all semester, students then refined and revised their thoughts before posting them for all to see on Blackboard. Each student was also responsible for posting a comment on at least one other paper, posted by a student from a different team. In addition to promoting engagement with other learners, I expected this exercise to encourage students to see the relevance of economics to their lives and the world around them, and also help them take a step toward becoming the kind of "informed skeptics" we seek to develop in the course.

Evaluation

My impression is that in some respects, this was the most successful CAT adopted. I think it was very important to have the students post their final observations to Blackboard as a part of an "e-poster session." I suspect that because each post was open to peer scrutiny/response, they were of much higher quality, given their 10 percent weight in the final grade, than if they were submitted only to me; Miami students seem to care not just about their grades but about their intellectual reputation among their peers as well. Mostly, the assignment reinforced my impression that students want to see relevance of what they are studying to their everyday lives. Fortunately, in a microeconomics course, this should be a reasonably easy goal to accomplish. I adopted this assignment in my spring macroeconomics course, and again it seemed to be the highlight of the semester for the students and for me. During the semester, I talked about the assignment and gave hints and tips about current events that students could write about. Interestingly, almost no one used the ideas I offered, which I took as a very positive signal about the degree to which students were finding the course to be personally relevant.

Students would frequently come to class wanting to discuss the very same news stories that I was planning to cover myself. They also raised a number of personal observations throughout the semester that helped expand my repertoire of examples and to which their peers could easily relate – for example: dating as a sunk cost; surplus extraction and NFL seat licenses; the inefficiency of class scheduling; the relationship between university parking fines and total parking revenues; the implications of a semester fee versus per-copy charges in student labs; in-state versus out-of-state tuition rates; the incentive effects and efficiency implications of different grading standards across departments and divisions; and, detailed negative externality and public good examples from shared apartments and dorm rooms. This will forever remain a part of my principles courses.

Student Evaluations and Concluding Remarks

In addition to the standard end-of-semester course evaluations, I also surveyed students at mid-semester about the degree to which the course was promoting the four Miami Plan goals. Since there were still several key assessments yet to be completed (the final quiz; additional muddiest points;

the final personal reflection), I suspect that the results paint a fairly conservative picture.

All of the students in the class either strongly agreed (64%) or agreed (36%) that the course was promoting critical thinking. On a 4-point scale, with a 4 being strongly agree, the class average was 3.64, which compares favorably to the overall historical average for the course (around 3.40). With respect to understanding contexts – a goal that the department feels is inexorably linked to critical thinking – 18 percent of the class strongly agreed that the goal was being promoted and 64 percent agreed; the average was quite close to the historical norm for the course (around 2.9). The reflecting and acting goal probably comes closest to capturing the department's desire to create informed skeptics, and almost all of the student agreed (57% strongly agreed; 39% agreed) that the course was effectively promoting this goal – numbers way above the historical norm for the course (roughly 2.45). I suspect, but cannot prove, that this improvement was related to the class emphasis on personal reflection. Finally, in light of the team structure adopted, I was a bit surprised that only 43 percent either agreed or strongly agreed that the course was promoting the goal of engaging with other learners. This reinforces my suspicion that more than one team may have turned the muddiest point exercise into a rotating individual exercise.

While my end-of-semester instructor evaluation scores were mostly in line with my long-run trend, student responses to two questions stood out. First, on a 5-point scale, with a 5 being strongly agree, students felt that they were challenged to think (4.67). Students also felt strongly that class attendance was important (4.89). While my assessment innovations may not be solely responsible for these high scores, they were certainly adopted, at least in part, to challenge students and to make class time more valuable and relevant.

The TIP innovations experience started a lengthy conversation in my department about assessment, and the focus eventually moved on to issues of compliance relative to divisional program goals and AACSB Assurance of Learning requirements. This dialogue centered on student learning outcomes and departmental learning goals as opposed to narrow compliance concerns in large part because of this project. We learned that "having the conversation" – either taking the time to deliberately reflect on your own course as an instructor, or talking about these issues as a department or a committee – is one of the most valuable parts of an exercise such as this.

As this process made me reflect more on my teaching and my students' learning, I also explicitly defined learning objectives not just for the course, but for each class. Each day, I prepared a handout with the learning goals for that class, along with one objective and one subjective question related to those goals. This turned out to be the change my students embraced most enthusiastically. By better articulating my goals for the course it helped me think about more effective ways to promote them; by better communicating expectations to my students, I feel as if I significantly improved the learning environment in the class.

Finally, the changes I adopted in my course did not lend themselves, individually or collectively, to empirical tests of their overall effectiveness. To me, this was a personal confirmation of one of the most important lessons I have learned about assessment – keep it simple, at least initially. Learning by doing suggests it may be easier to iterate to a truly meaningful assessment regimen rather than trying to get there on the first step.

II. ASSESSMENT IN STATISTICS AND ECONOMETRICS

Katherine Silz Carson

Most econometricians will agree that the best way to learn econometrics is to do it. At some point or another in our careers, we have all struggled with problems with our data, apparently irresolvable error messages, or having to implement a new and unfamiliar type of modeling technique or hypothesis test. Many of us would agree that it was during these struggles that we learned the most. Although these types of learning experiences are ideal, it is often not possible to implement them in one-semester courses on econometrics or statistics due to constraints arising from time, space, data availability, or the students' prerequisite knowledge in mathematics and statistics. The challenge is to create miniature learning experiences which can recreate some of the "Aha!" moments we all have had. This section of the chapter describes classroom assessment techniques implemented in two courses at the United States Air Force Academy: Analysis of Economic Data and Introduction to Econometrics. These techniques were designed to address specific gaps in student learning in order to help them identify their own misconceptions and improve their mastery of basic statistical concepts.

Economics 365, Analysis of Economic Data, is a required course for all economics majors at the Air Force Academy. Cadets normally take this course during the spring semester of their junior year. In the semester prior to taking this course, cadets complete a semester of introductory statistics that is a part of the Academy's core curriculum. Because Econ 365 is designed to serve as a bridge between the core statistics course and the econometrics course that cadets take during the fall of their senior year, the emphasis is on the problems typically present in real-world economic data, applying basic statistical analysis to economic data, and interpreting the results in an economic context. Section sizes are between 15 and 20 students. At the time that these assessment techniques were implemented, students were expected to be able to do the following things by the end of the course: (1) Articulate the different types of economic data and know where to find them; (2) Apply basic statistical analysis techniques to economic data series; (3) Test economic data series to determine whether or not they support alternative economic hypotheses; (4) Explain the role that data analysis plays in a program of economic research. The first assessment tool was designed to help students meet the first objective. In particular, it was designed to help students correct mistakes they were making in distinguishing between time series and panel data sets. The second assessment tool focused on the third objective. Although it did not ask students to conduct formal hypothesis tests, it did help them to hone their ability to think critically about using economic data to support or refute an argument.

Assessment #1: Who? What? How Often?

In order to know what type of data analysis is appropriate, it is necessary to know whether the data set contains time series, cross-sectional, or panel data. Objective 1 of Econ 365 requires students to be able to distinguish among these three types of data, as well as identify whether a data set contains microeconomic data or macroeconomic data. Students also should be able to locate major economic data series on the Internet. Most of us have been categorizing economic data for so long that we do it without even thinking. We look at a data set and instantly know whether it contains time series, cross-sectional, or panel data. But how did we get to this point? Many students do not find that this skill comes easily, and giving students definitions of the different types of data and expecting them to be able to recognize the difference without additional practice is often unrealistic. This assessment exercise was designed to help students identify the key characteristics of a data set so that they can determine how to categorize it. The exercise was originally developed after results from a midterm examination revealed that students frequently confused time series data with panel data, primarily because they had difficulty distinguishing between an economic unit and a variable. For the purposes of clarity, the following definitions apply to the discussion below:

Economic unit: A country, state, county, city, individual consumer, individual producer, or other unit about whom economic data is collected
Variable: The information that is measured about the economic unit(s)
Cross-sectional data: Multiple economic units, measured at a single point in time
Time series data: A single economic unit, measured at multiple points in time
Panel data: Multiple economic units, measured at multiple points in time

Although these relatively standard definitions make perfect sense to economists, students often find it difficult to apply these definitions to actual data sets. Often, students confuse the economic unit(s) with the things that are being measured about the economic unit(s). This exercise addresses this confusion by presenting students with a data set and asking them to answer the following three questions:

Who is being measured? (the economic unit(s))
What is being measured? (the variable(s))
How often are the measurements taken? (the frequency in time)

Once students distinguish between the who (the economic unit(s)) and the what (the variable(s)), it is a trivial exercise to determine whether a data set contains time series, cross-sectional, or panel data. As originally implemented, the exercise presented students with the following three data sets: (1) Table B-3, Quantity and Price Indices for Gross Domestic Product and % Changes, 1959–2006, from the 2007 *Economic Report of the President* (time series data); (2) World Bank data reporting GDP, the GDP growth rate, and exports and imports as a percentage of GDP in 2005 for 226 countries (cross-sectional data); (3) Per capita personal income and the unemployment rate from 1976–2006 for the states in the St. Louis Fed's district (panel data). As all these data sets contain multiple variables, they force students to distinguish between an economic unit and a variable. Students worked in pairs to answer the three questions above and categorize each data set as cross-sectional, time series or panel. After the exercise, students commented that they found the who/what/how often tool to be useful in figuring out how to categorize an economic data set, and they wished that they had done the exercise earlier in the semester. This exercise is still part of the assessment toolkit in Econ 365. It has been modified to employ one data set per week in the weeks preceding the midterm exam. This enables the students to get repeated practice with applying these concepts, and allows them to be exposed to a wider variety of economic data sets. Generally, the last few times students complete this exercise, they find it to be so simple that their attitude is, "Duh, this is easy," which is, of course, the desired outcome.

Assessment #2: What Does This Graph Show?

One purpose of Economics 365 is to help students develop their abilities to think critically about the use of economic data to support or refute arguments about economic policy. As a part of the course, students must critically assess op–ed pieces which include citations of economic statistics to support the point of view expressed in the article. The purpose of this exercise is to help students assess their ability to think critically about economic data presented in graphical format so that they can practice and improve these skills prior to writing their critical assessments. It was inspired by Walstad's (2006) statement that it can be enlightening to observe how students misinterpret data presented in tables or charts. On the lesson preceding the exercise, students completed two readings in which the authors cited the same economic data to espouse opposing viewpoints. Students generated lists of the claims about the state of the economy made by each author. On the day of the exercise, students were shown a series of graphs which displayed the data cited in the articles. For each graph, students voted via a show of hands on whether the graph could be used to support/refute each claim. Individual students were then asked to explain the reason for their vote, and a class discussion of each graph typically ensued. As a result of this exercise, students were able to hone their abilities to determine what information a graph displays, and whether that information was or was not consistent with a particular argument. By helping students to talk through their reasoning and confront any misconceptions that arise during the discussion, it is possible for the instructor to assess what additional practice students might need to further develop their critical thinking skills. After this exercise, one student commented, "That was a fun way to learn." Based on the quality of work in the critical analyses which students turned in at the end of the semester, it appears that this exercise served as a useful warm-up for students and helped them to practice thinking about economic data critically and systematically.

These assessment tools provided useful and engaging ways to help students learn about economic data. They also help the professor to determine where students are in the learning process. During these exercises, students appeared to learn in spite of themselves. Later versions of this course have included modified versions of these exercises as well as additional ones. Furthermore, the success of these exercises was a motivation for developing additional classroom assessment tools for the follow-on course: Economics 465, Introduction to Econometrics. Two of these tools are discussed below.

Classroom Assessment in Econometrics

Economic 465, Introduction to Econometrics, is a required course for all economics and operations research majors at the Air Force Academy. Students typically take this course during the fall semester of their senior year. Most students have completed either two semesters of statistics (operations research majors) or one semester of statistics and one semester of analysis of economic data (economics majors) prior to taking this course. The typical section size is between 15 and 20 students. By the end of the course, students are expected to be able to: (1) Create and estimate regression models using economic data; (2) Interpret and explain the meaning of the results of the model using layperson's language; (3) Use the model to make quantitative predictions about economic behavior; (4) Analyze the model using appropriate hypothesis testing techniques; (5) Evaluate whether the standard model is applicable to their problem and data; (6) Write a one-paragraph summary of the model and results in layperson's language. The first assessment tool discussed below is designed to help students learn to correctly interpret the meaning of a confidence interval, part of objective two. The second one helps students assess their ability to correctly set up hypothesis tests, part of objective four.

Assessment #3: Confidence Interval Simulation

Monte Carlo simulations are one way to help students learn abstract econometric concepts like unbiasedness and efficiency. Kennedy (1998) presents some ideas for using Monte Carlo studies to teach econometrics and some textbooks (e.g., Barreto and Howland 2006) use Monte Carlo simulations as the primary tool for teaching econometrics. This Monte Carlo simulation is designed to help students learn the proper interpretation of a confidence interval. If the exercise is successful, students will be able to come up with the correct interpretation of a confidence interval on their own, as well as assess deficiencies in alternative explanations which some of their classmates or the instructor may offer.

This assessment exercise employs a Microsoft Excel spreadsheet and a simple set of steps that the students complete either in class or prior to coming to class. In the spreadsheet, students generate 10 samples of data (10 observations per sample) which meet the Gauss-Markov assumptions. For each sample, they calculate a slope and a 95-percent confidence interval for the slope. Each student then counts how many of his or her intervals contain the true value of the slope from the simulated population. The instructor then polls each student about the number of intervals which contained the population slope and keeps a running tally on the board of the total number of intervals which contain the true slope. In a class of 20 students, typically around 190 of 200 intervals (95%) contain the population slope. The instructor then asks students to relate this result to the phrase "95-percent confidence interval." Students typically quickly recognize that this phrase corresponds to the fact that 95 percent of the intervals that the class calculated contain the population slope. The exercise concludes with the instructor asking students, "What is wrong with this explanation?" and presenting the students with alternative incorrect explanations of the interval (such as the probability that the parameter is in the interval is 0.95). Sometimes, students will offer these incorrect explanations spontaneously, and will often be corrected by other students. Because this exercise illustrates the point that the population slope is fixed, and it is the interval that changes from sample to sample, it allows students to confront their misconceptions about the meaning of probability statements about confidence intervals.

Assessment #4: Setting Up Hypothesis Tests

In order to meet objective four, students in Economics 465 must be able to convert statements about the economic relationship between two variables into a null and alternative hypothesis which they then test using an appropriate hypothesis-testing technique. After two semesters of statistics, most students are quite good at setting up null and alternative hypotheses when they are asked a question like, "Test whether the coefficient of X is negative." However, they often stumble when this same problem is phrased as, "Test whether quantity falls when price increases." In this exercise, students translate economic statements into null and alternative hypotheses, then assess the correctness of their answers.

First, the instructor presents the students with some regression output. It can be new, but it may be helpful if the students have seen the data and results previously so that they can focus on the hypotheses. For the most recent implementation of this example, a data set from Ashenfelter, Levine, and Zimmerman (2003) was used for a model which relates an index number for the price of 27 different Bordeaux wines to each wine's age. Students are given the following three statements about the relationship between a wine's age and the index of its price, which they must translate into null and alternative hypotheses: (1) Test whether a wine's age has an effect on its price; (2) Test whether older wines have higher prices; (3) Test whether a wine's price index goes up by 0.05 for each year that a wine ages. These three statements are designed to reflect three different types of hypothesis tests that students are expected to be able to do: a two-tailed test, a one-tailed test, and a test centered on a number other than zero. Students may work in pairs, and write down what they think an appropriate null and alternative hypothesis is for each statement. The instructor then chooses three teams to put their null and alternative hypotheses on the board. Afterwards, the instructor presents students the following rules one at a time for setting up null and alternative hypotheses:

Rule 1: Hypotheses are always about the population parameter
Rule 2: Always put equality in the null hypothesis.
Rule 3: If possible, put what you'd like to conclude in the alternative hypothesis.

As each rule is presented, students discuss whether the three hypotheses on the board conform to these rules, and what changes, if any, need to be made to the hypothesis statement to make it correct. This method appears to work better than presenting the rules first and then having the students set up the null and alternative hypotheses, as the students seem to gain a better understanding of the concepts when they have concrete examples to which to apply the rules, particularly when these examples contain errors which they can easily determine how to correct. It seems that once students correct errors in someone else's work, they are less likely to make them in their own.

Concluding Comments

The challenge in teaching undergraduate econometrics is to create an environment in which students can learn from their mistakes, but to split these learning experiences into bite-sized chunks. Many of us probably made these same mistakes at one time or another, but they occurred so long ago that we have forgotten how we found our way around them. These simple exercises which take at most a 50-minute class period to implement, allow students to confront their misconceptions and learn from each other. They are designed to allow the students to observe where their own learning is falling short and identify where they need improvement, while at the same time providing the faculty member with feedback about areas in which students may require additional practice in future lessons. Lastly, these exercises require students to be engaged with the material, thus generating a more rewarding classroom experience for both teacher and student.

III. SMALL GROUP WRITING IN MONEY, BANKING, AND FINANCIAL MARKETS

Indradeep Ghosh

At Haverford College, I teach a variety of courses in macroeconomics and finance. In the past three years, I have taught introductory courses in macroeconomics, as well as upper-level electives in Money and Banking, International Macroeconomics, and Computational Methods in Macroeconomics and Finance. In these courses, I have used a range of different assessment techniques, ranging from periodic problem sets, midterm and final exams, to small group writing assignments and group projects. In what follows, I will describe my experience with using small group writing assignments for the "Money, Banking and Financial Markets" course. First, I will describe the course, and set it in the context of the wider economics curriculum at Haverford College. Then, I will provide some context for the use of small group writing assignments as an innovative assessment technique in this course that I implemented in fall 2008. Finally, I will describe the outcome of this innovation, and offer some reflections on how the use of this innovation could be sharpened and made more effective in future versions of the course.

Course Description

Money, Banking and Financial Markets is a 200-level elective course. Most of the students who take this course are either majoring or minoring in economics, although I also get the occasional student who belongs to neither category but is interested in a job in the financial sector and so decides to take the course. Enrollment in the course varies from year to year, but is rarely large. It averaged about 16 students from 2006 to 2009.

Introductory micro and introductory macro are prerequisites for Money, Banking, and Financial Markets. The introductory macro course, which is the more relevant prerequisite, is designed for first- and second-year students who are unsure whether they wish to major in economics. As such, the objective of the introductory course is to stimulate interest in economics as an academic discipline, and at the same time, present a roadmap for what a student can expect in more advanced classes, should he or she choose to major in the subject. This means that even at the introductory level, I use quite a bit of mathematics and graphical analysis.

Money, Banking and Financial Markets is more analytical and taught at a more advanced level, covering concepts in monetary economics, asset pricing, and banking theory. The content involves an understanding of basic asset pricing (bonds/stocks), an understanding of how these rules of asset pricing might apply in practice in real-world financial markets (a discussion of the efficient markets hypothesis, the limits of rationality and a foray into behavioral finance), a discussion of derivatives and foreign exchange markets (in the light of the crisis, this particular topic took up more than the usual time in Fall 2008), and finally, the introduction of money and an analysis of how monetary policy works and interacts with financial markets.

As a textbook for the course, I have used *Money, Banking & Financial Markets* (Mishkin 2006). In Fall 2008, I assigned the textbook at the start of the semester, but because the financial crisis began to unfold at a rapid pace during this time, I de-emphasized the textbook, and added on a large number of mandatory readings drawn from economics blog articles (such as those posted at blogs written by Greg Mankiw and Brad De Long, as well as *Marginal Revolution*), financial newspapers (such as *The Economist*, *The Financial Times*, and *The Wall Street Journal*), and online financial news websites (such as CNN Money.com and Yahoo Finance).

Small Group Writing Assignments

As stated above, the course is designed to have a strong analytical component, and for the assignments, students are expected to supplement their learning of the textbook material with information reported in the financial press. When I taught the course in prior years, students typically were assigned periodic problem sets, an in-class midterm exam, and one individual writing assignment.

In Fall 2008, I added two small group writing assignments (henceforth SGW) to complete the follow-on assessment module for Teaching Innovations Program (TIP). The financial crisis of 2008 made it imperative that some kind of writing assignment should be included as part of the course assessment because the textbook was clearly inadequate for engaging students on what was happening in the real world as the crisis unfolded. In fact, many students had begun to raise questions in class about various aspects of the crisis, very early on in the semester. I was fortunate to have learned about SGW assignments during the San Antonio TIP workshop in May 2008. I felt comfortable introducing this innovation with the hope that it would serve two broad objectives – give students the opportunity to connect theory to real world markets, and give me the opportunity to test them in a way that problem sets and exams don't allow.

The SGW assignments were designed to have students read news articles and then answer questions based on the articles. Before I could assign the SGW, I had to ensure that enough conceptual material had been covered in class that students might be able to relate the concepts to what they were reading. Consequently, the first SGW assignment was given only in the first week of November, and the second one in the final week of November.

The time allotted to each of the two SGW assignments was two weeks. Together, these two assignments contributed to 30 percent of the final grade. I graded each assignment along the following lines: 50 percent of the grade was based on my judgment of whether the group had tackled effectively the questions I had asked, and whether they had been able to articulate clearly their answers. This part of the grade was based on my subjective assessment of content as well as style, and each person in a group received the same score for this part of the grading process. The remaining 50 percent of the grade was based on peer-evaluations of how each student performed as part of the group. I asked each student to rate his or her group members on a scale of 0 to 10 (with 10 representing "excellent group participation"), and also to provide comments about such participation. I then aggregated these responses to determine the remaining 50 percent of the student's grade on each assignment.

For the first SGW, the article assigned (from *The Economist*) was approximately 3000 words long. I divided up the 11 students in the class into 3 groups (4/4/3) based on random matching, and then assigned the same article and the same questions to each group. Rather than leave the questions very broad, I asked very specific questions based on the text of the article.

The structure of the second SGW assignment was similar. I assigned the same article (the text of a speech by Senator Ron Paul before Congress, approximately 2000 words long) to all groups, except now I divided up the class into 4 groups (3/3/3/2). The group composition was no longer random. Instead, I attempted to balance ability across groups after considering each individual's grade from the first assignment. Here, I considered both portions of the grade – the part based on pure written content, and the part based on peer evaluations. Even though the peer evaluations were anonymous, I was still able to use them to identify who had done the work, and who had not participated fully. Thus, in choosing groups for the second assignment, I was careful not to assign to the same group two individuals who had both been identified as slackers in the first assignment, or two individuals who had both performed exceedingly well on the written part (as part of their group efforts).

Outcome of SGW Innovation

Students reported to me that they liked the idea of having to write short pieces in groups rather than answer multiple-choice or purely analytical problems as they do in the more traditional types of assessment. Based on their positive feedback, I structured the final exam as a writing assignment as well, except that the final was an individual writing assignment.

As I mentioned earlier, I had students fill out peer evaluation forms. In these forms I also asked students to comment on how the SGW assignment had worked for them, whether they had any comments or suggestions about whether it could have been more effective. A few students (about 60%) responded to this question. Most of the responses stated that the SGW assignment had forced them to think outside of the material presented in the textbook and lectures, and had been a good break from the normal routine of problem sets and exams that economics courses at Haverford usually use for assessment.

One student, however, complained that the first SGW assignment was too easy and that he or she (the responses were anonymous – students were asked to rate themselves along with their peers to ensure this) did not see the point of working in a group since the questions were simple enough for him or her to have tackled alone. I realized that perhaps the first SGW had been too simple, but also that because the SGW assignment had been structured in such a way that students in a group could divide up the work, some groups had not spent much time discussing the answers before writing them up (that is, each student just cut and pasted his or her part of the work into the group document, without necessarily confirming that the work done by others in the group was in fact satisfactory).

To address this issue, I made the second SGW more difficult, and insisted that group members schedule a meeting specifically to discuss and debate responses before writing up the final product. I emphasized that this was particularly important from the perspective of style because in comparing answers to different questions by the same group, it was easy to ascertain if the group had collectively aimed at a homogeneous style of presentation in the final written responses. This change seemed to work as the second SGW assignment produced much more homogeneity in terms of style.

I did not find any major differences in performance across groups, so the portion of the grade that depended on group output (the final written answers) did not vary a lot across students from different groups (within a group, this portion did not vary by construction). There was, however, some variation in the portion of the grade that was based on peer evaluation because a few students were not deemed to have participated fully by their peers (e.g., the person may have missed a group meeting, or had not delivered his or her portion of the group assignment on schedule). This was an issue only with the first assignment, though, because I personally approached each such student and communicated the importance of participation. I found that the peer evaluations were much more uniform for the second assignment.

As mentioned earlier, each of the two assignments contributed 15 percent to the final grade. In terms of assessment, the first assignment played a more formative role, since it allowed students to learn by doing, and also provided me with information that I found helpful in designing the second assignment. Both assignments also were graded by me and counted as part of the course grade, and therefore served as summative assessments as well.

I retained all the written pieces and draw upon them in the next couple of paragraphs, to comment on the quality of student responses and what I inferred from such quality about students' facility with the material that I was teaching. I illustrate with two examples drawn from the first assignment, which required each group to read and answer questions based on an article entitled "A Short History of Modern Finance: Link by Link" published in the October 16, 2008, issue of *The Economist* magazine.

Example 1

The first question required students to provide a real-world example of hedging through currency options. I had already covered the basics of derivatives markets in class, so this question was designed to force students to confront how a real-world company might use options contracts to hedge.

Moreover, in class, I only covered stock options and currency swaps, and hedging possibilities in these markets, so in answering the question, students were expected to extend their understanding of how hedging might work in these two markets to an understanding of how it might work for currency options. I insisted that the group identify a real company with real hedging needs, and then construct a specific options contract that would satisfy such hedging demand. While the contract itself could be fictitious, it had to demonstrate the specific industry and market concerns faced by the company that the group had chosen. The responses by the groups demonstrated that students were able to identify multinational companies or companies engaged in extensive world trade as an important source of demand for currency options contracts (the three groups picked Merck, Aston Martin and Sony Corp.). Only two of the three groups, however, were able to answer the second part adequately – i.e., describe a very specific situation which would call for hedging, and then describe how the contract might play out under different scenarios. The third group provided the basic ideas of how a currency options contract might be used to hedge by the corporation of their choice, but their answer was thin on details such as: what is the precise amount that is hedged, what specific options contract might be used to hedge this amount and, where would the company buy such options?

Example 2

The second question in this assignment specifically addressed the fact that I had not had time to cover currency markets in the lectures. But I had covered stock and bond markets in enough detail that I was confident about requiring students to study the basics of currency markets on their own. The question was therefore designed to test whether students could leverage their knowledge of asset pricing in stock and bond markets to understand asset pricing in currency markets. All the groups performed very well on this question, and their performance gave me confidence that students had learned the fundamentals of asset pricing adequately.

Some Final Reflections

I think the addition of the SGW assignments to the course was a success, both for me and my students. For me, it was a success because the innovation greatly enthused students to learn about the crisis, and also allowed me to demonstrate to students how one could use the concepts I was teaching to think about real-world financial markets. For the students it was a success because they got to work with each other and because they came away feeling like they had learned something useful. My first experience with SGW assignments convinced me that I should use them again in my courses at

Haverford. I now include a component in each of the courses I teach now, including the current version of Money, Banking and Financial Markets.

Relative to my Fall 2008 experience and based on student feedback, I have made two changes to the way I implement this SGW assessment technique. First, given some students' concerns that the first SGW assignment in Fall 2008 was too easy, I have started assigning tougher questions, which require the groups to extrapolate from lecture material and the content of the assigned article, to a greater extent than was the case with the first SGW assignment I used. The questions I now use test the students' ability to think critically about what they were being assigned to read so the assignment is more than a test of reading comprehension. Second, I have each group present the answers to their questions before the entire class. This change allows me to cross-examine their understanding of the material and also their own answers.

IV. CONCLUSION

As the above personal accounts reveal, formative assessment activities and assignments can require students to use all forms of intellectual engagement such as writing, discussing, graphing, calculating, estimating, surveying, critiquing, solving, or something else. They add richness and vitality to a course and help instructors interact with students in positive ways that foster economic achievement and greater participation by students in the learning process. They also have the capacity to show students the complexities and subtleties of economic thinking, deepening their economic understanding.

Most formative assessment techniques are relatively easy to adapt for use in any undergraduate economics course. How much time they require to implement will depend on how extensively the instructor wants to use a technique in a course or whether they decide to incorporate multiple assessment techniques as part of instruction. The best advice for an economics instructor who is new to formative assessment is to start out simply and experiment with one or two new techniques and spend instructional time making sure they work in one quarter or semester. They can then build on their prior experience and expand their assessment repertoire in the next quarter or semester.

REFERENCES

Angelo, T.A., and K.P. Cross (1993), *Classroom Assessment Techniques: A Handbook for College Teachers* (2nd ed.), San Francisco: Jossey-Bass.

Ashenfelter, O., P.B. Levine, and D.J. Zimmerman (2003), *Statistics and Econometrics: Methods and Applications*, Hoboken, NJ: John Wiley and Sons.

Barreto, H., and F.M. Howland (2006), *Introductory Econometrics Using Monte Carlo Simulation with Microsoft Excel®*, New York: Cambridge University Press.

Frank, R.H., and B.S. Bernanke, (2005), *Principles of Microeconomics* (2nd ed.), New York: McGraw-Hill.

Kennedy, P.E. (1998), "Using Monte Carlo studies for teaching econometrics," in W.E. Becker and M. Watts (eds), *Teaching Undergraduate Economics: Alternatives to Chalk and Talk*, Cheltenham, UK and Lyme, USA: Edward Elgar, 141–59.

Mishkin. F.S. (2006), *Money Banking & Financial Markets* (8th ed.), Boston: Pearson/Addison-Wesley.

Walstad, W.B. (2006), "Assessment of student learning in economics," in W. Becker, M. Watts and S.R. Becker (eds), *Teaching Undergraduate Economics: More Alternatives to Chalk and Talk*, Cheltenham, UK and Northampton, MA, USA: Edward Elgar, 193–212.

Wheelan, C.J. (2002), *Naked Economics*, New York: W.W. Norton.

CHAPTER 8

Context-rich Problems in Economics

Mark Maier
Joann Bangs
Niels-Hugo Blunch
Brian Peterson

Graduation-gowned Harvard students interviewed in the films *A Private Universe* and *Minds of Our Own*,[1] reveal embarrassing lapses in scientific understanding: "it is hotter [in summer] when the earth gets nearer to the sun"; tree wood forms when matter "is sucked up from the ground." In our experience, economics students give similarly ill-informed answers to fundamental economics questions even though, as in the case of Harvard science students, they had only recently "learned" the same concept in the classroom. Research on learning suggests that transfer of knowledge from inside the classroom to outside the classroom is not an automatic process. It is most likely to occur if students practice new understanding repeatedly in a variety of contexts (Bransford, Brown, and Cocking 2000).

In this chapter we describe an instructional innovation called context-rich problems that aims to help students transfer their learning to new situations. Developed by the University of Minnesota Physics Education Research group,[2] context-rich problems were extended to economics instruction by the Teaching Innovations Program (TIP) in which all chapter authors were participants. In Section I, Joann Bangs and Mark Maier summarize the context-rich problem approach. In Sections II and III, Bangs and Maier explore the relationship between context-rich problems and other interactive learning strategies and summarize the research on context rich problems. In Section IV, Niels-Hugo Blunch outlines the steps taken in TIP to write and use context-rich problems and discusses recent experiences related to the implementation of context-rich problems. In Section V, Brian Peterson explains how context-rich problems can be used as an assessment tool. Section VI provides our conclusions.

I. WHAT ARE CONTEXT-RICH PROBLEMS?

Context-rich problems are designed to move students away from a "plug and chug" mentality: finding the right equation for the problem, substituting numbers for variables in the equation, and calculating the answer. This approach may allow students to succeed on traditional tests, but is not helpful for most problems encountered outside the classroom and does not replicate expert-like thinking by economists. Context-rich problems include a short story in which the student is the major character with a plausible motivation for deriving a solution. The problem requires a series of decisions to be made about fundamental concepts before mathematical manipulation of formulas, and then a self-conscious reflection on how the problem was solved.

Consider the traditional problem:

Calculate the present value of $10,000 received in ten years. Assume a discount rate of 4 percent.

A context-rich alternative to the traditional problem is:

You and your brother have inherited a U.S. government bond that will pay $10,000 in ten years, but will not pay any interest before that time. You agree to share the bond equally, but your brother would like to receive his one-half of the bond's value now. How will you explain to your brother, who has not studied economics, how much you should pay him for his share?

Context-rich problems are not the only pedagogy to incorporate real-world situations in problems; problem-based learning and case methods offer a rich source for pedagogical innovation adopted by economists.[3] Context-rich problems' design is what differentiates them: an easy-to-use structure for transforming traditional problems in ways to facilitate transfer of knowledge. Specifically, the approach asks instructors to design problems that:

1. Are based on one core concept.
2. Begin with a personalized story, often in a non-standard application.
3. Ask the student to choose the appropriate concept and to create the relevant diagrams.

4. May have excess or missing information.
5. May lack cues and may have no explicit target.

Identify the Core Concept to be Investigated in the Problem

Even though there is not widespread consensus on the content appropriate for college-level economics, there is agreement that each instructor *should* identify core concepts so that there will be cohesiveness within that introductory course, if not across courses taught everywhere (Hansen, Salemi, and Siegfried 2002). These concepts should flow from the student learning objectives created for the course. The following context-rich problem requires students to use the core concept of tax incidence:

> *You own a grocery store in the city of Minneapolis. As you read the paper this morning you discover that a proposal to fund a new football stadium in Minneapolis includes raising the sales tax in the city of Minneapolis by making it 0.5 percent higher for all sales within the city limits. Compose a letter to the editor of your newspaper to explain your point of view on this proposal.*

Begin with a Personalized Short Story, Perhaps in a Non-standard Application

Research on writing in college courses suggests that students write better if assignments offer a motivation for the task and specify the audience to whom the student is writing (Bean 2001; Graff 2004). The context-rich problem format provides a number of prompts with clear motivation and audience that, in our experience, lead to longer and more substantive essays.

Most context-rich problems begin with "You…," and places the student in a specific circumstance that provides a motivation for solving the problem. The following prompts suggest the range used in context-rich problems:

- You are…(in some everyday situation) and need to figure out…
- You are on vacation and observe/notice…and wonder…
- You are watching TV or reading an article about…and wonder…
- Because of your knowledge of economics, your friend asks you to help him/her…
- You are writing a science fiction or adventure story for your English class about…and need to figure out…
- Because of your interest in the environment and your knowledge of economics, you are a member of a citizens' committee investigating…
- You have a summer job with a company that… Because of your knowledge of economics, your boss asks you to…

- You have been hired by a college research group that is investigating… Your job is to determine…
- You have been hired as a technical advisor for a TV (or movie) production to make sure the economics is correct. In the script…, but is this correct?
- You have been hired to write scripts of short dramatizations that will teach high school students important concepts. The concept for this script is…
- You are a police detective solving a crime. Because of your knowledge of economics you are able to solve the crime by…
- You have hired to write the text for a radio commercial that will use an economic concept to argue…

The following is a personal short story that targets economic concepts.

You have been hired as an economics consultant by a friend who is writing a science fiction novel. (You remember that this is how Alan Greenspan got his start, so you agree.) In this novel set in the future, the air is so polluted that people must buy air like they buy water or gasoline today. Your friend wants to write an interesting and complex novel in which outcomes aren't simple or predictable. She asks you for a list of economic concepts she might use, for each one explaining how it might lead to an interesting plot.

Ask the Student to Choose the Appropriate Concept and to Create the Relevant Diagrams

Context-rich problems often do not specify the concept or diagram to be used. If a topic was recently studied, students may be able to guess which concept is needed. In this case, it may be beneficial to use context-rich problems for periodic review after a number of concepts have been studied. Nonetheless, we repeatedly find that students are unable to note the applicability of a concept that, in theory, had just been "learned." In the following problem, the student is expected to recognize the appropriateness of a supply/demand diagram, whether or not it will show market clearing, and how to illustrate the proposed policy solutions:

Your uncle is very upset because after a recent snowstorm he was charged $300 by a private snow-removal company to clear his driveway. He wants to petition the local village government to pass a law to put a cap on how much firms can charge for clearing driveways. As a student of economics, he asks your advice for wording his petition. What do you tell him? Is there a better solution?

The Problem has Excess Data or Missing Information

To replicate the real-world situation in which appropriate data must be selected before using a formula or concept, some context-rich problems have excess numerical data. Alternatively, the problem can have missing information, expecting students to recognize the need for readily-available data, or to make reasonable estimates based on experience. For example:

> *Your uncle reminisces about the good old days in 1973 when the price of gasoline was only 40 cents a gallon. But you know that everything has gone up in price since then and you wonder if gasoline has really increased in price if we take into account inflation. Write a one-page response to your uncle, explaining whether or not gasoline really costs more today.*

In this problem, the missing information is the price of gasoline today and the relevant price indices for 1973 and today, all available to the student either in a textbook or online.

The Problem Lacks Cues and May Have No Explicit Target

As practitioners, economists often face general questions about a decision that do not initially specify which variables will be used to make the decision. Context-rich problems are especially effective when the student is placed in a similar situation and must select the problem-solving criteria. For example:

> *You have been asked by the President of the College and his Cabinet for assistance as they reevaluate the current pricing strategy of the College, which is to raise tuition annually by 5 percent for all students. You are not sure that this is the best strategy for the College. Prepare a three-page memo for the President and Cabinet describing what kind of information you need to help them determine a new strategy, and what conclusions you will draw on the basis of this information.*

To answer this question, students will need to recall not only the laws of supply and demand, but also elasticity. If the problem is assigned later in a principles of microeconomics course, students should also consider market structure. In addition, the student will need to decide the target variable, likely the impact on tuition revenue.

Context-rich problems have a number of benefits for student learning. The format, beginning with "you" in a novel situation, engages students more readily than standard textbook problems. Typically the quantity of student writing increases substantially, more than double in our experience in comparison with non-context-rich problems. Because there is a clear audience and situation, student writing is better focused and also less error-prone (Bean 2001, 63–64).

Context-rich problems often reveal that students lack deep understanding of course concepts. For example, when solving the previous problem, students typically reveal that they are unable to use price elasticity of demand in a correct and appropriate way even though they had recently studied elasticity. In my experience, context-rich problems do a better job of revealing such shortcomings than do traditional problems.

When a context-rich problem reveals that students do not understand an important concept, repeated use of context-rich problems reinforce the underlying concept and deepen student retention and understanding of it. By focusing on one concept put in a new context, the problem requires students to transfer understanding from one situation to another, a step identified as critical for sustained learning (Bransford, Brown, and Cocking 2000).

In our experience, students sometimes object to context-rich problems, preferring problems with single, correct answers. In such cases, students need direct explanation of the rationale for course goals. Most students usually appreciate that the course will be of long-term benefit only if they are able to apply concepts in real-world situations. Student attitudes toward context-rich problems and success in solving them can be improved if the problems are sequenced in terms of complexity. Instructors can begin with a problem that has a target variable and no missing or extra information, followed by problems that add these potentially more difficult characteristics.

II. USING CONTEXT-RICH PROBLEMS WITH OTHER ACTIVE LEARNING STRATEGIES

The difficulties in implementing context-rich problems also can be alleviated if they are used in combination with other active learning techniques. For example, context-rich problems are well-suited to in-class cooperative learning exercises. The following context-rich problem was written for a principles of microeconomics class:

> *You have been hired to be a consultant on pricing strategies for two different companies. Both of the companies have similar customer bases in that their customers fall into two well-defined groups: college students and young well-paid professionals. The first company is a trendy bar. The bar is currently seeing many young, well-paid professionals as customers, but quite a bit fewer college students. The bar has run a marketing campaign to attract more college students, but that only caused a small increase in the number of those customers. The second company is an electronics store selling items such as iPods. This company is also*

currently seeing many young well-paid professionals as customers, but quite a bit fewer college students. The electronics store has also run a marketing campaign to attract more college students, but that also only caused a small increase in the number of those customers. Both of these companies want to know if they could make some changes in their pricing strategy to increase their sales to college students and thereby increase their overall profits. Prepare a report for each company. Each report should be one-half page in length. In each report, make a recommendation to the company detailing what they must do to follow your recommendation and explain why they should follow your recommendation.

This was one of three context-rich problems assigned by Joann Bangs. Each student was required to come to the next class with her typed solution to the problem she was assigned. At that class period, one name was drawn from a hat to determine who would present her solution to the class. Subsequent class discussion was quite engaged as students shared additional analyses and students asked clarifying questions to make certain they understood how the economic concepts applied to the problem. For the context-rich problem shown above, all students recognized the need for price discrimination. In addition, a number of creative solutions were suggested for dealing with the potential for resale, including advertising only in student publications to limiting the number of purchases per student.

Alternatively, context-rich problems can be used as a follow-up to cooperative learning. For example, Jennifer Rhoads (2009) used a context-rich problem as the final step in a cooperative learning exercise. In her upper-level health economics course, students first completed a cooperative learning round table on health care policy options and then developed their own comprehensive health care policy recommendations.

Context-rich problems are especially effective in combination with the just-in-time teaching (JiTT) approach – short assignments typically focusing on material that will be covered in the next class and submitted electronically via a course management system hours before class (Simkins and Maier 2009). Consider the following context-rich problem written by Stephen Schmidt, Union College.

You walk into a convenience store and observe a police officer talking to the cashier and a customer. You infer from what is being said that \$50 is missing from the register. The police officer, talking to the customer, says, "Let me get this straight. Yesterday, you came into this store with \$50, and bought four big bags of chips for \$8 each and three six-packs of beer for \$6 each. Is that right?" The customer nods. The police officer turns to the cashier and says, "Now, this morning you changed the prices?"

The cashier says, "Yes. We lowered the price of chips to $5 and raised the price of beer to $10." The police officer asks, "At those prices, how much did you sell before he came in?" The cashier replies, "We sold 60 bags of chips and 50 six-packs of beer." The officer asks, "So what happened when he came in today?" The cashier replies, "He bought two big bags of chips and four six-packs of beer. He paid me with a $50 bill. Another customer behind me asked me a question and, when I turned around to answer, he swiped the bill off the counter!" The customer exclaims, "That's a lie! I bought only two six-packs of beer and six bags of chips. When I gave him the $50 bill, he grabbed it and stuffed it in his wallet." The cashier replies, "There's a $50 bill in my wallet, but it's mine; I had it when I came to work this morning." The police officer thinks for a second, then tells the cashier, "You lied to me. You're under arrest!" As the cashier is led off in handcuffs, the customer turns to you and says, "How did the officer know the cashier lied?" How do you, as a diligent student of consumer behavior, explain to the customer how the police officer reached this conclusion?[4]

By practicing first with a complex context-rich problem such as the one above, students will gain experience and confidence to solve context-rich problems in high-stakes, more heavily graded situations. Student responses submitted before class can be used as the basis for in-class activities. For example, in the problem above case, the instructor could display (anonymously) student answers and ask students, working in small groups, to evaluate different explanations for the cashier's arrest.

III. RESEARCH ON CONTEXT-RICH PROBLEMS

Much of the work done on context-rich problems has been done in physics education. Most notably, the two-part paper (Heller, Keith and Anderson 1992; Heller and Hollabaugh 1992) examined both the role of context-rich problems and cooperative learning in an introductory physics course.

In these two studies, the goal of the introductory physics course was to improve the problem-solving skills of physics students. Class time was set aside specifically to model a problem-solving strategy and a grading scheme was devised to encourage the use of this problem-solving strategy. Student groups were then observed solving both traditional textbook problems and context-rich problems. When solving traditional textbook problems, the students spent their time searching for formulas to use rather than spending time discussing what physics concepts to apply to the problem.

As a matter of fact, the students did not want to apply the problem-solving strategy they had been taught to these traditional textbook problems. The students felt that following this process was unnecessary because it required them to write out more information than they felt was required to solve the problem. It should be noted that the students frequently were not successful at solving these traditional textbook problems with their formula-searching strategy, but this lack of success did not seem to encourage them to look for alternative problem-solving strategies.

Heller and Hollabaugh's observations of students solving traditional textbook problems are consistent with the work of Chi, Feltovich, and Glaser (1981) regarding novice-like problem solving. They noted that experts tend to analyze a problem by thinking about what information they will need to solve the problem while novices tend to search for formulas that incorporate the variables they have been given. Heller and Hollabaugh believe this reliance on novice-like problem solving occurs because traditional textbook problems do not require that students make important problem-solving decisions. In these types of problems, all of the information given is relevant to the problem, and none of the necessary information is missing. In addition, these problems always let the students know exactly what should be solved for – generally in the last sentence.

Students in Heller and Hollabaugh's inquiry were much more likely to engage in discussions about physics concepts (rather than searching for formulas) when they were given context-rich problems to solve. Context-rich problems discourage novice problem-solving techniques because the students must make decisions. When working with context-rich problems, students are forced to determine which information is relevant, which information is missing, and how they might obtain such information. Like the expert problem solvers noted by Chi, Feltovich, and Glaser (1981), they must ask themselves what is needed in order to solve the problem. In addition, Heller and Hollabaugh's students were much more satisfied with the problem-solving process they had been shown when asked to solve context-rich problems. When confronted with the need to make decisions, these students understood the value of the expert-like problem-solving process.

Additional evidence for context-rich problems relies on research about learning in which there is both theoretical and empirical support for learning in context. For example, a 1987 study by Miller and Gildea (as reported in Brown, Collins, and Duguid 1989) on teaching vocabulary found that an average 17-year-old had been able to learn roughly 5000 words a year by learning them in context by reading, talking and listening. By contrast, however, a traditional vocabulary teaching method of giving a dictionary definition and example sentences was not nearly as effective, allowing students to learn only 100 to 200 words a year. Even more problematic than the slow pace of learning is that this process often leads to incorrect use of the new vocabulary words because the students do not have the opportunity to understand the context needed for the words. Brown, Collins, and Duguid (1989) liken this experience to acquiring tools (buying hammers, screwdrivers, etc.), but having no idea how to use them. By providing context to the learning, context-rich problems help our students go beyond merely acquiring the tools of economics, to being able to actually use those tools in the right way in the right situation.

Certainly the idea of learning in a context is not a new idea. For centuries, apprentices have learned in context. Brown, Collins, and Duguid (1989) suggest we put the context back into learning by using an approach they label as cognitive apprenticeship. They suggest that educators bring the three key steps of the apprenticeship process (modeling, coaching and fading) into our classrooms. Just as the traditional apprentice begins by observing the master working, our students should begin by watching experts working. Context-rich problems provide the opportunity for instructors to model the problem-solving process. By going through the step-by-step process that we as economists follow to solve realistic problems, we model how to "think like an economist."

After observing the master, the apprentice will begin independent work. However, the apprentice is coached through the process. Over time less and less coaching is required (fading) until the apprentice is ready to complete the entire process independently. In cognitive apprenticeship we accomplish the coaching and fading by starting the students with heavily scaffolded problems, then progressing to problems with less and less scaffolding. The level of difficulty is easily manipulated in context-rich problems by varying the amount of excess information given and the amount of missing information. We also can make use of cooperative learning groups to give the students the opportunity to help coach each other. While context-rich problems are not the only way to implement a cognitive apprenticeship approach, they do allow us to put the students into situations where they learn from experience. We can help our students to "think like economists" by modeling, coaching and fading with context-rich problems. In fact, context-rich problems can be quite useful in allowing us to see that our students are truly understanding how to use economic tools, rather than simply repeating information from the textbook.

IV. CREATING A CONTEXT-RICH PROBLEM
Niels-Hugo Blunch

The context-rich problem discussed below was created for an introductory statistics class with enrollment of 23 students in a small private liberal arts college. Enrolled students came mostly from the business school and were majoring in accounting, business, politics, or economics. All of these factors need to be taken into account when developing the context-rich problems – some providing challenges, others providing opportunities. For example, while student backgrounds are somewhat heterogeneous, the small class size makes for more interaction, facilitating in-class use of context-rich problems.

I began by taking a more traditional-type problem used in class and converting it into a context-rich problem. My problem already in use was:

Suppose the number of cars that arrive at a car wash during one hour on weekend evenings is Poisson distributed, with mean (and therefore also variance) 6. What is the probability of 4 arrivals in 30 minutes (i.e., a half hour) on a weekend evening?

Completing TIP's "One-Sentence-Summary Objective Setting Exercise" helped make it clear "what I was after" as I converted the traditional problem into a context-rich alternative.

Who: I, the economics instructor;
Does what: Develops my students' skill in recognizing when probability distributions are applicable to help solve problems from everyday situations;
For whom: My students;
When: During the course part devoted to discrete probability distributions;
Where: In small-group work in class, on homework assignments, on tests;
How: By having students practice with context-rich problems;
Why: To help students use probability distributions in real-life situations.

In the end, my learning objective is that students will be able to apply the concept of probability distributions in a real-life situation. The Hansen proficiencies that I expect students will demonstrate are the ability to interpret and manipulate data and apply existing knowledge (Hansen 1986; 2001).

Developing the context-rich problem from the more traditional problem therefore was much more straightforward – and resulted in the following:

Your old friend from high school, who is now a mechanic, has recently started a car wash on the side. He doesn't know much about statistics – but since you told him about how excited you were about taking this course he knows that you do!

He therefore asks you if you can help him decide whether the current capacity is ok or not. On weekdays it's not much of a problem, but on weekend evenings he noticed that cars sometimes have to wait in line.

Specifically, since the capacity of the carwash is 2 cars per 30 minutes and he doesn't want to have more than one car waiting in line at any one time, he is interested in how likely it is that there will be 4 arrivals in 30 minutes.

To help you (and therefore also himself!) with your analysis he has collected data on the average number of cars arriving in one hour on weekend evenings (which turned out to be 6 cars per hour), but he is not sure what to do with that data and whether it is sufficient for what he wants to know.

What do you tell him? More specifically, is the probability of maxing out on capacity – i.e., having four cars arriving in 30 minutes – sufficiently low that he doesn't need to worry about that happening in practice? (Hint: Briefly explain the relevant statistical technique/test and then perform it – a few lines should do.)

This context-rich problem explicitly incorporates three characteristics of context-rich problems. The problem is personalized: "Your old friend from high school…" "What do you tell him?" It omits the information that the relevant distribution is the Poisson so that mean and variance are the same. It adds irrelevant details about performance of the carwash on weekdays and weekends.

The lessons learned from the implementation of this context-rich problem, along with two other context-rich problems implemented later in the term, as part of the midterm and final exams, respectively, can be divided into four main lessons:

First, context-rich problems (CPR) are more demanding on the instructor than traditional problems, requiring more work than more traditional problems: First, at least initially, the preparation of problems takes a bit more time and effort than more traditional problems although with practice, this gets easier. Second, the execution may be a bit more involved, helping students understand exactly what is required of them. Third, grading of the context-rich problems can be challenging. This is both true if trying to compare student learning from context-rich problems relative to either similar more traditional problems or to other context-rich problems later on in the term using a "pre/post" set-up.

Second, the CRP is a flexible tool in economics instruction: Despite the challenges faced by the instructor in implementing context-rich problems as part of economics instruction, there also are obviously strong advantages with using them. Foremost, in my experience, is their flexibility. They can be combined with several of the other TIP-based innovations discussed in this book, including cooperative learning, case studies, and interactive learning in large enrollment courses. Such flexibility allows the instructor to mix and match among the various components of TIP, thus making classes more engaging for students and, ultimately, improving learning outcomes.

Third, students benefit. Review of student answers from midterm and final exams suggests that students gave more detailed answers to context-rich problems than to more traditional problems. In addition, students responded favorably when it was explained that context-rich problems prepared them for tasks they may encounter in future careers.

Fourth, student frustration and confusion with context-rich problems is not necessarily bad. The mix of deliberately missing and excess information that is part of the creation of context-rich problems can cause frustrations for students. In a survey taken after the midterm exam, students reported that they were confused and frustrated because of missing and excess information – two of the very components intentionally built into context-rich problems!

I used this opportunity constructively by first assessing the amount of frustration and confusion through informal probing of students and then explaining to students how context-rich problems were indeed very similar to what they would later experience out there in the real world when having to sift through and combine information as interns and, later, as regular employees. That way students understood that their frustration and confusion had not been in vain, but instead gave them a perspective on the learning objectives for the course as well as their education more generally.

V. CONTEXT-RICH PROBLEMS AS AN ASSESSMENT TOOL **Brian Peterson**

Context-rich problems can be usefully integrated into the course or program assessment process to find out what students have learned as opposed to what they have remembered. Or, as described at the institutional level by the Collegiate Learning Assessment, the goal of their use in the classroom is to "gauge summative performance authentically…"[5] Consider the following two student learning objectives taken from the economics program assessment at a small private liberal arts school in the Midwest:[6]

1. *Demonstrate the ability to recognize economic applications in everyday life.*
2. *Demonstrate the ability to utilize cost–benefit analysis to solve economic problems.*

Traditional economic assessment mechanisms often only determine if students can reproduce economic concepts in a constrained context. They do not address whether students have mastered the information so that they can respond to a more open-ended inquiry of the material. For example, the following short-answer question is typical in a public finance course:

What is the relationship between domestic investment and the federal government's decision to increase deficit spending?

Obviously, the question deals with the potential crowding out of private investment as a result of federal deficit financing: Will interest rate increases resulting from the government's decision to borrow cause private domestic investment to fall, assuming Ricardian equivalence does not hold? In a fully correct answer the student could have memorized the relationship, but not necessarily mastered the economic content or the underlying relationships between economic variables. However, consider that problem reworded as a context-rich problem:

You are an economic analyst with a small company. At the start of the recession, the federal government indicated that it was planning to significantly increase its spending to help out those in need. Your boss and president of the company came into your office ranting about the fact that investment by his and other firms would dry up, slowing economic growth. He asks you for a "fair and balanced" appraisal of the government spending increase. What do you say to him?

The focus of the problem has shifted from the student's understanding of the crowding-out effect to the impact of government spending on businesses in general or a particular type of business (depending on the wording of the question), including the notion of Ricardian equivalence. The student could bring in additional information about the changes in interest rates, potential changes in tax rates, or long-term benefits from the increased spending. The context-rich problem's value lies with the requirement that students must explain their answers rather than simply restate something from a textbook.

Additionally, context-rich problems easily can be used to assess one program-specific goal at a time or several at once. For example, I modified the original deficit finance question in the following way in a recent public finance course:

Walking down the street one day, you see a college classmate speaking to a group of people gathered on a street corner. Walking closer, you hear that your friend is protesting the high level of government debt accumulated to this point. His principal arguments are that government indebtedness is preventing our country from doing what needs to be done socially, and that the increasing level of debt will eventually bankrupt us as a nation.

Suddenly, he sees you in the audience, and says, "Look, there is my friend from college who is an economics major. This person has studied the matter closely, and can provide an expert's opinion on the matter." All eyes turn to you, and the crowd falls silent.

You clear your throat, and begin talking. Write a short, five-minute presentation detailing what you would say to this crowd.

Context-rich problems are able to address student learning objectives set for the course. This particular context-rich problem addresses objective 2 as it requires an understanding not only of cost–benefit analysis, but also the underlying notion of opportunity cost. At the same time, it could address objective 1 by adding a requirement that your friend wanted you to discuss what the popular press has been reporting with regard to government programs. Here, the value is not in the specific answer given; some students will agree with this friend, and others will not. The value of this kind of problem lies in the student's ability to craft an argument based on what has been learned in class. This pushes the students past the ability to simply recall and apply economic concepts into the realm of integration of economic concepts in everyday life.

In addition, student writing will be improved because the intended audience is now clear. The original problem did not specify to whom the answer should be addressed and implicitly asks the student to re-create the textbook's explanation with no guidance as to the detail required. Experts on college-level writing agree that such vague directions often lead to poor writing (Bean 2001; Graff 2004). The new problem puts the student in a plausible real-life situation in which writing has an audience and a purpose. As a result, the students must not only put the answer "in their own words," but also think about which words are appropriate and how much detail is needed. The result, in my experience, is longer, more-focused and better-written answers.

The following excerpts are representative of student work with this context-rich problem:

This act – the Balanced Budget and Emergency Control Act – was flawed from the start as the government realized it would be better to adjust the targets than automatically cut spending on important government programs.

Blaming the government for our current situation is not entirely fair; we have all contributed to our government's debt one way or another, and it is up to the government to successfully allocate funds to programs that will target increasing long-run costs and to us to behave sustainably by being more environmentally conscious as well as health conscious.

If we want to sustain our private investment during times of deficit, in order for it to be completely stable, it is necessary to find a way to sustain it with private saving alone because we will have no control over foreign saving which tends to be rather unstable.

The average score on this problem was a B−. While students generally followed the required format, and created arguments in one particular direction, they did not create the focused argument I wanted.[7] The responses had an "everything but the kitchen sink" feel because students included as much as they could remember, instead of making a specific argument using course information. It was clear that students needed additional practice in providing solutions to these problems. Consequently, I introduced several other context-rich problems later in the course, including the following, which was based on a series of popular articles on a particular election race in fall 2009 (Bendavid 2009; Nagourney and Peters 2009; Peters 2009).

> *Suppose you are the chief political strategist for Doug Hoffman, Conservative Party candidate for the open seat in NY's 23rd Congressional district. In a fit of despair after the election, he approaches you and says, "(Name), please, please explain to me why we lost. I thought we had it in the bag. We demonized the Democrat, made the Republican look like a Democrat, and appealed to traditional Republican bases. What happened?" In a brief (250 words maximum) essay, explain to him why he lost the NY election. Note: You may assume he understands key terms, so there is no need to explain them in your response.*

On this follow-up context-rich problem, the average grade was an A−, reflecting much improved arguments. Students now felt more comfortable with the open-ended nature of the responses. Even those students who expressed frustration at the ambiguity of the problem, understood their value as preparation for tasks they likely would encounter in future jobs.

Grading

Because context-rich problems are open-ended, the instructor faces challenges in grading. Rubrics can serve as a helpful tool in grading these problems, providing a way of letting the student know a priori how the question will be graded, and helps the instructor maintain consistency of grading across what will ultimately be dissimilar responses to the context-rich problem. For example, consider the following game-theoretic context-rich problem based on an episode from the *West Wing:*

> *You just finished watching the West Wing episode (from Season 3), "Hartsfield's Landing," in which President Bartlett (played by Martin Sheen) plays two extended chess games: one with Sam Seaborne (played by Rob Lowe) while discussing turmoil between China and Taiwan; and*

another with Toby Ziegler (played by Richard Schiff) while discussing the role of negative campaigning in presidential elections.

Immediately following that episode you wrote a letter to your pen pal in Russia and described how amazing you found that particular episode, and how closely you found it tied to your economics instruction. Your pen pal, however, has never seen the episode, nor has she taken an economics course in her life, but is curious how those concepts fit together. She's asked you to explain to her exactly what you mean. In your next 1–2 page letter to her, explain to her how chess, negative campaigning, and armed conflict are connected to your understanding of economic theory.

While there are specific cues in the problem that guide the student, there is no specific path that the student must take in answering this context-rich problem. A rubric that outlines specific targets the instructor requires will help facilitate grading problems like these as shown below.

	A	B	C	D	F
Economic Analysis (up to 10 points)	Accurately relates chess, campaigning, conflict and strategic behavior to economics analysis. Uses correct terminology.	Accurately relates at least two of the components to economic analysis. Terminology is appropriate	Incorrectly relates at least two of the four components to economic analysis. Correct economic terminology is not present.	Incorrectly relates at least three of the four components to economic analysis. Correct economic terminology is not present.	Does not write to the proscribed assignment.
Mechanics (up to 10 points)	Written analysis coherently relates the four components. Few typographical errors.	Written analysis is less coherent; minor typos.	Written analysis is less coherent, and there are significant grammatical errors.	Written analysis is difficult to follow.	Written analysis raises major literacy concerns.

Students should be shown the rubric in advance so that they have an understanding of how the problem will be graded. Since there is no particular "right" answer, showing them the rubric does not provide anyone with any particular advantage. Seeing the rubric in advance helps them understand that a portion of their grade will be based on mechanics and a portion on context. In discussing the rubric with students, I emphasize that I want them to integrate, not just reproduce information from the class.

VI. CONCLUSION

The framework for context-rich problems, originally developed for physics courses, is readily adaptable to economics instruction. Students in both physics and economics courses often start with novice problem-solving skills, looking for quick, "plug and chug" answers based on a recently learned formula. Context-rich problems help students to understand when and how core concepts can be applied to problems similar to those encountered by economic practitioners. As a result, students practice expert-like problem-solving skills: identifying relevant information, recalling information that should be common knowledge but was not included in the problem, and determining the target variable, also often not explicitly stated. Additional examples and information on how to write context-rich problems are available at the National Science Foundation-sponsored web portal Starting Point: Teaching and Learning Economics.[8]

In addition, context-rich problems can prompt better writing than often occurs when students answer traditional problems. Because the audience and purpose are specified, the student has a clearer sense of length, detail, and tone to be used. The result is not only improved writing but also answers that can be assessed more accurately by the instructor. Instead of repeating expressions used in the textbook, students answer context-rich problems with more authentic language revealing whether or not a concept was fully comprehended.

Despite their extensive use for more than two decades in physics education, there has been little empirical research on the impact of context-rich problems. Economic educators face a challenge and an opportunity to document the ways in which context-rich problems improve student learning. The potential clearly is there; the evidence has yet to be collected.

NOTES

1. *A Private Universe* and "Lessons from Thin Air" in *Minds of Our Own* produced by Harvard-Smithsonian Center for Astrophysics, Science Education Department, Science Media Group.
2. http://groups.physics.umn.edu/physed/Research/CRP/crintro.html.
3. On case studies, see Starting Point: Teaching and Learning Economics module on the Case Method at http://serc.carleton.edu/econ/cases/ index.html.
4. Context-rich problem written by Stephen Schmidt, Union College. Used with permission.
5. http://www.collegiatelearningassessment.org/ (accessed December 22, 2009).
6. While specific student learning outcomes may vary from institution to institution, the spirit of the learning outcomes may be fairly consistent across institutions.

Indeed, as Myers, Nelson, and Stratton (2009) suggest, such learning outcomes are never far removed from Hansen's (1986; 2001) proficiencies for the economics major.

7. A more comprehensive treatment of this assessment process is detailed in Peterson (2010).
8. http://serc.carleton.edu/econ/context_rich/index.html.

REFERENCES

Bean, J.C. (2001), *Engaging Ideas: The Professor's Guide to Integrating Writing, Critical Thinking, and Active Learning in the Classroom*, San Francisco: Jossey-Bass.

Bendavid, N. (2009), "Tea-party activists complicate Republican comeback strategy," *The Wall Street Journal*, October 16, A-1.

Bransford, J.D., A.L. Brown, and R.R. Cocking (eds) (2000), *How People Learn: Brain, Mind, Experience, and School*, Washington, D.C: National Academy Press.

Brown, J.S., A. Collins, and P. Duguid (1989), "Situated cognition and the culture of learning," *Educational Researcher*, **18** (1), 32–42.

Chi, M.T.H., P.J. Feltovich, and R. Glaser (1981), "Categorization and representation of physics problems by experts and novices," *Cognitive Science*, **5** (2), 121–52.

Graff, G. (2004), *Clueless in Academe: How Schooling Obscures the Life of the Mind*, New Haven, CT: Yale University Press.

Hansen, W.L. (1986), "What knowledge is most worth knowing? – For economics majors?," *American Economic Review*, **76** (2), 149–52.

Hansen, W.L. (2001), "Expected proficiencies for undergraduate economics majors," *Journal of Economic Education*, **32** (3), 231–42.

Hansen, W.L., M. Salemi, and J.J. Siegfried (2002), "Use it or lose it: Teaching literacy in the economics principles course," *American Economic Review*, **92** (2), 463–72.

Heller, P., and M. Hollabaugh (1992), "Teaching problem solving through cooperative grouping. Part 2: Designing problems and structuring groups," *American Journal of Physics*, **60** (7), 637–44.

Heller, P., R. Keith, and S. Anderson (1992), "Teaching problem solving through cooperative grouping. Part 1: Group versus individual problem solving," *American Journal of Physics*, **60** (7), 627–36.

Myers, S.C., M.A. Nelson, and R.W. Stratton (2009), "Assessing an economics programme: Hansen proficiencies, ePortfolio, and undergraduate research," *International Review of Economic Education*, **8** (1), 87–105.

Nagourney, A., and J.W. Peters (2009), "G.O.P. moderate, pressed by right, abandons race," *The New York Times*, November 1, A-1.

Peters, J. (2009), "Democrat wins a narrow victory," *The New York Times*, November 4, A-24.

Peterson, B. (2010), *Context-Rich Problems in Public Finance: Reverse Engineering an Upper-Level Policy Course*, Unpublished working paper.

Rhoads, J.K. (2009), *Cooperative Learning in a Health Economics Course: 2008 U.S. Presidential Campaign and Health Care Reform*, available at: http://cee.econ.uic.edu/workingpapers.html (accessed March 14, 2010).

Simkins, S., and M.H. Maier (2009), *Just-in-Time Teaching: Across the Disciplines, Across the Academy*, Sterling, VA: Stylus Publishing.

CHAPTER 9

Case Use in Economics Instruction

Patrick Conway
Derek Stimel
Ann E. Davis
Monica Hartmann

Walstad and Saunders stated in their handbook that: "Effective instruction in economics depends upon more than deciding what content to teach or the selection of course objectives" (1998, 5). We can perhaps make this point more precise: every instructor has the meta-objective that his (or her) students must learn. Selection of course objectives and decisions on content to include (or exclude) define what will be taught. What does the instructor do to ensure that the students learn?

Researchers in cognitive psychology, education, neuroscience and other fields have uncovered many of the important pathways for learning.[1] Our goal in this chapter is not to extend this original research, but to bring its lessons to bear on economics instruction. Specifically, we will answer the question: "Given that you know what you want to teach in a course, will incorporating cases in the syllabus improve student learning?" Our evidence is drawn from our own experience in case use in economics courses at our universities and colleges. We answer in the affirmative: incorporating cases into the curriculum does improve the learning outcomes of our students.

We will address this question in five sections. Section I defines the case as an instructional tool. It describes the five characteristics of a "star quality" case, and discusses appropriate placement of cases in the syllabus.[2] Section II addresses the importance of achieving higher-order (in the sense of Bloom et al. 1956) learning outcomes for our meta-objective in the classroom and describes the unique suitability of cases in achieving those outcomes. Section III highlights the importance of discussion and debate in the classroom in encouraging student learning, and highlights the uses of cases in facilitating such discussion and debate. Section IV introduces the affective nature of learning: our students learn more when they find the material interesting. Cases enhance learning by bringing real-world problem-solving to the classroom. Section V summarizes and concludes.

I. WHAT ARE CASES?

We've all heard of cases due to the popularity of their use at graduate schools of business: Harvard Business School provides some of the first and best-known examples.[3] A. Hansen (Christensen, Hansen, and Moore 1987, 7) summarizes a case as "an edited version of a real and thought-provoking event which occurred in some teacher's professional experience." J. Boehrer (1994) offers a related definition: "A teaching case is essentially a story, a brief account, for example, of a crisis in foreign policy decision-making. Like any story, a case presents a conflict, typically the tension between alternative courses of action that bring different viewpoints, interests, and values into contention and that must be resolved by a decision."

After considering these and other definitions, we chose to work with the following operationalization. *A case is a group of source materials on a single subject, drawn from real experience, that places the participants in a decision-making analytical role.* The group of source materials may be a short written summary. It also could include an image, a video, a collection of news articles, a cloud of tweets, or any other representation of real events.

Why this definition? Most importantly, because it makes precise the difference between a case and a case study. We are all familiar with case studies: summaries of individual historical events that provide background information, analysis or synthesis of that information, and the evaluation drawn by the author. A case study would seem to satisfy the Hansen and Boehrer definitions, but it would have limited use in facilitating learning. If the goal of the course is to stimulate the ability to analyze, synthesize and evaluate, the case study does all the work for the student – the analysis, synthesis and evaluation are all presented there. The case, by contrast, presents the background information and the substantive dilemma. The participants then use that information to create their own analysis (or synthesis, or evaluation). As our definition states, "it places the participant in a decision-making analytical role."

The advantage of using cases in the classroom is similar to the advantage of "learning by doing" over "learning by observing." We have all experienced the conversation with the student who explained, "I understood it when you said it in class, but I didn't understand it anymore when asked about it on the test." New developments in the science of learning emphasize the importance of helping people recognize when they understand and when they need more information. (Bransford, Brown, and Cocking [2000, 12] refer to this as "metacognition".) In the pursuit of active learning, the student who does the analysis is more likely to recognize the important components of the process than the student who simply reads the analysis in a case study.

Not all cases are created equal. Lynn (1999) proposes five key characteristics for a successful case – characteristics he calls the "five points of a star-quality case." They are:

1. Poses problem or decision that has no obvious answer;
2. Requires reader to use information provided in the case;
3. Has enough information for analysis, synthesis, or evaluation;
4. Evaluating the problem and reaching a solution requires reader to think and analyze;
5. Identifies actors who must solve the problem.

A case with these characteristics will provide the raw materials for learning by doing. We present three reasons why incorporating cases in your syllabus will lead to enhanced learning in the classroom relative to a syllabus without cases. First, Derek Stimel argues that our goals in the typical economics class include the student's ability to analyze, synthesize and evaluate economic phenomena and policies. These "higher-order" skills can best be learned through doing, and the case provides the framework for that action. Second, Ann Davis argues that learning will be most effective when students are put in the position to defend their thinking. Classroom discussion and debate provide the context for that defense, and cases offer excellent frameworks for facilitating that defense in a nonthreatening way. Third, Monica Hartmann states that learning is best encouraged when the students can see the practical application of classroom tools. Cases are both real-world in nature and place the students in a decision-making role. If properly designed, they provide the students with the affective incentives to participate and learn.

II. CASES ENCOURAGE "HIGHER-ORDER" LEARNING
Derek Stimel

I believe using cases in the classroom facilitates higher-order learning. To explain that point I will first define higher-order learning using Bloom's taxonomy (Bloom et al. 1956; Saunders 1998). As an example, I focus on one of my basic goals in Principles of Macroeconomics: the goal of economic literacy. I argue that higher-order learning is required to accomplish that goal and that the active nature of a case is a key feature that pushes students towards that goal. I illustrate this by reviewing my experiences with a case I use at the beginning of my Principles of Macroeconomics courses.

Table 9.1: Description of Bloom's Taxonomy

Type	Concept	Illustration Related to GDP
Knowledge	Recitation of arguments, facts, and theories.	The four components of GDP are consumption, investment, government spending, and net exports.
Comprehension	Understanding of arguments, facts, and theories.	When new home sales fall, all else the same, investment falls, and GDP falls.
Application	Applying arguments, facts, and theories to new contexts.	In the third quarter of 2009, a rise in government spending contributed to an increase in GDP.
Analysis	Deconstructing arguments, facts, and theories into component parts.	GDP is both a measure of income and spending because income is derived from the sale of goods and services as illustrated by the circular flow diagram. Measurement error called statistical discrepancy is added to income to ensure both methods produce the same number.
Synthesis	Building arguments, facts, and theories from component parts.	Productivity is output per unit of labor. Average income is total income per capita. As a measure of both output and income, GDP per capita is an estimate of productivity as well as average income for an economy.
Evaluation	Justifying a decision or opinion with facts, arguments, and theories.	I believe GDP per capita is an accurate measure of living standards in a country because it is the broadest measure of income. Furthermore…

Source: Author's construction.

Bloom's Taxonomy

Bloom's taxonomy is a framework to distinguish between different types of learning or understanding (Bloom et al. 1956). Running from the lowest level to the highest level of understanding, there are six defined categories: knowledge, comprehension, application, analysis, synthesis, and evaluation. To illustrate, Table 9.1 provides a brief description and example related to gross domestic product (GDP) for each level of understanding. As the table suggests, the three highest levels of understanding, which I henceforth refer to as higher-order learning, require a relatively more complex or sophisticated reasoning process than the three lowest levels. In my Principles of Macroeconomics courses, I have observed it is difficult for students to demonstrate higher-order learning. I think this may be because of the oversimplification of the concepts in the course and a tendency to focus on basic definitions.

Economic Literacy

Teaching Principles of Economics is challenging regardless of whether the course focuses on microeconomics, macroeconomics, or a combination of the two. As reported in Siegfried (2003), about 40 percent of college students take at least one economics class in their college career. Because it is an introductory course and a common general education requirement, Principles is the "at least one" course they take. Given that students have heterogeneous learning styles, a varied approach to a principles class is appropriate (Lage, Platt, and Treglia 2000). That variation and the additional variation that comes from students with different majors and backgrounds suggests a narrow focus on the intricate details of economic models may not be the best way to motivate students in a principles course (Fitzpatrick, McConnell, and Sasse 2006). As a result, many have suggested that "economic literacy" should be a primary goal of a principles course (Saunders et al. 1993; Hansen, Salemi, and Siegfried 2002; Haskell and Jenkins 2003) and I have adopted that goal for my Principles of Macroeconomics course.

A simple way economists (myself included) state "economic literacy" is the ability of a student to read and understand news stories about the economy such as those that appear in the *Wall Street Journal* or similar news outlets. There is an implicit notion that students should be able not only to comprehend a news story but be able to form an informed opinion of one. However, readers of news stories are passive by nature. They are consumers of news. A clearer path to demonstrating economic literacy and hence higher-order learning would be as a producer of news; that is, the author, not the reader, is the active role. It is this active nature that a star-quality case (defined in the previous section) shares with a well-written news article. A star-quality case pushes the reader closer to that active role of the writer of an article and towards the evaluation level of higher-order learning. The reader is in effect inserted into the case and forced to make a recommendation or take some other action, and then to justify that recommendation or action. Further, much like the author of a *Wall Street Journal* or similar article, when the case reader formulates her opinion or makes her decision, the correctness of the choice is uncertain. A case has a sense of ambiguity. When the writer formulates her thesis, she also does not know ex ante the accuracy of her thesis and must rely on the evidence she gathers to support the thesis both to herself, to her editor, and to her readership.

Thus, if a student masters a case, the student has clearly demonstrated economic literacy by replicating a similar logical process that underlies the construction of a quality article about an economic issue. These differences between a case and a news article push a student beyond "learning by observation" from reading an article and towards "learning by doing" by actively wrestling with the material.

Example

In my Principles of Macroeconomics course I use a case during the first week of the semester. The case involves a decision about accepting a baseball card for payment or not. In the case, a college student named George runs a car-washing business to raise some extra money. After washing a car, he is offered a choice between $20 and a baseball card. An identical card sold on eBay for $21.55 the previous week. Students are placed in the role of George and must make his decision. For this short case, my goals are simply to introduce the case method to students, to have students understand that decisions involve tradeoffs, and to have students recognize that these tradeoffs can be complicated by uncertainty about the future (see Appendix 9A).

While admittedly simple, the case contains the five points of a star-quality case. The reader must make George's decision though there is no obvious "right" answer. The key actor is identified. "Being" George requires thought and analysis. There is enough information to make an informed choice. Information from the case (such as the eBay price of the card) must be used. I like to use this case at the start of the semester because it is short and allows students to gain familiarity with using cases.

To understand the level of reasoning involved, it is helpful to reverse-engineer the reasoning process required for accomplishing those goals. This largely involves the student's ability to recognize the tradeoffs. For example, choosing to accept the baseball card means George forgoes the $20 alternative. It is important in evaluating that decision to consider all opportunity costs. In addition to giving up the $20, choosing the baseball card requires giving up time needed to sell the card on eBay. Of course the final sale price of the card is unknown. This makes the benefits of selling the card uncertain, which also affects George's decision. Thus, the case relies on two separate but related concepts: opportunity cost and choice under uncertainty. If students are able to use those two concepts in order to justify what they believe George should decide, that is the higher-order learning of Bloom's taxonomy. From Table 9.1, we see that evaluation involves providing justification of an opinion. Here students will be synthesizing two concepts to support their opinion as to George's dilemma. If they simply can recognize those two concepts are at the heart of George's dilemma, then they will have achieved the analytic goal of the exercise.

Of course I recognize that not every student is going to achieve an "evaluation" level of understanding during the course of a case discussion. Some students may only be able to describe opportunity cost and have a general sense as to its relevance to George's decision. At best, these students achieve the "application" level of learning on Bloom's taxonomy. Some students may not be able to do more than provide a definition of opportunity cost when prompted, only demonstrating "knowledge" on Bloom's taxonomy. The point is that a case and a case discussion afford the opportunity for a student to understand economic concepts and achieve higher-order learning. The ultimate learning outcome for a particular student depends upon the student's engagement with the material. As Monica points out in a later section, using cases with a "real world" setting also enhances that engagement.

Classroom Experience

I teach Principles of Macroeconomics sections that usually have 20–25 students. I provide the case to students at least one class period prior to the day it will be discussed. On the day of the discussion, I provide students with a set of questions related to the case. Those questions are as follows:

1. What issue or dilemma is George faced with?
2. In evaluating this dilemma, what are the relevant pros and cons of George's choice?
3. Construct an argument (a paragraph) for the decision you feel is best for George.
4. Can you think of an additional piece of information that George would like to know that will aid his decision but doesn't currently have?
5. In the problem, the card sold on eBay last week for $21.55. How would your advice to George change (if at all) if the card had sold for $23.30 instead?

Normally, I break students into smaller groups of four or five depending on the class size. The typical rhythm of the class period is for each small group to answer one question then we discuss that question as a class, then the small groups move on to the next question and so forth. I typically teach an 80-minute class session, and this process often leaves room for a brief summary of the main ideas at the end.

In using this case, I have commonly found that how students answer the first question greatly affects the nature of the subsequent discussion. Some students understand that George's dilemma is the choice about the baseball card versus money. Some students will focus instead on George's broader problem of raising money for his college experience. It is important to recognize that is not a "wrong" answer. What happens usually is the discussion becomes about George's options for raising money and the tradeoffs between a car-detailing business and an alternative. The same basic principles still apply, just the context changes. If the discussion proceeds down this broader path, it also tends to make the last question irrelevant (although it can be interesting to discuss whether there is a different dollar amount – something absurd such as $100,000 – that would affect George's choice about how to raise money for college).

In my experience, students are better able to demonstrate higher-order learning and economic literacy through use of this case than through strictly lecture or discussion settings. I'm often impressed how students are able to understand the issue of opportunity cost of time quickly by recognizing the hassle of selling the baseball card. They less frequently tie that in to the uncertainty about the price for selling the card. They also often bring in other relevant issues such as George's like or dislike of baseball cards and whether the card is genuine or not. In the latter case, while students do not use the phrase, the fact that offering the card seems to violate a social norm makes students more reluctant to want to accept the card. Students are often able to put those two concepts together and argue that George should take the cash, which is higher-order learning.

In my most recent semester I used this case except that I changed George to Jane, the car-detailing business to a tutoring business, and the baseball card offer to a video game offer (Madden 2010 for the Xbox 360). I largely observed the same results. I also ask exam questions that either directly relate to the case discussion or involve a scenario that is similar to a case. My anecdotal observations of student performance on those exam questions are that they perform as well if not better. At the very least students seem to enjoy the change of pace a case offers from lecture and remember the details of the case better than some of the abstract concepts of the course.

III. CASES FACILITATE DISCUSSION, INDEPENDENT DECISION-MAKING AND DEBATE

Ann E. Davis

After learning to use cases in TIP, I have introduced case modules in all of my courses.[4] I have found that cases facilitate discussion, debate, direct observation, and independent decision-making by students, resulting in improved learning outcomes. I also have found that cases can play a useful role in the context of an economics curriculum which is based on abstract, highly structured concepts and precisely formulated assumptions. Cases can facilitate a comparison between those assumptions and actual circumstances. The specific actor identified in each case must understand the significance of these assumptions in order to make effective use of economic theory, and to address the ambiguities and particularities of each specific context. Then, even applying precise economic models, the predicted outcomes may vary, opening up the potential for debate and discussion among students in each situation. Further, the objective consideration of multiple points of view occurs more naturally, based upon the conflict among actors within the context of the actual case. That is, debate among different points of view is no longer just an "academic" matter. I recount my experiences with two of these cases in the paragraphs below and then provide an overall assessment.

I developed a structure for the case modules in my courses to assure "star quality" (Lynn 1999). First, I begin with a review of an economics concept, as formally defined with strict assumptions. Then I provide information sources related to a specific case and/or assign the students to collect information within a structured methodology in specific steps. Then I pose the problem, with a specific actor identified, and assign the specific question to be answered. The instrument for evaluating the student's performance can be a class discussion, a short paper with references, an essay question on an exam, or some combination of these.

The Coffee Shop Business Plan is an interactive case I developed for my Principles of Microeconomics course. The goal for this case was to establish the conditions of perfect competition and the differences that emerge when products are differentiated. We began in the classroom with the reference concept of perfect competition. Then the students were assigned to map the coffee shops in the vicinity of campus with an information form to be completed, making note of their product differentiation by location, ambiance, varieties of coffee drinks and other food products, décor, and typical clientele. Students also measured the differences in unit price, which they found to be roughly correlated with the degree of product differentiation. Student observation revealed that the conditions of perfect competition did not fit the facts, and began their consideration of alternative "theories" and models. (See Appendix 9B for this first part of the case.)

The second part of the assignment was to develop a business plan for a new coffee shop within the vicinity of campus. For this exercise, I provided information regarding costs, including rental space, equipment, supplies, and labor. Based on potential market size, break-even price and volume of sales were calculated. Discerning the type of product differentiation which would appeal to a specifically student clientele then stimulated creativity among the competing student groups, including special ceramics, live music, and local food. Their specific proposals were judged by a local business mentor. Substitute products such as energy drinks and water became a focus of discussion, as tastes may have changed and new preferences developed. Competing strategies among off-campus local franchises, such as McDonald's, Applebee's, Starbucks, and Mobil On-the-Run, as well as locally-owned businesses (a coffee shop, two delicatessens and a family-owned diner), were considered. The dynamic nature of competition soon became apparent, including technical change (espresso machines at McDonald's) and new product development (most recently Starbucks VIA, a new instant coffee product).

Another lesson from this case is the essentially competitive and dynamic nature of the local coffee shop market. Even though the products are somewhat differentiated, especially the national brands, there is still relatively free entry and exit. Useful discussion questions for students included the definition of the market (coffee, beverage, energy drink) and the identification of the most appropriate model, perfect competition or monopolistic competition. In contrast to the static nature of textbook treatments, the continuing flux in market competition soon engaged the students in their own direct observations. Because the small strip mall where the coffee shops are located is just across the street from our classroom building, I continue to refer to these examples in subsequent years, even without the formal structure of the entire case.

This case engages the students in reflection on their own daily activities and consumer decisions, which becomes a form of "learning by doing." In this specific case, the students can see themselves as consumers, their familiar role, as patrons of a coffee shop. Reflection on their own experience becomes input into analyzing the "student consumer market." In addition, when considering the business plan aspect of the case, a new role, the entrepreneur, is added to their repertoire. One student in my first class using this case ultimately entered a local business plan competition, sponsored by the county economic development agency, and won second place. As an economics major, this class project had been her only prior "business" experience and gave her the confidence to take such an initiative. The application of the concept of perfect competition to a realistic situation enabled her to make full use of the insights of market forces, while also understanding the practical complexities of entry and exit.

In the context of this case, I felt that students fully understood the distinction between homogeneous and differentiated products for the first time. That is, they could directly address the question, "Is coffee just coffee," and only quantity matters, as the free coffee offered with McDonald's breakfasts? Or is coffee a distinctive product, differentiated by flavor, aroma, and geographic origin, as well as variations in preparation and "pairings," combined with an "experiential" component, as at Starbucks? While McDonald's emphasizes volume and speed, Starbucks encourages customers to linger and socialize, and to access the convenient Wifi Internet connections. Can the local "Casablanca" coffee shop, with comfortable chairs and exotic décor, compete? In this context, the company brand and logo become an understandable part of business strategy, providing instant recognition and differentiation along with higher price, compared with homogeneity, lower price, and higher volume of sales. Even the term "business strategy" only has meaning in the context of some degree of imperfect competition.

Another case I've created to spur discussion and debate is the Google Book project case. The objective was to develop a case which would encourage students in Principles of Microeconomics to bring their own use of information technology and the Internet into class discussion, to make use of active learning and observation of their own behavior in this context. The substantive subject matter is ownership of intellectual property. Economics textbooks describe such ownership as just another "property rights" example, but recent commentators on the Internet suggest that information "wants to be free." In this context, the zero marginal cost of reproduction of digital products, such as music and books, can help the students to interpret the distribution strategy of zero price. Further, the concept of network externalities, where a product is more useful the more users there are, helps to explain Google's continuous development of complementary products on its website. As a final tool for this analysis, cost concepts were very useful. For example, the high fixed costs of providing Internet access and software development for a competitive search algorithm helps to explain the drive for increased volume. That is, making use of network externalities can help Google to achieve large scale to reduce average fixed costs. The large user base then attracts advertisers and provides a revenue stream from third party payers. The Google Book Case provided an easily accessible example for examining these important microeconomics concepts in the context of the information technology industry.

I had three background sources for the case. First, I assigned several chapters of a free book by Harvard Law Professor Lawrence Lessig, *Remix*, (Lessig 2008) available on the web, along with short papers to review his basic concepts. The easy electronic availability and zero price of this particular book serve to illustrate some of the very points Lessig makes about the undue restrictions of copyright. Further, widely available discussions of Lessig's work on his and other blogs, and videos on YouTube, enabled students to use electronic media to follow the debates about copyright on electronic media. Second, during the semester we had a speaker – James A. Cannavino, a highly regarded business strategist formerly with IBM and more recently an Internet entrepreneur – address the economic impact of information technology. Mr. Cannavino's opening statement was "The Internet has changed everything." He described a new Internet business model, in which advertising paired with search enables the firm to get product information to the consumer just at the point of intended purchase. "The company knows exactly what the consumer is thinking because the consumer has just typed the terms into the search box on the screen," he explained. The shift of advertising from newspapers and magazines to online media then affects the economic viability of the traditional media, altering the industry in significant ways.

Third, there were background readings on the Google Book Project. In 2004, Google began to scan millions of books from various research libraries and to make them available on its website. In 2005 Google was subject to a class action lawsuit initiated by authors and publishers for violation of copyright. Although students make frequent use of Google search, the Google books option, which I demonstrated in class, was not yet known to many of them.[5] The revised settlement to this class action lawsuit was due in November, 2009, in the middle of the fall semester.

The book by Lessig provided a framework for the analysis of Internet companies such as Google. He describes the formation of Internet communities and the distribution of free products as a type of "sharing" economy, like families and churches. On the other hand, the Internet has also spawned a highly robust "commercial" economy, where the motive for operation is revenue and profit, like Google. He describes "hybrid" firms as a combination of the two, like Craigslist, which charge fees only for select products, while primarily existing for the purpose of the community of users. The first two short papers in this module served as an introduction to these concepts. Students were expected to explain these concepts accurately, with examples, and to address the question of the long-term viability of the "hybrid" model.

The third short paper in this module was more complex (see attachment). I created the case from these materials by assigning the students to advise the judge in the class-action lawsuit. The written assignment was a memo to the presiding judge from the Attorney General of the Anti-Trust Division of the Department of Justice. The student's task was to weigh the "public good" aspect of increased access to books by the public (and the potential commercial gain and enhanced monopoly power for Google) against the economic costs to authors and publishers of having free distribution of their intellectual property. This third short paper made use of Lessig's concepts of the "sharing" and the "commercial" economy, as well as demonstrated further the challenge to intellectual property rights in the Internet economy. Given its ubiquity, students could evaluate the Google books project as potential customers, and could also weigh the effects on Google's advertising revenue stream, market share, and Internet innovation. While the paper was structured with specific questions and a specific actor, the following class discussion was more open-ended.

The first example of the benefits of this integration of the information technology industry into the curriculum came early in the semester, in a discussion of supply and demand. I asked students to identify the impact of YouTube on the market for movies shown in theaters. Some correctly identified the shift in demand for theaters with the availability of a free substitute on the Internet. Then, spontaneously in both sections, other students called out the more important substitute for movies in theaters, a website called www.bootleg.com, among others. This volunteering of information more relevant to the students' own lives and beyond my own personal experience, was a real payoff for me, providing a vivid example of the application of a concept as well as two-way learning. A second informal discussion surrounded the identification of fixed and variable costs, in the context of cell phones and downloadable music services. That is, each call is free on a cell phone, at zero marginal costs, but the service contract which lasts for a given time period is a fixed cost. A third application of cell phone usage was the concept of "network externalities;" that is, a cell phone is more useful the more users there are.

The Google Book case clearly demonstrates the potential for debate and discussion in the pursuit of learning. Well-known authorities have different positions, so students are challenged to develop their own. For example, Lessig favors increased access and reduced protection of copyright for some specific purposes. Darnton and Auletta are more wary of Google's growing monopoly power. This assignment puts students in a decision-making role to weigh both positions and to articulate the aspects of the settlement which would balance the related "goods" of public good access, competition, and profitability. The subsequent class discussion revealed the diversity of views among students and the variety of proposed policy options regarding this case. Students successfully defended both sides in class, and had developed several creative policy alternatives. Some supported the public option of having Congress assume the book project and make it available to everyone. Others supported a regulatory structure to oversee the fees that Google would charge. Still others applauded Google's initiative and felt confident that continuing innovation and technological change would undermine any monopoly aspects at the present state of product development. All used (with varying degrees of sophistication) the economic concepts from class to organize their thinking. Certainly the topic of costs, usually obtuse and opaque to principles students, became highly relevant to company strategy and to the development of new products that are an integral part of their daily lives. This case generated more higher-order learning and discussion on these issues than I had observed in many prior semesters of lecturing about these topics.

In summary, the use of cases enabled me to supplement courses with relevant, timely material which illustrated key concepts in economics. By authoring these cases, I am more engaged in developing and presenting materials for students, with that enthusiasm obvious to students. This allows me to emphasize key issues which may receive little attention in the textbooks, and to incorporate current events in real time. This also allows me to illustrate the highly dynamic nature of economics, and the constant flux in markets, definitions of property, technology, and consumer preferences. I can present alternative positions on particular issues, and even alternative frameworks, for student consideration and debate. Students are more open to various points of view which are embedded in the case information, rather than reacting to the instructor's or the textbook author's particular perspectives. The evidence from the case discussions in class makes clear that the instructor authorizes multiple points of view, as long as each is logically defended, and this is an important lesson in critical thinking. The assigned problem for a specific actor within the context of each case also poses a real-world challenge, which helps to motivate learning and analysis at a higher level.

The use of materials relevant to the students' own lives also enhances their powers of observation, and their ability to see and articulate economic issues everywhere and in real time as they occur. Cases provide a structured and powerful tool to bring into the classroom a wider range of materials, from novels and movies to news media and personal experiences. The selection of dramatic examples, such as the market for human body parts and food safety, or ubiquitous examples, such as coffee shops and the Internet, increases the retention and application of economic concepts. The classroom itself can become more interactive, with examples emerging from all participants, with surprising and novel outcomes. Cases can help enrich economics classes, and in turn make economics classes a more memorable experience In open-ended anonymous student evaluations, students offered comments such as "great in-class discussions and modern day applications to microeconomic theory." According to my own observations, the classes were more lively, more engaged, more accepting of ambiguity and debate, and more effective in eliciting higher-order critical thinking.

IV. CASES ENHANCE UNDERSTANDING AND GENERATE ENTHUSIASM FOR LEARNING

Monica Hartmann

Cases enhance students' learning of economics and their enthusiasm for learning the subject material. This is due to the fact that cases rooted in real-world events provide students a rationale for why they would want to acquire the knowledge this discipline has to offer. Furthermore, cases make economic concepts less abstract for students and thus make it easier for them to understand the material. In this section, I will provide illustrations from my teaching experience to demonstrate this.

As the prominent economist, John Maynard Keynes, once wrote:

> The theory of economics does not furnish a body of settled conclusions immediately applicable to policy. It is a method rather than a doctrine, an apparatus of the mind, a technique of thinking which helps its possessor to draw correct conclusions. (Robertson 1922, v)

Many of us teach students this "apparatus of the mind," the economists' way of thinking to analyze an issue. The "real world" is the natural subject of our apparatus of the mind. For introductory courses in economics, though, the real world is a blessing and a curse. It is a blessing because students' excitement about economic tools rises to the extent that we demonstrate that the tools can be applied to real-world problems. It is a curse because the real world is messy; while concepts like "the law of demand" are stated "holding other things equal," in the real world other things are very rarely equal. Discussion of real-world events often gets us as instructors side-tracked onto discussion of interesting questions that are off the syllabus or more complex than the students can address with their current toolbox.

Using cases particularly in principles courses permits us to have the blessing while minimizing the curse. The students work through real-world problems, and thus are motivated to learn. The cases, though, are structured to emphasize the features of the historical record most relevant to the economic concept under study. The students' efforts are more focused and lead to greater learning of the concepts on the syllabus. I provide two examples of cases in this section, both of which I created for my courses: the multi-part case on hyperinflation in Zimbabwe and the case for (or against) Health Saving Accounts (HSA).

Cases motivate students to learn in different ways. The basic characteristics of a case require students to *experience* a situation by taking on a role and using the information provided to solve a problem and reach a solution. They are asked to simulate the decisions a person must make in a similar situation. In the two cases I will present in this section, the manner in which students are motivated to learn is tied to the decision they are simulating. In the Zimbabwe cases, the students are motivated because they can sympathize with the Zimbabweans, even if they never anticipate living in a hyperinflationary economy. Through the simulation, students identify trade-offs Zimbabweans must face in each decision, and they come to recognize that they would make similar decisions when faced with similar economic circumstances. In the health saving account case, the students are motivated because they recognize the analytical activity of the case to be something that they will do in their future careers, and the case is a good chance to practice these tasks prior to entering the work world.

Given my desire to demonstrate the relevance of economics to my Principles students, a series of four cases was written to allow students to apply macroeconomic concepts discussed throughout the semester to a real-world example of hyperinflation in Zimbabwe in 2007 (Hartmann and Werner 2009).[6] The first case, "Zimbabwean Economy – Day 1," was written with the intention of giving students an opportunity to apply the economic concepts of opportunity cost and production possibility frontier to the Zimbabwean economy. The first pedagogical goal for this case was for students to recognize there are scarce resources and one cannot satisfy all wants. As such there is an opportunity cost for each choice one makes. The second goal is for students to be able to identify the location for which a country is operating with respect to its possibility frontier and how its choices affect its position in the future.

The second case, "Zimbabwean Economy – Day 2," is based upon the price ceiling imposed on domestic goods sold in Zimbabwe in 2007. Students are asked to identify store owners' short-run and long-run responses to enacting a price ceiling. Students are not told that a price ceiling was imposed, but rather that the government declared the prices had to be reduced by half. I do not use this case right after the supply–demand lectures. I wait a few lectures so that it is not completely obvious what economic concepts are being demonstrated in the case, more closely reflecting how students will encounter economic issues in their daily life.

For the third case, "Zimbabwean Economy – Day 3," students evaluate the effectiveness of using fiscal and monetary policy to promote economic growth in an economy experiencing hyperinflation. This case is assigned after they have learned about the tools the government and the Federal Reserve has to manipulate the economy. This case is also used to introduce to students the link between money supply and inflation before formal notes are given. It provides a rationale for the importance of understanding the role of money supply in a functioning economy.

In the final case, "Zimbabwean Economy – Day 4," students learn about the historical lack of respect for property rights and a weak judicial system in Zimbabwe. They are asked a series of question so they can see how this can adversely affect incentives to produce, lead to inefficiency, and slow economic growth. This case is meant to illustrate how political/legal factors influence market forces (Colander 2009). Because this case requires students to engage in higher orders of learning, this case is done near the end of the semester despite the fact that the economic concepts were introduced in the first few weeks of class.

These four Zimbabwean cases consist of short readings (done in class), guided questions, small-group discussion and a classroom discussion of the answers. Each case takes approximately 30 minutes of class time with the third case only requiring 10 minutes. A PowerPoint presentation also was shown to provide students the current and historical context of the political situation in Zimbabwe. Although this presentation is optional, it does provide students an opportunity to ask additional questions on what can and is being done in response to the economic situation facing Zimbabweans.

Hyperinflation is a topic typically discussed in an introductory macroeconomics course, but it can be very difficult to help students to understand the magnitude of the problems created by hyperinflation and how it affects every facet of one's daily life. Inflation in Zimbabwe during 2007 was 108,000 percent per annum; this imposed significant costs on the Zimbabwean citizen (International Monetary Fund 2008). The case exercises I developed put the students in the position of these Zimbabweans, adjusting their economic choices to minimize those costs. Furthermore, the students recognize that a variety of different problems stem from hyperinflation. Having the four cases linked allows the knowledge obtained in one case to be applied in the next case. Each case builds upon the concepts of the previous case(s). Students see the interrelatedness of the concepts given that one is using the same illustration.

For the first case, "Zimbabwean Economy – Day 1," students are given a list of prices for items a typical Zimbabwean household may want to purchase each month. Students must allocate the household's income of two million Zimbabwean dollars among different competing needs. Students determine that there is only enough money to pay for rent, water, a month's supply of mealy meal and two eggs. They also realize there is no money for AIDS vaccinations for the sister, schooling for the children, or meat to get some protein. Then the students proceed to determine the short-run and long-run effects of their budget decisions for the household and the macro economy as a whole (given that many households across the country are making similar budgetary decisions).

When going over the answers as a class, I asked a question not part of the case: Why did they spend everything and not save money so they could purchase a bigger ticket item next month? Immediately many students raised their hands to respond that the value of the Zimbabwean dollar is declining so fast the household would not be able to purchase anything with it next month. They said it so matter of factly. Based upon past student exam answers, this is a concept I could not get across to many of their predecessors when I lectured on the subject. This time, with a case that required them to think through the steps, it just made sense to them. My observations are consistent with the literature (among others, Dale [1969] and Stice [1987]) that students retain 90 percent of what they do (e.g., simulate a real experience) versus only 50 percent of what they hear and see (e.g., lectures and movies).

The case also requires students to determine if Zimbabwe is producing on its production possibilities frontier (PPF) or at an interior point. They are able to determine this based upon the description of the Zimbabwean economy students read prior to answering case questions. Having students do this makes an abstract concept like the production possibility frontier more concrete and forces students to think about what the PPF really represents (e.g., how it is constructed, and what shifts it). When we discuss the answers as a class, I link this discussion of tradeoffs to the students' decision to attend college instead of working in construction or attending community college, for instance. Many of the decisions we make require trading off current for future benefits and thus have consequences in the future.

Students observe macroeconomic phenomena through many lenses prior to enrolling in my principles course, including news media, household discussions and participation in other (non-economics) courses. These observations often left them curious and confused. A case like this one provides my students a venue to ask questions about those phenomena. As we noted in the introduction, each student comes to the classroom with a unique set of prior knowledge. When I present a theoretical model, it is often too abstract for the students to connect with their prior knowledge. The set of circumstances provided in the case allows the students to make connections, whether correct or incorrect, with what they've previously observed. Yes, a case may "sidetrack" the discussion to issues not on the syllabus. This is not necessarily a bad thing, since the "sidetrack" is an attempt by a student to connect the phenomenon under discussion with her prior knowledge. (If the discussion goes on too long or the issues are too complex, one can continue the dialogue after class or in office hours for the interested student.)

In the second case, "Zimbabwean Economy – Day 2," students examine the short-run and long-term effect of President Mugabe's declaration that prices on domestic goods had to be slashed in half (Wines 2007). Students *discover* on their own that this presidential decree is essentially a price ceiling that leads to shortages and shutdown of firms as discussed in our formal lectures on price controls. This case is particularly helpful for those students who have difficulty depicting graphically how a price ceiling affects market price and output, or for those students who simply memorize the graphs. By working through the case questions, students obtain intuition on why price ceilings lead to market distortions. Given that students will not typically be graphing supply and demand curves after their principles courses conclude, it is very important to me that all of my students can articulate why consumers are worse off with price ceilings. Assigning the case for class was helpful when a student later on the semester argued that price ceilings helped consumers. I just referred to this case and asked him what happened in Zimbabwe when they instituted price ceilings. I did not correct his answer, rather he corrected himself once he was able to recall the elements of the case scenario he simulated.

But why is analyzing Zimbabwe's economy, a place about which my students have limited knowledge, so attractive to my principles students? First, it demonstrates the usefulness of economics in a real world situation. To the extent that I demonstrate this, they are apt to pay more attention and thus to learn more. Second, providing concrete examples as done with cases mirrors my students' learning styles. Based upon Myers-Briggs tests, 75 percent of the U.S. population relies on inductive reasoning (i.e., arguing from specific facts to more general principles) in their learning (Ziegert 2000). But, economics is a discipline that is traditionally taught through deductive reasoning (i.e., arguing from general principles to specific instances). Thus, my economics lecture that discusses concepts in abstract, theoretical terms first is not an effective way to convey economic concepts to a majority of my principles students. These cases allow me to provide my inductive learners concrete examples that facilitate their learning.

One of my primary goals is for my students to be able to take an abstract economic concept, such as comparative advantage, and apply it to circumstances when all other things are not held constant, contrary to the assumptions in the theory. Beyond illustrating the usefulness of economics, I employ cases to give students an opportunity to practice using economic concepts to come up with a solution or to evaluate a business practice.

Here is one illustration of a case I wrote to challenge my Managerial students to identify primary and unintended secondary effects of a policy change. Health care cost management is the number one human resource issue for virtually every U.S. employer. Costs are rising 10–15 percent a year and companies are either absorbing the costs internally via reduced or no salary increases and/or headcount reductions, or they are moving their operations overseas. My case, entitled "Consumer Driven Health Care Demand," facilitates the students' learning that misalignment of employer and employee incentives may drive up health care costs. Companies have adopted health saving accounts (HSAs) in an attempt to slow down cost increases. Prior to class, students are asked to read a series of newspaper articles on HSAs. In class, I provide students a brief overview of our current health insurance system, comparing it to how it would operate under HSAs. This is similar to a presentation that would be given by the head of the Human Resources Department to the Board of Directors.

This case is assigned after I have presented in lecture the principal–agent model as well as models on asymmetric information, including adverse selection and moral hazard. These key economic concepts are not explicitly identified for the students in the case. Rather the students must recognize on their own the relevancy of these concepts in evaluating HSA plans. Students identify the key economic issues in this scenario and then use theory to evaluate the situation (see Appendix 9C). Students are then given the task to determine if they should adopt a HSA plan as a means to address their hypothetical business's rising health care costs. Students are broken into groups where each student takes on a role of an employee with different health care needs (e.g., a young single person, a middle-aged married employee with sick kids, an employee near retirement). Students must first anticipate how their assigned employee will respond to the employer's proposed shifting of the cost and responsibility to them. For example, this policy change may reduce health care expenses in the short run, but if employees cut back on routine health care maintenance, expenses may rise in the future. Thus, the secondary negative unintended consequences may outweigh the primary benefits of lower health care costs today.

Then the students are asked to identify modifications to the proposed HSA to alleviate or eliminate the problems they just have anticipated. At the end of the case, students have a deeper understanding of the benefits and drawbacks of adopting consumer-driven health care plans (e.g., HSA and high-deductible insurance plans) as a means to reduce businesses' rising health care expenses. Students have identified many (if not the majority) of the problems that businesses encountered implementing HSAs in the early days of their usage. In the debriefing of the case, they are reminded that thinking through how each type of employee will respond to their business proposal allowed them to anticipate employee reactions and respond to the unintended secondary effects before implementation. Thus, a case can challenge students to apply all stages of Bloom's taxonomy of higher-order learning, as Derek showed in an earlier section. This case also puts the students in the position of analyzing the importance of economic incentives for business and other policy decisions.

All of my students were aware of the health care reform debate that took place in 2009 and 2010. As a result, they have heard about the "previous condition" exclusion and are very motivated to learn about the concept of moral hazard. The specifics of the case lead the students to analyze/synthesize/evaluate with the goal of solving moral hazard problems in health care. Because the majority of my students intend to work in management, they are quite interested in learning how to align employee incentives with the employers' objectives. Given that the current health care reform is in part about lowering health care costs, they have heard about people who have used great amounts of health care, while others use too little. This observation and interest in correcting principal–agent problems motivates them to learn more about the incentives that drive the patients to these extremes.

Another feature of this case (and cases in general) is the opportunity for feedback on student learning in "real time." Often I do not get this information until the exam, and by then it is much more difficult to bridge the gap in student understanding. Through cases, students also get feedback for themselves on how thoroughly they know the models. They are forced to look through their notes and start asking questions about different features of the mathematical models. They cannot simply "plug and chug" by taking a derivative and solving for an answer. They must understand the underlying elements of an adverse selection model, for instance, if they are going to be able to answer the questions.

Fostering student interest in the subject material is also an important component in student learning. This is particularly important for students who enroll in principles courses because they tend to enroll for curriculum requirements rather than any interest in the subject. Thus, not only do we have to teach students economic theory, but we must demonstrate to them why these courses are useful to them beyond their value for obtaining entrance into business school, for instance. Cases can be an effective tool to demonstrate the applicability of economics. When students can see the relevance of what they are learning, they are more likely to undertake the time investment to learn the subject material. And we know from experience the students who put more effort into their studies *learn* the material *better*. Bloom et al. (1956) observed as well that students learn more when they are interested in what they are studying. They referred to harvesting of this knowledge as acquisition of skills in the "affective domain." The best way to demonstrate to students the relevance of economics and thus motivate studying the subject is to root the cases in real-world examples.

My series of four cases on Zimbabwe allows students to apply macroeconomic concepts to a real-world example of hyperinflation. In the third part, "Zimbabwean Economy – Day 3," students examine the role money growth had in creating inflation. They are shown the actual magnitude of the changes in the money supply in Zimbabwe. Once students see how mismanagement of the money supply led to economic chaos in Zimbabwe, they understand and are concerned about whether the Federal Reserve Chairman Ben Bernanke can contract the money supply fast enough in the current economy to avoid inflation when economic growth begins again. In addition, student interest was sparked by seeing the actual changes in money supply and inflation levels in Zimbabwe over the last two decades. They asked me additional questions about the economic and political situation. They were not passive in their learning, but created their own understanding. Some even asked me more questions after class (and in office hours) about what can be done about Zimbabwe suggesting that their thinking about the topic did not stop when the class ended.

One final comment: Cases are continually under construction. Students were asked to provide feedback on the most and least valuable aspects of the cases and any modifications they would suggest to improve them. While the most popular response for improvements was "none," two of the comments are quite illustrative of what we need to address in cases we develop for our own courses. First, one student asked for "suggestions on how to solve economic problems like Zimbabwe." In the initial version of the case, we discussed the problems hyperinflation created, but we did not discuss what could be done to address them. The case piqued the student's intellectual curiosity, but he needed to spend more time in debriefing at the end to answer questions the case created. Second, the case provided all of the key information needed to evaluate how hyperinflation affects economic choices. But, students wanted to know more about how Zimbabwe got itself into this situation. More specifically, one student requested "more historical background before hand to get students more interested in the material/assignment" before proceeding to the economic analysis. These students needed more historical context to understand the economic problems of Zimbabwe beyond what the initial version of the case provided. In future uses of the case I provide that information, thus improving the "real world" nature of the learning experience.

In summary, cases allow students to simulate the economic way of thinking similar to how they would use economic theory in the real world. Given that simulation of an activity has a higher retention rate than for standard lectures, cases can provide instructors a tool to have a longer-lasting impact on student learning (Dale 1969). Because many students primarily rely on inductive reasoning, they need to start with a specific set of facts before they can form a general conclusion. By their very nature of being rooted in real-world scenarios, cases allow students to build their economic knowledge that mirrors their learning style. Finally, the real-world aspects of cases also enhance student enthusiasm for learning. Economics is no longer just a theoretical intellectual exercise, but relevant for their personal and business decisions.

V. CONCLUSION

We conclude that cases improve the learning outcomes of our students when compared to more traditional teaching techniques. There are four reasons we hold this view.

First, use of a case facilitates active learning in the classroom. The nature of a case places a student in an active role, and appropriate classroom activities based on these cases will stimulate discussion and debate among the students. Students remember 90 percent of what they "do," but a much smaller percentage of what they "hear." The simple activity of case use will improve learning outcomes.

Second, students are interested in cases because they have real-world characteristics. This interest leads to greater attentiveness and effort, and these pay off in improved learning. We have our own corollary to Stice (1987): Students remember 0 percent of material when they're not listening. The real-world, decision-making nature of cases leads to greater attention, greater effort – and greater learning.

Third, case instruction has a comparative advantage in stimulating higher-order inquiry in our students. If our goal of "economic literacy" implies that students should be able to apply/analyze/synthesize/evaluate economic phenomena using economic concepts, then case instruction is a relatively effective way to stimulate that learning.

Fourth, the most effective learning strategies involve frequent formative assessment, including self-assessment. The instructor has the responsibility to build opportunities for these assessments into the syllabus. Case use in the classroom is an excellent tool for introducing formative assessment in a meaningful and non-threatening fashion.

Ultimately we recognize that student learning depends on a number of factors, many of which are not directly observable. The stock of knowledge, skills, and aptitude of a student matters. The general interest level a student has for economics matters. The ability of the instructor to explain economic concepts clearly matters. Even seemingly minor factors like the time of day the class is scheduled for can matter.

We've made a compelling argument that case use is an effective instructional technique. The natural follow-up question is: Should we switch to exclusive use of cases in the classroom? This has been the Harvard Business School approach, after all. As true academics, we argue yes – and no. *Yes*, we should incorporate the active-learning characteristics of case-use instruction into our daily classroom work. The benefits can be had through very frequent use of these techniques. *No*, we shouldn't use cases exclusively in instruction. They provide real-world applications, engage the students and encourage discussion, as we've pointed out. In instruction, the true comparative advantage of case use comes in achieving higher-order learning. There are many topics that we cover in our economics classes for which our learning goals are not the achievement of higher-order understanding. For these topics, lecture or less formal active-learning strategies may be preferred.

This leads us to a topic we've neglected in this chapter: the opportunity cost of using cases in the classroom. This is typically measured in our scarcest resource: classroom time. Case instruction is time-consuming relative to lecture, primarily because of its advantages: it builds in time for higher-order reasoning by the students, and it builds in time for formative assessment. This time could be used covering more material. The balance on depth versus breadth of coverage will be one for each instructor to define, but for those instructors with "economic literacy" as a goal we advise frequent use of cases in the syllabus.

NOTES

1. Bransford, Brown, and Cocking (2000) is an excellent, though already somewhat dated, summary of these research findings.
2. The "star quality"concept is drawn from Lynn (1999).
3. Christensen and Hansen (1987) provides a good summary of that usage.
4. These are all cases I created myself. Examples include the Coffee Shop Business Case (Principles of Microeconomics), Markets for Human Organs (Principles of Microeconomics), Los Angeles and the Water Rights of Owens Valley (Environmental Economics), the environmental impact of industrial food systems (Environmental Economics), and the Google Book Project (Principles of Microeconomics). I will discuss only the first and last in this section, but can provide details of the other cases on request.
5. In this case, I made support materials available to the students on the website associated with my course (Brin 2009; Helft 2009; Hyde 2009). Included in the materials was Lawrence Lessig's chapter on copyright in the *Remix* book, as well as recent news articles on the case. The students were also assigned to use the Google search facility for the term "Google book settlement," making clear the role of Google in information access for many purposes, even related to the legality of its own operations. Additional optional resources included Auletta (2009) and Darnton (2009).

6. The four-part case on Zimbabwe is currently under consideration for publication, and thus cannot be reprinted here. Readers interested in learning more about that case should contact Monica Hartmann directly at mehartmann@stthomas.edu

REFERENCES

Auletta, K. (2009), *Googled: The End of the World as We Know It*, New York: Penguin Press.

Bloom, B., M. Engelhart, E. Furst, W. Hill, and D. Krathwohl (1956), *Taxonomy of Educational Objectives Handbook I: Cognitive Domain*, New York: David McKay.

Boehrer, J. (1994), "On teaching a case," *International Studies Notes*, **19** (2), 14–20.

Bransford, J.D., A.L. Brown, and R.R. Cocking (eds) (2000), *How People Learn*, Washington, DC: National Academy Press.

Brin, S. (2009), "A library to last forever," *New York Times*, October 9.

Christensen, C., and A. Hansen (1987), *Teaching and the Case Method*, Cambridge, MA: Harvard Business School.

Christensen, C., A. Hansen, and J. Moore (1987), *Teaching and the Case Method: Instructor's Guide*, Cambridge, MA: Harvard Business School.

Colander, D.C. (2009), *Economics* (8th ed.), New York: McGraw-Hill Irwin.

Dale, E. (1969), *Audio-Visual Methods in Teaching* (3rd ed.), New York: The Dryden Press; Holt, Reinhart, and Winston.

Darnton, R. (2009), *The Case for Books: Past, Present, and Future*, New York: Public Affairs.

Fitzpatrick, L., C. McConnell, and C. Sasse (2006), "Motivating the reluctant novice learner: Principles of macroeconomics," *Journal of Economics and Economics Education Research*, **7** (2), 23.

Hansen, W.L., M. Salemi, and J. Siegfried (2002), "Use it or lose it: Teaching literacy in the economics principles course," *American Economic Review*, **92** (2), 463–72.

Hartmann, M., and R. Werner (2009), "Hyperinflation: What can Zimbabwe teach us?," working paper, St. Paul, MN: University of St. Thomas.

Haskell, J., and S. Jenkins (2003), "Teaching economic principles through literacy methods," *Journal of Economics and Economic Education Research*, **4** (2), 19–25.

Helft, M. (2009), "U.S. presses antitrust inquiry into Google Book settlement," *New York Times*, June 10.

Hyde, L. (2009), "Advantage Google," *New York Times*, October 4.

International Monetary Fund (2008), *World Economic Outlook*, April 2008, Washington, DC.

Lage, M., G. Platt, and M. Treglia (2000), "Inverting the classroom: A gateway to creating an inclusive learning environment," *Journal of Economic Education*, **31** (1), 30–43.

Lessig, L. (2008), *Remix: Making Art and Commerce Thrive in the Hybrid Economy*, New York: Penguin Press.

Lynn, L. (1999), *Teaching and Learning with Cases: A Guidebook*, Washington, DC: Sage Press.

Robertson, D. (1922), *Money*, Cambridge, UK: Cambridge University Press.

Saunders, P. (1998), "Learning theory and instructional objectives," in W.B. Walstad and P. Saunders (eds), *Teaching Undergraduate Economics*, New York: Irwin-McGraw-Hill, 85–108.

Saunders, P., G. Bach, J. Caulderwood, and W.L. Hansen (1993), *A Framework for Teaching the Basic Concepts*, New York: Council for Economic Education.

Siegfried, J. (2003), "How many college students are exposed to economics?," *Journal of Economic Education*, **31** (2), 202–4.

Stice, J. (1987), *Developing Critical Thinking and Problem-Solving Abilities,* New Directions in Learning and Teaching Series, No. 30, San Francisco, CA: Jossey-Bass.

Walstad, W.B., and P. Saunders (eds) (1998), *Teaching Undergraduate Economics*, New York: Irwin-McGraw-Hill.

Wines, M. (2007), "Zimbabwe price controls cause chaos," *The New York Times*, July 3.

Ziegert, A. (2000), "The role of personality temperament and student learning in principles of economics: Further evidence," *Journal of Economic Education*, **31** (4), 307–22.

APPENDIX 9A
Time is Money, but what about Baseball Cards?
Derek Stimel

George was amazed at how expensive it was to attend the university. Although his parents paid for the meal plan, he found that getting to know his classmates was expensive. Between the movies and the designer coffees, he managed to exhaust his budget by the 15th of every month.

George came up with an ingenious solution to this problem. He started an auto-detailing business on the side. He charges $20 per car to wash, wax and vacuum the interior. He found that if he worked on five cars per month, he could make it to the end of the month with his social schedule unhindered. Saving isn't in his game plan yet, and he hasn't started worrying about taxes.

Today's job was no picnic: a Ford Expedition that looked as if it had been driven through the La Brea Tar Pits. When he finished, the owner made him an intriguing offer: "Since you did such a great job I'll give you a choice. You can have this $20 bill. Alternatively, I'll give you this 1968 Roberto Clemente Topps baseball card #150. It's in mint condition, see? One just like it sold on eBay for $21.55 last week."

George is an eBay fan, and he remembered that auction – it did sell for $21.55. In fact, the same card had sold last year for $19.75. The Expedition owner is waiting, cash in one hand and baseball card in the other. Which should George take?

Source: Patrick Conway, Teaching Innovations Program

APPENDIX 9B
The Coffee Shop Case
Ann E. Davis

This case requires a number of steps to be completed outside of class. Review these instructions carefully, exchange personal contact information with your group members. You are responsible for completing each step, and reporting to class on the day designated for discussion of this case, and actively contributing to the analysis.

Context: You are gathering market information for a business plan. An entrepreneur wants to start a coffee shop near campus, and needs relevant information. The bank has hired you to make an assessment of the market, based on your knowledge of the student market. Your task is to make use of your own experience and your observations of other students. Is this coffee shop a promising, viable business opportunity, or not a good investment?

Gather as a group and plan a specific day and time to visit one retail outlet where coffee is available, *within walking distance from campus*. During your visit observe and record information about the coffee shop such as the décor, clientele, the numbers of coffee options available, size of coffee cups, price of coffee (before taxes), and the extent of other items on the menu.

Discuss with your group before class the unit price you observed. Does the price seem reasonable, high, or low, compared to your experience elsewhere (home, other dining options in the vicinity, other experiences). Develop hypotheses regarding the price, to explain the determinants of price. Make use of your text book and concepts from the course. Consider supply (costs of production, economies of scale, degree of competition (local and national), size and number of firms, materials prices, technology), and demand (degree of product differentiation, price and availability of substitutes, size and nature of the market including income), and other relevant considerations.

Assignment: Write a concise, well-organized typewritten report, 250 words, summarizing your hypotheses and your reasoning regarding the explanation of the prices that you observed, due November 7–8, for class discussion. Organize observations under the categories of supply and demand. Attach a data form that records your observations.

In class discussion, the groups will compare their information regarding the prices observed. Based on this comparison, the instructor will ask students such questions as: (1) Is there one price for a regular cup of coffee, or many prices? (2) What is the degree of price divergence or convergence, if any? (3) How strong is market competition? (How many competitors are there within walking distance? How variable is customer base or niche clientele among the different types of shops?) (4) How important is market structure (the number of competitors and the degree of product differentiation)? (5) How important is advertising and brand image? (6) How important is cost of production and competitive prices? (7) What additional information or methodologies would be useful? (8) Will this information affect your own buying habits?

APPENDIX 9C
Economic Analysis of a Health Savings Account Plan
Monica Hartmann

Memo from the Human Resource Director: We are facing a 29 percent increase in the annual price tag for our employees' health insurance coverage. We cannot sustain this cost increase and still maintain our market competitiveness. One option is to raise the monthly insurance premiums by

$95 for singles and $165 for families. Alternatively, we can adopt a health savings account (HSA) plan as promoted by President Bush to keep our health care costs under control. In theory, because consumers will have to pay more of non-catastrophic medical costs rather than relying on insurance, they will become more informed and cost conscious purchasers of medical services. As a result, employee and employer incentives would be more aligned and reduce the growth rate in employee health care expenses.

Under our current system, we pay the full premiums for our employees' health care coverage. However, employees do share in some of the costs, in the form of a $20 co-payment and a $300 and $700 deductible for singles and families, respectively. Under the proposed HSA plan, we will continue to pay premiums, but now there will be a high deductible: $2,900 for singles and $5,000 for families (the maximum amount allowed by law; the minimum is $1,000 for individuals and $2,220 for families). Employees can contribute their own money each pay period to fund their individual HSA until their annual contribution reaches the deductible. To lower health care costs, we also will cut back on our financing of basic preventive care (e.g., annual check-ups, shots). Because we are shifting some of the medical costs onto employees, we anticipate that 20 percent of our employees will strongly resist the coverage change, potentially leaving the company for another firm that provides a more traditional form of insurance.

Your task is to conduct an economic analysis of adopting an HSA plan starting June 1st. To do this, one must be cognizant of how your employees will respond to the shift toward consumer-driven health care. Because the shift will affect individuals differently, you will need to analyze the HSA plan from the perspective of many. For this reason, four representative employees have been profiled as described below.

Legal counsel: You are in your 40s, married, have one nine-year-old child, and have a combined household income of over $100,000 a year. Despite this high income, you are still concerned about the policy change. In addition to paying your law school loans, you must pay for medical treatments for your daughter that exceed $10,000 a year. You and your wife do not have any pre-existing health conditions beyond what is associated with your age.

Market Analyst: You are 22 years old, single, have no children, and make $25,000 a year. Money is tight because you are working full time to pay your college tuition. In the past you have seen the doctor once a year for check-ups. You do not have any pre-existing health conditions.

Accountant: You are in your 40s, married, have 4 children, and earn $50,000 a year. You are also married to a doctor (and have many friends who are doctors). Because of this, you are not worried about determining which doctor is the best value for the dollar for any medical procedure you or anyone in your family might need. However, you are worried about the time it will take to collect this information. In addition to the standard medical issues you and your spouse face as you age, you have four healthy children who suffer the numerous standard childhood sicknesses and injuries from playing sports. With six people, you will be constantly seeing doctors for one health issue or another.

Factory worker: You are in your 50s, married with no children at home, and earn $25,000 a year. Your monthly prescription-drug expenses will increase to about $400 under the HSA, compared with about $100 under the previous plan. (Insurance does not cover anything until the annual accumulated health care expense exceeds the deductible.) You are frustrated. You have finally gotten to a point in your life that you need insurance and you feel it is being taken from you. When you are only being paid $25,000 a year, every pill or test can bust the household budget. You and your wife do not have any pre-existing health conditions other than ones that are expected with age.

Each group member should take on one role and answer these questions: (1) Explain how each employee potentially may react (positively and negatively) to a shift toward a consumer-driven health care system. *(15–20 minutes) (Write-up may consist of bullet points).* (2) How will the company's profits be affected by the behavioral changes identified in your answer to question 1? *(5 minutes)* (3) Given your answers to question 2, what features would you want to add, drop, or modify in order to reduce long term health care costs, but still maintain worker morale and productivity? *(10–15 minutes)* (3) Should we adopt an HSA plan as a means to address our rising health care costs? *(10-15 minutes)*

Keep in mind the following as you prepare your answers: (1) Many people who have "high health care deductible" policies never open HSAs that go with them, or they neglect to fund them. (2) It is difficult to get prices from doctors and hospitals in advance. (3) The median household income in the United States is $48,000. (4) This company is a small one that employs 200 workers, of which 75 percent are factory workers. There is only one person in the human resource department. Only 80 percent of workers have internet access.

CHAPTER 10

Interactive Large Enrollment Economics Courses

Gail Hoyt
Mary Kassis
David Vera
Jennifer Imazeki

Economists who are given the charge to teach a large class often look at the task with fear and trepidation. Whether transitioning to a large class means making the change from 20 to 50 students or moving from 50 to 500, teaching a class larger than that to which you are accustomed can be a daunting and anxiety-inducing task. Many of us conjure the image of a sea of students, sitting passively with eyes glazed over, listening to a lecturer in the front of the room. Even instructors who are very innovative in their classroom techniques often feel that the move to a large class will be the death knell of the things they enjoy most about teaching. And while large class size does increase the likelihood of barriers related to student passivity and anonymity, with effective classroom management, careful planning, and ingenuity, teaching a large enrollment course can actually turn out to be a very engaging and productive learning experience for students and a rewarding experience for the instructor.

In this chapter, we first explain the goals of the interactive large enrollment course module. We also outline the structure and content of the module while including an explanation of the various tasks that module participants are required to complete. The main section of the chapter highlights the work of three TIP participants who designed and implemented innovations in their own large classes to increase the degree of interaction, engagement and learning. You will find that while their institution type and class sizes vary, each ably introduces effective innovations into their classrooms. Mary Kassis at the University of West Georgia is the first to share her experience. Mary found ways to systematically integrate the "think–pair–share" technique in her Principles of Macroeconomics classes with approximately fifty students of varying majors and backgrounds and in multiple sections. David Vera from Kent State also finds creative ways to use "think–pair–share" techniques, but additionally introduces a mix of evocative visual and textual passages and participatory lecture/student notes. Finally, Jennifer Imazeki of San Diego State University explains how she has incorporated personal response systems (clickers) in combination with other interactive techniques to enhance student intellectual engagement in her large sections.

It is our hope that the large enrollment instructors who read this chapter, especially the newcomers, might follow the steps provided by the module, ponder the content and suggestions, and find guidance and inspiration that leads to a fruitful large-course experience.

I. GOALS OF THE INTERACTIVE LARGE ENROLLMENT MODULE

The module on interactive learning in large enrollment classes is designed to help participants learn about and use techniques which add interactive learning to large enrollment courses in economics with the intent of more fully engaging students and helping them learn economics better. But when we discuss courses with a larger than normal number of students, what size constitutes "large"? Certainly most of us would agree that, in absolute terms, a class of 500 students is large. However, if you are at an institution with an average class size of 20, then a class with 50 students is large. Perhaps it is this relative definition of size that matters most to each of us and so we leave the definition of what counts as large to you. While designed to work within the constraints imposed by higher volume, the suggestions offered in this chapter could certainly be applied in a class of any size.

Module activities are designed to help instructors evaluate their teaching situation so they can identify and overcome obstacles to incorporating interactive techniques in their specific large enrollment course. Participants are encouraged to evaluate and assess available resources and institution-specific constraints. After considering obstacles and constraints, familiarizing themselves with the relevant literature, and forming learning objectives and other pedagogical goals, participants determine an optimal combination of interactive learning activities and adjust grading structure accordingly. After a test run of the innovation in their classroom, participants assess the implementation of the innovation and reflect upon its effectiveness and potential modifications for subsequent semesters.

Module Content, Structure, and Tasks: Background and Reflection

The goals of the module are met through exposure to a variety of relevant content and the completion of several specific tasks. A participant begins with background exercises designed to set the stage for interactive learning in his/her large enrollment course. Participants consider impediments to interactive learning in large classes along with personal fears and concerns about the large enrollment experience. Next, a self-evaluation of relevant past experience takes place. Following this reflection, the instructor takes inventory of classroom and campus resources and constraints. This leads to consideration of classroom management issues and a review of the relevant literature.

Participants begin by answering a series of reflective questions that the reader might want to consider as well if embarking upon teaching a large enrollment course. The questions follow:

- What do you see as the unique challenges to teaching a large enrollment course?
- What are your fears and concerns about the specific course you will be teaching in a large enrollment setting?
- Have you taught a large enrollment course in the past? If so, describe that experience.
- What things have you tried in classes that you think might work well in a large class setting and what things have you tried that you think will not work well and why?
- What do you see as the impediments to using interactive strategies in your large enrollment class?

Answering these questions can help instructors identify and tackle their fears with regard to the large enrollment experience as well as anticipate potential impediments enabling the instructor to design workable strategies. Also, instructors consider answers to these questions before reading relevant literature, increasing the odds that they might find many of their concerns addressed on those pages.

It might not be surprising that when articulating their concerns and fears about teaching a large enrollment course, most people mention student passivity and the likelihood that students will feel and behave as though they are anonymous. In a survey of economists who are experienced and well-renowned large-course teachers, Helen Roberts at the University of Illinois at

Chicago says, "My biggest challenge is making the really large classes feel small to students, to connect so they don't get lost in the large group."[1] Many also mention the fear of losing control of a large class. Ali Akarca, also at the University of Illinois at Chicago, when describing what he views as the greatest challenge to teaching a large enrollment course, mentions his concerns about "keeping order in the classroom without intimidating students, coming up with interesting anecdotes, analogies, and metaphors to make topics interesting and digestible for the students."

Another series of questions forces an assessment of constraints related to resources on campus and classroom space. As class size increases, so does the importance of these factors and their impact on pedagogical outcomes.

- How big is big on your campus? What is the average class size on your campus and how does your class compare?
- What are the structural requirements and/or constraints for how you teach your large enrollment course? Are you the only one working with students or are there recitation sections led by teaching assistants? How much assistance with grading will you have? What electronic grading resources are available to you?
- What classroom on your campus will you be using for your large enrollment course? Is technical support provided and if so, who provides the support and what does the support include?
- What technological resources are available in your classroom? Will you need a sound system? If so, is the current system adequate? What audiovisual capacity do you have in the room? (Do you have whiteboards, overhead projection, computer projection, document camera, tablet PC, remote mouse, etc.?) Are there resources that are unavailable, but that you could request from campus administrators?

While instructors should not let class size hinder the use of certain techniques, specific resource constraints and other practical considerations may be unavoidable. It will require additional thought and effort on the instructor's part to navigate these issues, but they are often manageable.

It is crucial for a teacher to visit the room in which he or she will be teaching long before the semester starts, allowing for an assessment of available pedagogical resources while there is still time to make adjustments. Participants are encouraged to speak with other instructors on their campuses who have taught large enrollment courses. This is an invaluable exercise as many issues related to teaching large classes can be campus specific. On many campuses, most large enrollment courses are taught in the same rooms every semester. Speaking with someone who has taught in that room for many years can be extraordinarily helpful. It also can be beneficial to ask students who the best large-course teachers are on campus and to subsequently ask two or three of these people for their advice. Factors related to classroom resources and management make up a very large portion of the energy and focus of the large enrollment teacher and when these factors have not been considered it is virtually impossible for effective economic instruction to take place. The answers to these questions will help the instructor anticipate the managerial issues that must be sorted out for the classroom activities to run smoothly.

Three of the experienced large enrollment teachers who were surveyed emphasize the vital importance of planning and paying attention to managerial details and logistics. Ken Elzinga, from the University of Virginia, states, "The lectures/classroom material (what I'll call the public part of the course) must be super-prepared and thought through. Large groups of students are much less forgiving of something going wrong (whether it is a software failure or mixing up the organization of a presentation) than a smaller group of students."

From the University of Wisconsin, Lee Hansen says, "Make clear the conditions of what I call the 'teaching/learning contract.' I believe firmly in setting out the ground rules in not only the syllabus but in the first class meeting as to what I expect of them, what they can expect of me, and what they must demand of each other."

And finally, Beth Bogan at Princeton comments "Any visuals must be clear to every seat. If you use chalk, use big sidewalk chalk. If you use PowerPoint, don't put too much on a slide. Have handouts ready in multiple piles at every door so students can quickly pick up copies of notes and graphs. Be really well-prepared, so you can lecture without error."

These comments emphasize the importance of anticipating the classroom management issues that might arise and the necessity of paying attention to detail so the instructor can prepare accordingly for a successful experience. Often when teaching smaller classes, instructors do not devote a lot of thought to where to place handouts for students to pick up without forming a "bottleneck." Nor do they spend time thinking about avenues for mobility around the room through rows and isles. But in a large enrollment class, these matters become vital considerations.

II. REVIEW OF THE LITERATURE UNDERLYING MODULE CONTENT, STRUCTURE, AND TASKS

The literature on teaching large enrollment courses in the economics discipline is limited to a chapter by Buckles and Hoyt (2006). This is a general survey piece offering advice to instructors of large courses in economics. There are additional resources found in the general education literature including Carbone (1998), Gedalof (1998), MacGregor et al.

(2000), McKeachie (1999), Stanley and Porter (2002), and Weimer (1987). A quick Internet search also reveals that most campuses with teaching and learning centers offer some advice to large-course teachers on their websites. Given the limited literature in economics, prior to the 2006 TIP workshop, a survey of nationally renowned large enrollment teachers of economics was conducted by Hoyt (2010). These experts offered their thoughts on the difficulties of the large enrollment classes and their best advice on overcoming those obstacles. Survey responses are included in the module reading list and several comments have been put forth in this chapter.

After reading selected portions from the reading list, instructors answer questions with the goal of alleviating some of the concerns that might have been identified while answering the initial reflective questions. This exercise also allows the reader to begin to plan for an appropriate classroom atmosphere and rapport, formulate learning objectives, and design strategies and techniques to implement. The reader also might consider these questions:

- What type of classroom atmosphere do you hope to achieve and how will this be conducive to interactive learning? List and explain three specific things you will do this semester to achieve this atmosphere.
- Based on the various readings and workshop materials, identify at least three common elements that reappear with regard to general advice for the successful implementation of interactive learning techniques in large lectures. Explain why each of these elements is essential for effective interactive learning in the large lecture setting.
- List the four pedagogical techniques that you think you would be most likely to try in your own class. For each one, why did you select it? What do you see as the strengths of each technique and what do you see as the challenges in implementing each technique? Describe the specific form the activity might take.

One piece of advice that consistently appears in the literature is the importance of breaking the class meeting into smaller pieces. From the survey of experts, Jim Gwartney at Florida State University comments, "Perhaps the biggest challenge is to develop a style that engages the students and makes the class interesting. Among other things, this means that you need to keep your segments relatively short. It is a good idea to shift regularly from lecture to engaging questions to videos to in-class activities and so on." Allen Sanderson who teaches large enrollment courses at the University of Chicago states, "I can't imagine listening to myself (or anyone else) talk for 80 minutes (I meet my class twice a week). My lectures are really "interactive." I don't mind being interrupted – in fact, I encourage it. I like the give-and-take from the group to energize me – and them."

Module participants are introduced to a wide array of potential pedagogical techniques that can be used to make the large enrollment course interactive. In fact, any of the techniques described in this volume are suitable including cooperative learning, discussion, experiments, assessment, context-rich problems, and cases, in addition to many others. However, it appears that some techniques are called upon again and again for those teaching larger classes. Most are techniques that an instructor might use in a traditionally smaller size class, but they are modified for the larger setting.

One of the more commonly called-upon techniques in the interactive large enrollment course is the demonstration. In a large class, this often involves a subset of students demonstrating something like diminishing marginal utility in front of the rest of the class or all students engaging in a demonstration of the construction of a demand curve.

Also, when using collaborative learning pedagogies, it appears repeatedly that the think–pair–share structure works best in the larger setting and is the most popular among large-course teachers. Individual student attendance is often less consistent in the larger class and unless there is a seating chart, students rarely sit in the same seat making it difficult to form a student group that might work together in more than one class period. However, the more informal structure of a think–pair–share group is appealing as the group is formed quickly with students sitting near each other and varies from class period to class period and even from one activity to the next within the same class period.

In large classes, instructors also often use evocative visuals, textual passages, or other attention-getting aids to lead into student interaction through discussion or collaborative work. Often the visual impact on a larger screen or the audio impact using the microphone system has a more powerful effect on students in the large enrollment course than it might have in a smaller setting.

Another popular tool for increasing interaction and punctuating the lecture is the use of "student notes" in which students use handouts with some of the content included, but some is missing and students must complete them as they follow lecture and course discussion. An alternative to the incomplete lecture note handout is the guided practice sheet upon which the student completes a problem in stages, alone or in groups, as different parts of the content are presented in lecture or discussion. Short quizzes in which students use clickers (personal response devices), index cards, or other media to answer are also popular for interaction and format change, and the quiz is often completed in collaboration with other students. Different forms of the two-minute write are widely employed as an opening tool for student engagement at the beginning of class and also to engage and solicit feedback at the end of a class period.

Large Enrollment Innovation Plan, Implementation, and Assessment

Keeping in mind the importance of breaking up the class meeting with frequent changes in format, two options or routes are offered to module participants in developing their actual innovation plan for their course.

In the first option, participants teach one week of their course that is planned and structured to incorporate a mix of short and long activities and format changes (a minimum of six) to make the class periods more engaging and learning more interactive. Participants provide a thorough description of the content they plan to cover in this one-week period and then list the readings, articles, etc., that they plan to assign. Participants are asked to formulate learning goals for the innovation, and then a technique is structured to teach these goals in an interactive way. It is during this stage that the many logistical details of the activity are determined, including any change in incentive structure or other means to provide students motivation to participate.

The alternative route is for the participant to implement one or two specific interactive techniques throughout the semester repeatedly with the same goal of increasing the level of interactive learning. Participants choosing this route must provide a minimum of six specific instances of using these techniques. The first route has the benefit of variety in format while the latter helps the students develop of sense of familiarity and comfort with a specific technique.

III. THINK–PAIR–SHARE
Mary Kassis

The University of West Georgia (UWG) is a state university in the University System of Georgia with approximately 11,000 students. Although UWG does not have exceptionally large classes by the standards of many other institutions, UWG's economics principles courses generally have 50–65 students and are often taught in lecture halls. This class size is large enough that it can be difficult to get students to participate actively in class. The semester I used the think–pair–share innovation in my class, I taught three sections of principles of macroeconomics with approximately 50 students enrolled in each section. All three of the sections were taught in the same lecture hall, which was equipped with a tablet computer and a projector. Most of the students in these classes were freshman or sophomores, and most were traditional-age college students. Many of the students were business majors, although this course can be used to fulfill the core social science requirement at the University, so there were also students from other majors in the course.

Description of the Innovation

My goal in incorporating think–pair–share activities in my course was to give students the opportunity to practice problems in class as well as get students more actively involved in class material. Throughout the semester after a topic was covered in class, students were given a problem on that topic to work in class. I specifically chose topics that I knew students had found difficult in the past. For the first few minutes students were asked to work independently on the problem. After students had been given the opportunity to work the problem individually, they were asked to pair off and share and explain their answers to each other. Finally we came back together as a class to work through the problem.

Quick response think–pair–share

The length of the think–pair–share activities depended on the subject matter. Some of the activities were fairly short and took less than five minutes. For a quick think–pair–share activity, I would usually either put the problem on the board or have it integrated into my PowerPoint lecture for that day. Students were not graded on these exercises, but I walked around the classroom to make sure all students were participating. For example, after introducing the concepts of the marginal propensity to consume and the marginal propensity to save, I had students assume that when disposable income increases by $20 billion, consumption increases by $15 billion. Students were asked to calculate the marginal propensity to consume and the marginal propensity to save. They also were asked to explain what must happen to the marginal propensity to save if the marginal propensity to consume increases.[2] This was a quick exercise designed as a checkpoint to make sure that all students understood this important concept before I continued with the lecture.

Extended response think–pair–share

Other think–pair–share activities involved more complicated problems that would take 10–15 minutes of class time. For these problems, I would have a worksheet to hand out to the students. The worksheet would contain one or more problems that we would complete in class that day. Sometimes there would be multiple questions on the worksheet, and we would stop at two different points in the lecture to work the problems at different times.

Since my classes were 75 minutes long, it was useful to break the lecture up to keep the students engaged, especially when the material was more difficult. Students individually answered the questions on the worksheet and then discussed the answers in pairs before going over the questions in class.

Students would turn the worksheet in at the end of class to receive credit. These problems counted as part of the student's in-class exercise grade, and students also were told that they would see similar questions on the test. Since we had gone over the question in class, I did not grade the answer but students got credit for having participated.

I also walked around the lecture hall while the students were working on a problem to answer questions and to help keep students on task. I would return the worksheets to the students the next class, so they would have them to study, but there would be no discussion of the worksheets when they were handed back because we had gone over them in the previous class period.

An example of this type of more complicated problem was used in the lecture that covered the simple spending multiplier. After the concept of the simple spending multiplier was introduced, students were asked to calculate a simple spending multiplier and use it to determine the amount of government spending needed to achieve a given increase in GDP. Later in the lecture, after we had discussed the relationship between the multiplier and shifts in the aggregate demand curve, students were asked to use the simple spending multiplier to determine the size and direction of the impact on aggregate expenditures, real GDP demanded, and the aggregate demand curve that would result from an increase in autonomous investment.

The think–pair–share activities worked well to promote interactive learning for the students. Most students were actively engaged while they worked on the activities, discussing the problem with their classmates. Students also were very willing to talk during the class discussion of the problems at the end of the activity. This willingness to participate in class discussion also seemed to carry over into class discussions on policy issues.

Assessment of the Innovation

To evaluate the effectiveness of the think–pair–share activities, I collected data on student performance on exam questions related to one of the graded exercises covering fiscal policy in two sections. I compared the performance of students who completed the activity in class (77 students) with those who did not complete the activity in class (20 students) using four exam questions covering the material from the exercise. The students who completed the activity got 64 percent of the questions correct while the students who did not complete the exercise only got 39 percent of the questions correct. Although the percentage for both groups was relatively low, the material I chose for the think–pair–share activity was some of the more difficult material in the course. The difference in the performance of these two groups was statistically significant ($z = 4.14$). Although there are self-selection issues because the students who come to class regularly may be better students than the students who do not come to class, the difference in performance still suggests that the think–pair–share activity did contribute to student learning.

Lessons Learned and Advice to Others

Overall I think the use of the think–pair–share activities accomplished my goal of giving students the opportunity to practice problems in class as well as getting students more actively involved in the course material. Although some students did not like the idea of pairing off, most students seemed to enjoy the opportunity to work problems and discuss them with other students, and it provided a good break from the lecture and gave me immediate feedback with regard to their understanding of the content. One thing I learned in implementing this innovation was that the instructor needs to make sure that all students participate the first few times you do the exercises. To encourage full participation, I walked around the classroom while the students were working and made sure that all students were paired off and actively participating. If they did not have a partner, I found one for them. Participation became less of a problem after the first few exercises as students realized what was expected of them as they worked on the classroom problems.

Another issue to consider when implementing the think–pair–share activities is that it will result in less lecture time. One way I dealt with this was that I changed the way I lectured and spent less time solving problems on the board and instead had the students do the problems as part of a think–pair–share exercise. It also helps to design the activities carefully. I tried to choose topics that I knew students had found difficult in the past, so that the additional class time was justified and would hopefully result in a better understanding of these difficult concepts. In addition, I found that setting a time limit (1–2 minutes) for the small group discussions among students helped me manage the class time and helped the students stay focused on the classroom exercise.

One change I made in a later semester was to use clickers as a way to grade the students on the think–pair–share activities. Rather than collecting the worksheets, I would ask a few clicker questions about the problem before we went over it in class. This way I did not have to collect and return the worksheets, which had used up class time and created a problem when students were not there to get the worksheet in the next class period. One additional benefit that I had not expected from the think–pair–share activities was that using these activities seemed to help promote student interaction throughout the semester. As students got to know each other better during these activities, they became more willing to participate in class discussions on economic policy issues and other topics so that I had more actively engaged students even when we were not participating in a specific think–pair–share activity.

IV. THINK–PAIR–SHARE, EVOCATIVE VISUAL, TEXTUAL PASSAGES, AND PARTICIPATORY LECTURE

David Vera

I have had the opportunity to implement innovations in a large-lecture setting at Kent State University (KSU). KSU is the third largest public university in Ohio, serving more than 34,000 students university-wide. At the main campus in Kent large-lecture courses offered by the economics department range in size from 150 to 220 students. I implemented pedagogical enhancements in a principles of macroeconomics class with an enrollment of 215 students that I taught in a large auditorium with seating capacity for 250 students. Since both principles of macroeconomics and principles of microeconomics are required for many majors at Kent State, the students enrolled in the course are very diverse in terms of major. Since principles of microeconomics is required for the macro class, the students were mostly sophomores and juniors.

We met in a large lecture hall for 75 minutes twice a week. Due to class size, I used PowerPoint, and posted a version of the notes online before class each day. The students had access to the notes before class and could print them and bring them to class. One important feature of the notes is that the students must fill in certain gaps during the lecture. For instance, in the implementation of the innovations described below, I provided most of the information during the lecture. The advantage of a "student version" class notes is that they will have to stay engaged in order to get the complete material for each lecture. Over time, I have received significant feedback from the students allowing me to adjust the content of the student version of the class notes to balance note-taking with interactive participation. Also, for the principles classes at KSU, there are supplemental instruction sessions where students can get help with the material. These sessions are led by a student who has mastered the material. Students are encouraged to attend, but because it is not required, attendance tends to be low.

Description of the Innovations

The main goal of the innovations I implemented was to better connect to students in a large class. The innovations used alternatively were the technique of think–pair–share, the use of evocative visual and textual passages, and participatory lecture. In the case of the innovations that were structured around think–pair–share, students were given data in order to estimate the value of variables (e.g., total GDP, nominal and real GDP, price of a bond) or answer a specific question (e,g., the relationship between current account and capital account transactions). The innovations were introduced after discussing the relevant theory and going through the intuition behind the specific concept. Below I describe three different interactive innovations for large lectures that I implemented.

Extended response think–pair–share: Calculating GDP

The main objective of this innovation is for the students to learn the concept of GDP through the think–pair–share approach. The students should be able to use the definition of GDP to determine which items from a list should be included in the estimation of the GDP. Using a list of items that will make up the different components of GDP, students should come up with the correct value for GDP, and each of its components according to the expenditure approach. After providing the list on a PowerPoint slide, students are given the following instructions. First, each student should individually determine which items from the list should be considered in the estimation of GDP. For example, should the sales of existing homes be included? Should the value of inventories be included, and if so, how? After five minutes, each student will discuss his/her results with a classmate sitting to his/her right. Then they should be able to provide feedback to the class on which items should be considered in the estimation.

In the second step, the students also work individually in classifying each of the items as a component of GDP (private consumption, private investment, government expenditure, net exports) and estimate the value of aggregate GDP. After spending five minutes working individually, each student shares his/her result with the classmate sitting on his/her left. I allow two more minutes for sharing and then proceed to get feedback on their results. At this point, I not only discuss the correct numerical values, but I also underline certain features of the data. For example, students will be able to understand how important private consumption is for the economy. The activity lasts 12 to 15 minutes.

No additional materials are needed for this innovation. I post the lists of items on PowerPoint slides and provide this list in class. This material is not included in the notes posted online that students print before class. In order to determine the answer, students need to know the definition of GDP and the different approaches to estimate it. Students also need to know the definition of each component included in the expenditure approach for the estimation of GDP. I do not collect the final product from the students. However, students can use their results for exam preparation since I include questions with similar format in the practice question for the exams as well as in the exams.

This technique allows students to grasp the concept of GDP from a different perspective than just memorizing it. They also enjoy coming up with the right number and explaining it to their classmates. An important motivation for active participation is that the exam will have similar questions, and students must use the definition of GDP to identify the different components and determine an estimate for the value of GDP.

Extended response think–pair–share: The difference between nominal and real GDP

The objective of this innovation is for students to learn the difference between nominal and real GDP. Also, students should understand the concept of a base year. I provide data on prices and quantities of a list of items for two years that students will use to estimate real as well nominal GDP for each year. In this case the students will have data for two years where the price and quantity of three goods are provided. Each student will have to first estimate nominal GDP for each year; this is relatively straightforward. At this point, I ask each student to discuss with a classmate sitting to his/her left, how to come up with a number for the real GDP for each year. Afterwards I ask for feedback; the point I am trying to make is that in order for them to estimate real GDP they need to select a base year.

After we have discussed the idea of a base year and agree on which year to use as the base year, the students will individually estimate real GDP for each year. The students then are told to share his/her results with the classmate sitting on his/her right. Finally, I ask for estimates of real GDP. It is interesting to see whether the students pick up the idea that real and nominal GDP are the same for the base year. This innovation takes about 15 minutes to implement. No additional material is needed from what we use in class. Before the innovation we discuss the definition of real and nominal GDP as well as the definition of base year. Nothing is collected from the students.

By using think–pair–share students can see more clearly why it is important to take into account price difference when estimating GDP. A by-product of this example is a discussion on the GDP deflator as a price index. As a motivation for student participation, students are told that a similar question will be included in the test, so students have an incentive to work through the example in class and understand it.

Evocative visual and textual passages and participatory lecture: Understanding international capital flows

The goal of this innovation is to get students to think how an open economy like the United States benefits from trade and capital inflows. The idea is to provide the class with evocative visual and textual passages that illustrate the capital investment that the United States receives from abroad. For this innovation, I used a blend of textual passages and participatory lecture. I provide at least two controversial real examples where foreign investors get involved in the U.S. economy by buying (or attempting to buy) American assets: (1) Dubai Ports World, a company owned by a United Arab Emirates sheikdom, tries to buy terminal operations in six U.S. ports. (2) An Australian-Spanish consortium bids to lease the Indiana Toll. There are many examples available in newspapers.

I present both examples and ask students about their impressions of these transactions. I obtain input from the students about the importance of foreign investors and post the following question: People in China, Dubai, Australia and Spain seem to have a lot of U.S. dollars to spend on American assets. Where are they getting all these U.S. dollars? The students read the examples and discuss each one before we deal with the major question. It takes about ten minutes. In order to participate in the activity, students need to know how investment is financed in a closed economy. They also should understand the importance of national saving. I do not collect anything from the students.

Most of the students are unaware of how much the United States depends on foreign investment. They know that the average American consumer buys many goods from abroad, but are not aware of how trade and capital flows relate. By understanding this example they are able to grasp the importance of capital inflows. Different from previous innovations, this innovation is used to introduce a new topic: the relationship between trade and capital accounts. As incentive and motivation, in the exam, students are asked to identify how certain transactions affect the trade account and the current account.

Assessment of the Innovations

The main outcome of the innovations is that students were more involved in class than they may have expected. It is important to point out that this outcome was attained gradually. Student participation, particularly in sharing their results, increased as more innovations were implemented. The innovations affected my teaching in a positive way. I believe students felt more at ease after trying to solve a problem with a classmate, and with time they enjoyed providing their feedback. Students understood early that they would be facing similar problems in the exams and quizzes, which provided an incentive to work harder during the innovations. The effectiveness of the innovations was determined through exams and quizzes. Two things that made the innovations effective learning exercises were that students were more involved than in previous semesters, and due to this experience the students felt that they could ask more questions regarding the material.

Lessons Learned and Advice to Others

Using think–pair–share, as well as evocative visual and textual passages and participatory lecture, provides a setting for students to get involved in the lecture. I also think that through these innovations students eventually feel that their contribution to the class is important. One particular issue about the think–pair–share technique is how it is structured so that students do not lose focus. Timing of the exercise and clear instructions are particularly important. A general point is to be extremely organized and prepare the innovation in detail; the innovation will not work unless you clearly describe what you want students to do. If instructions are to be read, read them slowly, and allow students time to answer the questions. In my experience, students are not used to being active in class. Although many students would ask for a more active or entertaining class, few students are willing to participate in a large lecture. It is important to implement several innovations during the semester or quarter; the process will be smoother as students become accustomed to the innovations' dynamics. After the second time we did think–pair–share, students looked forward to doing more of it.

Another point that I did not quite get when I started teaching large sections is that students in large lectures very often do not know other students in the class. I always ask students to say hello to the persons sitting to his/her right and to his/her left early in the semester. They always like that part. This also makes the implementation of certain innovations like think–pair–share easier.

Another point to take from innovations in a large class setting is that they work very well in smaller classes too. Since I first used these innovations in the large lectures, I started using them in other courses such as upper-division intermediate macro. The content of the course will need to be adjusted to the new material, but the benefits of the innovation are still there. Remember in small classes, many students would prefer to be invisible like in large lectures. Using innovations such as think–pair–share is a non-threatening way to engage students in the classroom. Some final advice is the following:

- Plan the interactive technique carefully before implementing it. This will allow the instructor to assess beforehand how the technique may work and whether it will be successful.
- Provide clear guidelines as to what the activity will be to students. In a large class it is important for students to clearly understand what is being asked, to be able to learn from the activity.
- Try using interactive learning techniques in spite of the initial fears and concerns. Even though interactive techniques can be intimidating to implement in large-lecture settings they do work.

V. CLICKERS
Jennifer Imazeki

I teach at San Diego State University (SDSU), one of the largest campuses in the California State University system (30,000 undergraduates), with a diverse student body, both in demographics and academic preparation. The large enrollment course I teach is Principles of Microeconomics, with an enrollment of 500 students. Most (80%) of the enrolled students are pre-business majors who are taking the course to satisfy a requirement to gain entrance to their major; about one quarter of the students have already taken Principles of Macroeconomics (also required for pre-business majors but the two courses are not required to be taken in a particular order).

Over the last six or seven years, SDSU has added several 500-seat sections across the University, in various departments (prior to that, the largest classes were generally 120 and most classes are still closer to 50), so students are slowly getting used to them but aren't generally happy about them. The move to larger sections has been accompanied by strong support from Instructional Technology Services and many of the large sections are taught with various forms of technology. All of the large classrooms have relatively user-friendly consoles for controlling the sound system, computers and projectors. They also have document cameras with whiteboards and headset microphones so it's possible to walk around the classroom.

For a long time, I purposely avoided teaching large classes because my teaching style has always been relatively interactive, and I could not imagine how to adapt that style to effectively reach more than roughly 50–55 students (and even that was larger than I considered ideal). So when I first began teaching the 500-seat section, my top priority was finding a way to maintain my 'small-class' style and keep the class as interactive as possible.

Part of my solution was to adopt classroom response devices (commonly referred to as clickers). Clickers are handheld devices that communicate with a receiver attached to the professor's computer. When a question is asked, students use the clickers to submit their responses (multiple-choice or numeric); the software compiles the responses and can show the answer distribution within a few seconds, thus providing instant feedback. In 2006, SDSU adopted a single clicker vendor so students can buy the hardware and use the same clicker in any class where faculty members use the system.

Description of the Innovation

I use clickers to facilitate interactive learning in several different ways.[3] The most basic is asking three to five daily quiz questions. Some of the questions review material covered in the previous class meeting, or check that students have completed assigned reading. Other questions test understanding of new material just covered (that is, I lecture for a short period and then ask a clicker question on that material). I also use the clickers to poll student opinions; for example, asking students why they are in college as an introduction to cost–benefit analysis, or asking whether they support or oppose California's recent 1 percent increase in the sales tax as an introduction to a discussion of equity. After showing the poll responses, I often ask for a volunteer to explain his/her response and that is the kick-off for the discussion of the more theoretical concepts.

Peer instruction

With questions that test understanding of new material, the instant feedback provided by the system allows me to proceed in one of two ways. If the majority of the class selects the correct answer, I move on to new material. If a large proportion (I use one-third as my usual guideline) of the class selects an incorrect answer, I do not tell the students which answer is correct but instead ask students to discuss the question with their neighbors and to explain why they selected the answer they did. I then ask the question again. Typically, more students get the answer correct the second time. This peer instruction allows students to explain concepts in their own words (which may be more understandable to their peers than the explanation of the instructor), as well as reveal to students the flaws in their original thought process. I sometimes ask for volunteers who got the question wrong the first time and correct the second time to explain their thinking to the class.

Open-ended questions

Clickers have also facilitated student work on more open-ended questions, such as drawing graphs to show the impact of a policy on a market. Although I do not collect or grade the answers to the open-ended questions, I can pose a multiple-choice version of the question directly after they work on the open-ended version. That is, students are first given a scenario to analyze and instructed to show the effect of an event on a market. An example of the type of question posed is: "Assume that a year ago, the market for handyman services was in equilibrium at a price of $40/hour. At that price, 1000 hours were bought and sold each month. But with the declining economy, more people are choosing to fix things themselves. Draw the supply and demand diagram for handyman services and show the effect of the declining economy on the market." Students may discuss their work with others, but are not required to do so. After the students have had time to work on the open-ended graphing problem, I pose a multiple-choice version of the question:

"The declining economy will lead to _____ prices and _____ quantity in the market for handyman services."

A. Higher, higher B. Lower, lower C. Higher, lower D. Lower, higher

I give them significantly less time to respond than with other clicker questions; for most quizzes, students have up to 1 minute to think about and submit their response (I start the time after reading the question) but because they have already worked out the answer by working on the open-ended question, I give them no more than 15 seconds.

Generating demand curves

I also use the clickers for at least one in-class activity: generating demand curves. In addition to multiple-choice responses, students can input numeric responses so I have the students use their clickers to indicate how many candy bars they would purchase at different prices. Specifically, the question posed is: "The University has purchased a new candy vending machine that randomly assigns a different price each day. How many candy bars would you buy if the price were ___? (an answer of zero is OK)."

The question is asked several times (that is, each price is a separate question in the system), each time filling in the blank with a different price (I use \$0.20, \$0.75, \$1.25 \$3.00, \$5.00).[4] I also instruct students to write down their responses in their notes. After collecting the data with the clickers, I randomly select four or five students to report the quantities they demanded at each price and I write those on the whiteboard. I ask the students to use this data to calculate the total market quantity demanded at each price and to draw the market demand curve, assuming these four or five students are the only consumers in the market, and to compare their graphs to those of their neighbors (i.e., think–pair–share). I usually randomly select one student to describe what the market demand curve looks like as I draw it for the class.[5]

Details of Implementation

Bruff (2009) discusses several practical issues that faculty will want to consider when adopting clickers. An important one is whether, and how, to grade questions. Some faculty choose not to grade clicker questions at all, or to give credit only for participation. In my class, if the questions address material the students are expected to know (e.g., material discussed in the previous class or part of the assigned reading), students must answer correctly to get full credit (although they get partial credit for answering anything). If the material is new (e.g., just covered in class directly before asking the question), or if there is no "right" answer (e.g., opinion polls), students receive full credit for submitting any answer. My policy is to make every class worth the same number of points (e.g., three for a MWF class) and if I happen to ask more questions, I randomly select three; other colleagues at SDSU adjust the points on each question or make every question worth the same so the points per day could vary.

It is also important to have a policy for dealing with clicker mishaps (i.e., dead batteries, forgotten clickers, etc.). With a large class, I believe the easiest policy is to drop a few scores at the end of the semester.[6] I generally figure out how many classes we might possibly have scores for and then subtract five or six; however, I have found that it is better to tell students that I will KEEP the top 25 scores (or however many works for your course), rather than telling them I will DROP the lowest X scores, because X may have to change over the course of the semester. I also have started making a quiz available on Blackboard that students can take if they miss class; I take the higher of their clicker score or quiz score for a given day. It is easier for students to get full credit if they come to class but by offering the quiz, (a) students who attend class get a little extra practice if they want it, and (b) I believe there were fewer disruptive students in class (i.e., students who were only coming to class to get the points but *really* did not want to be there tended to talk more. With the online quiz, they were less likely to come to class, which I feel is ultimately better for the other students, but I still felt reassured that they were staying on top of the material).

Assessment of the Innovation

I definitely believe that clickers lead to higher student engagement in the class. Aside from the incentive for students to merely attend class, the questions allow students to *do* economics in a way that also gives them instant feedback on their progress. When students seem to be struggling with particular concepts, the peer instruction approach almost always leads to a larger proportion of students getting the right answer after discussion with their classmates (the exceptions have tended to be because of poorly worded questions rather than real student confusion about the concepts). Clickers have not really changed the way I teach as much as they have allowed me to continue teaching in a 'small-class style' with the much larger section. With smaller sections I also gave daily quizzes and had students work on graphing in small groups in class; with clickers, I can still do that in the large class.

Although I do not have direct evidence of how clickers impact student learning, I have survey responses to several questions about clickers (SDSU's Instructional Technology Services provides a survey that they ask all clicker-using faculty to administer at the end of each semester). Responses to these questions suggest that students believe clickers help them learn and make them feel more involved:

- Class clicker usage helps me to remember important course content: 80.6 percent strongly or somewhat agree; 7.3 percent strongly or somewhat disagree.
- Class clicker usage helps me focus on course content I should study outside of class: 70.9 percent strongly or somewhat agree; 9.7 percent strongly or somewhat disagree.

- Class clicker usage makes me more likely to attend class: 85 percent strongly or somewhat agree; 5.3 percent strongly or somewhat disagree.
- Class clicker usage helps me to feel more involved in class: 83.5 percent strongly or somewhat agree; 6.3 percent strongly or somewhat disagree.
- I understand why my professor is using clickers in this course: 94.7 percent strongly or somewhat agree; 0.97 percent strongly or somewhat disagree.
- My professor asks clicker questions which are important to my learning: 92.2 percent strongly or somewhat agree; 1.5 percent strongly or somewhat disagree.
- Buying the clicker and getting it working was worthwhile: 68 percent strongly or somewhat agree; 12.6 percent strongly or somewhat disagree.

These percentages are from Spring 2009 (n = 206, 56% of enrollment). The percentage agreeing with the statements rose in each of the three semesters I taught the 500-seat section, and the percentage disagreeing fell.

Lessons Learned and Advice to Others

Other than a small learning curve for using the technology, I think there are two main challenges for instructors adopting clickers for the first time. One is that, like many other interactive techniques, integrating clicker questions and activities into classes reduces time for lecturing. Instructors will need to think carefully about what they want to give up in terms of covering material.

The second major challenge is writing good questions, particularly questions that can be used for peer instruction. Since I write my own exams, I have partially solved this by using questions from the previous semester's exams. Not only do students appreciate seeing what exam questions look like, this has the added benefit that I can use the answer distribution from the previous semester to gauge which questions are likely to be good candidates for peer instruction. I also now have an end-of-semester assignment where students must write one multiple-choice question (with explanations of why the right answer is right and the wrong answers are wrong) and this provides at least a few additional questions I can use in future classes.

VI. CONCLUSIONS

The thought of teaching a large enrollment course can be a frightening prospect, but with efforts to incorporate interactive pedagogy, the actual experience can be both productive and rewarding. There is no doubt that a student sense of anonymity and the resulting tone of passivity are powerful obstacles, but with careful planning and classroom management, efforts to establish an interactive tone and environment can be successful. Once this environment is in place, carefully designed interactive learning techniques offer the best route to enhance student engagement and improve learning.

Our collective experiences all point toward the importance of being "ultra-organized" and training students to be in the active learning mindset. When a miscommunication occurs or guidelines are poorly designed, resulting problems are magnified in large enrollment courses. Any large enrollment instructor will tell you that classroom management and logistical issues claim at least 50 percent of their teaching time and effort. For this reason overall course guidelines and specific activity instructions must be very clear.

Also, students must become acclimated to an interactive learning environment, which requires thorough explanation and justification of pedagogical techniques from the instructor and activities being incorporated on a regular basis so they become a welcomed and comfortable habit for the student. Once the proper tone is set for interactive learning in organized activities and exercises, the eventual spillover effects to other aspects of the class can be profound with improvements to discussion and engagement even when not in the midst of a formal activity.

NOTES

1. The chapter authors appreciate the contributions of the following economists to the survey of large-lecture instructors: Ali Akarca (University of Illinois at Chicago), Beth Bogan (Princeton University), Ken Elzinga (University of Virginia), Jim Gwartney (Florida State University), W. Lee Hansen (University of Wisconsin), Evelyn L. Lehrer (University of Illinois at Chicago), Dirk Mateer (Pennsylvania State University), Helen Roberts (University of Illinois at Chicago), and Allen Sanderson (University of Chicago).
2. End of chapter problems are a good source of ideas for think–pair–share exercises. The examples I describe in this section were developed from similar problems in McEachern (2006).
3. See Salemi (2009) for additional examples of clicker use in a principles course.
4. Salemi (2009) describes a similar exercise but rather than solicit quantities at given prices, he uses clickers to hold an auction, thus collecting data on willingness to pay for a given quantity.
5. This also can lead into the discussion of determinants of demand, by asking the students to explain why they wanted so many/little at any given price.
6. Alternatively, faculty could have students turn in a hard copy of their answers but this requires inputting those grades by hand.

REFERENCES

Bruff, D. (2009), *Teaching with Classroom Response Systems: Creating Active Learning Environments*, San Francisco: Jossey-Bass.

Buckles, S., and G. Hoyt (2005), "Active learning in the large lecture economics class," in W.E. Becker, M. Watts, and S.R. Becker (eds), *Teaching Economics: More Alternatives to Chalk and Talk*, Cheltenham, UK and Northampton, MA, USA: Edward Elgar, 75–88.

Carbone, E. (1998), *Teaching Large Classes, Tools and Strategies,* Thousand Oaks, CA, USA, London, UK, and New Delhi, India: Sage Publications.

Gedalof, A.J. (1998), *Teaching Large Classes: Green Guide Number 1*, Halifax, Canada: Society for Teaching and Learning in Higher Education.

Hoyt, G. (2010), *Results of a Survey of Large Enrollment Course Experts from the Economics Profession*, working paper, Lexington, KY: University of Kentucky.

MacGregor, J., J.L. Cooper, K.A. Smith, and P. Robinson (2000), *Strategies for Energizing Large Classes: From Small Groups to Learning Communities*, San Francisco: Jossey-Bass.

McEachern, W.A. (2006), *Macroeconomics: A Contemporary Introduction* (7th ed.), Florence, KY: South-Western.

McKeachie, W.J. (1999), "Teaching Large Classes (You Can Still Get Active Learning)," in W.J. McKeachie, *Teaching Tips: Strategies, Research, and Theory for College and University Teachers*, Boston, MA: Houghton Mifflin Co., 209–15.

Salemi, M. (2009), "Clickenomics: Using a classroom response system to increase student engagement in the principles of economics course," *Journal of Economic Education*, **40** (4), 385–404.

Stanley, C.A., and E. Porter (eds) (2002), *Engaging Large Classes: Strategies and Techniques for College Faculty*, Bolton, MA: Anker.

Weimer, M.G. (ed.) (1987), *Teaching Large Classes Well*, San Francisco: Jossey-Bass.

CHAPTER 11

Findings from a Teaching Innovation Program for Economics Faculty

William B. Walstad

The Teaching Innovations Program (TIP) sought to improve undergraduate education in economics by offering instructors an opportunity to improve their teaching skills and participate in the scholarship of teaching and learning. TIP was funded by a five-year grant from the National Science Foundation and its Division of Undergraduate Education as part of its initiative for Course, Curriculum and Laboratory Improvement (DUE 0338482). TIP was co-sponsored by the Committee on Economic Education of the American Economic Association. It built on the long history of that committee's involvement in projects and activities to promote effective teaching of economics. That work included national and regional workshops on teaching economics, the holding of annual teaching sessions at the professional meetings of economists, and the encouragement of research and publications related to economics instruction (Salemi, Saunders, and Walstad 1996; Walstad and Saunders 1998; Salemi et al. 2001).

TIP offered economics instructors from colleges and universities an opportunity to participate in three phases of teaching activity. In the first phase, the faculty member applied to attend a three-day residential workshop, and if accepted, was introduced to different types of interactive teaching methods and strategies (e.g., interpretive discussion, classroom experiments, cooperative learning, cases, context-rich problems, assessment, and large-class activities). Ten workshops were offered between 2005 and 2009, two per year during May or June. The second phase of TIP was a follow-on program of web-based instruction and mentoring designed to help participants tailor interactive teaching strategies presented at the workshop for use in their classrooms. The third phase of TIP gave participants opportunities to engage in the scholarship of teaching and learning in economics by making presentations on their economics teaching at a national or regional conference or seminar on economic education, writing pedagogical papers on teaching, or doing some other academic work related to economic education, such as serving as a discussant or reviewing papers.

More details about the TIP workshops, online modules, and scholarly activities are provided in the first three chapters of this volume. What this chapter adds to those descriptions is an explanation of TIP assessment. The chapter offers a brief description of the assessment design and then presents some of the key assessment findings. These findings are based primarily on survey data collected from the participants and from records of participant activity that were kept by the TIP staff throughout the program.

I. ASSESSMENT DESIGN

As any educational program draws to a close, the focus often turns to questions related to assessment. The basic goal of TIP was to improve the teaching skills of economics faculty by enhancing or expanding their use of interactive teaching strategies. That goal is difficult to measure directly because it would require one or more valid and reliable measures of teaching skills that would be applicable to the many interactive teaching strategies taught in the program. Another assessment consideration is that teaching skills are but one input in the learning process for students, although certainly a major input in the minds of most economics instructors.

Presumably a comprehensive study of the effects of TIP would involve evaluating how TIP changed the teaching skills of economics faculty and how that change in turn influenced the learning of economics students. Such a study, however, is well beyond the scope and budget of this project. The complexities of this type of research are sizable because of the known difficulties of accurately measuring teaching skills, effectively assessing student learning in different types of economics courses over varying time periods, and controlling for all the other factors that could likely influence the learning outcomes of students. Instead, the assessment for this project is more limited and investigates the program participation of economics faculty members and what they thought of the TIP program. The evaluation evidence is largely based on records collected throughout the program and surveys administered to participants as they completed different phases.

The TIP assessment was designed to use a combination of formative and summative evaluation strategies (Fitzpatrick, Sanders, and Worthen 2004). Data were collected during each phase of the program. In the first phase, for example, an anonymous exit survey was administered to the participants from each workshop. The results were tabulated and analyzed and then discussed with the workshop staff to refine the content and format of workshops in subsequent years.

In phase two, TIP participants who completed follow-on modules were asked to complete an anonymous exit survey assessing the value of module instruction. These data were shared with module instructors to make any necessary changes in the module and to monitor module completion and eligibility to receive a teaching certificate awarded by the Committee on Economic Education of the American Economic Association.

For phase three, requests were made to TIP participants to report on their professional activities related to the scholarship of teaching and learning economics that likely arose from their involvement in TIP, such as presentations or papers. These records were used to document and ensure that there were sufficient opportunities to participate in pedagogical and scholarly activities focused on economics teaching and learning. This formative assessment data also was valuable to collect and analyze because it could be used for annual summative reports submitted to the National Science Foundation to document outcomes from the project.

II. RETROSPECTIVE SAMPLE

Near the end of the project, what appeared to be missing from the survey work for the assessment of the program was a longitudinal perspective from TIP participants. As TIP participants completed the workshop and module phases of the program, they could give their views of each activity, but what was unknown was how their evaluations would change over time as they finished their work and turned to their other tasks at their institutions. To address this concern, a survey was prepared and added to the assessment.[1] The results from the retrospective survey serve as the basis for analyzing and interpreting some of the key assessment findings from the project.

The online retrospective survey was sent in mid-fall 2008 to all of the TIP participants who had attended and completed one of the eight TIP workshops that were held from 2005 through summer 2008. A total of 128 TIP participants supplied responses from a pool of 268 possible respondents who had attended and completed a workshop by summer 2008 (a 47.9% response rate). In addition, in mid-fall 2009, the same online survey was administered to the current cohort of 67 TIP participants who had attended the two 2009 summer workshops. Among this group, 34 supplied a valid survey response

(50.7% response rate). For the purposes of this reporting of assessment findings, the responses from the two groups were combined because of the strong similarities in the characteristics of both TIP groups and their survey response rates. Aggregating the survey data from the two groups resulted in a total of 162 respondents out of a total possible 335 who had attended and completed a TIP workshop (a 48.4% response rate).

Table 11.1 shows the percentage distribution of survey respondents for each of the ten workshops that they reported attending. The response distribution for the workshop survey is spread fairly evenly across all ten workshops. This similarity in the distribution would be expected for the workshop sample because approximately 10 percent of the 335 TIP participants attended each workshop (n = 329 completing a workshop survey for a 98.2% response rate). The distribution by workshop in the responses to the retrospective survey also is fairly evenly spread although less so than for the workshop survey. Nevertheless, for seven of the ten workshops there is only a difference of two percentage points or less between the expected 10 percent response rates for a workshop and what was actually obtained in the retrospective sample. A chi-square test for equality in the proportion of response rates across the ten workshops for the retrospective sample and the workshop sample was not statistically significant (χ = 4.605, 9 d.f.).

Table 11.1: Workshop Attended

Responses	**Workshop (n=329)**	**Retro[a] (n=162)**
2005 North Carolina (UNC/Rizzo Center)	10.3%	11.1%
2005 Georgetown University (conference center)	10.3	6.8
2006 Santa Fe (Hotel Santa Fe)	10.0	7.4
2006 Chicago (O'Hare/Rosemont Marriott Suites)	9.4	10.5
2007 Santa Barbara (Hotel Mar Monte)	9.7	9.9
2007 Boston (MIT Endicott House)	9.9	8.8
2008 San Antonio (St. Anthony Hotel)	10.6	14.8
2008 North Carolina (UNC/Rizzo Center)	9.4	10.5
2009 Chicago (O'Hare/Rosemont Marriott Suites)	10.3	11.1
2009 Santa Fe (Hotel Santa Fe)	10.0	9.9

Note: [a]"Which TIP workshop did you attend?"

Of course, there is some variation in response rates by workshop for the retrospective sample because the rates ranged from a low of 6.8 percent (Georgetown 2005) to a high of 14.8 percent (San Antonio 2008). There are several possible reasons for the differences in response rates among the workshop groups that are worth exploring. The first is related to the workshop evaluations for each group. Workshop groups with higher workshop evaluations, on average, would be more likely to complete the retrospective survey than workshop groups with lower evaluations, on average, presumably because higher workshop evaluations would be associated with a more positive and lasting impression of a workshop program. There is some evidence to support this proposition, but the relationship is modest at best. The correlation between the workshop response rates and workshop evaluations was positive, but only 0.53. A test of the null hypothesis of a positive association between the two variables produced a *t*-value of 1.77, which was not statistically significant at the 0.05 level based on a one-tailed *t*-test and a sample size of 10.

A second factor that might affect the response rates is the year in which workshops were held. It could be argued that more recent workshop groups are more likely to have higher response rates than more distant workshop groups because an increasing time gap might erode the willingness of TIP attendees to respond. Here too there is some evidence to support that assertion because the response rate in each of the first three years (2005, 2006, and 2007) was 9.0 percent, but it was 12.7 percent in 2008 and 10.5 percent in 2009. This positive correlation, however, was a modest 0.66 and not statistically significant. Although the pattern of response rates across workshop groups or across years differs, there does not appear to be an easily identifiable factor associated with the variation in rates.

The demographics of the follow-up survey sample are similar to what would be expected with a complete census of TIP participants. The 162 survey respondents reported that they had been teaching an average of 9.49 years (standard deviation: 8.365) when they participated in the workshop. The same question was asked of all workshop participants in an exit survey administered at the end of each workshop.[2] The average number of years that this group reported teaching was 10.1 years (standard deviation: 8.539). The difference in years teaching reported in the retrospective and workshop surveys was not statistically significant (*t*-value = 0.807).[3]

Two other demographic comparisons show that the retrospective survey sample is similar to workshop attendees – gender and institution type. The workshop attendees were 51.5 percent male and 48.5 percent female. The gender of the retrospective sample was essentially reversed: 47.5 percent male and 52.5 percent female. Despite the differences, a chi-square test for the equality in proportion of the two samples based on gender was not statistically significant (χ = 0.686, 1 d.f.). Table 11.2 also shows that the retrospective sample is drawn from a similar distribution as the full sample of workshop attendees (n = 329) based on the type of institution at which the TIP participant worked. A chi-square test for differences in the response differences between the two groups was not significant (χ = 2.362, 4 d.f).

Table 11.2: Current Institution[a]

Responses	Workshop (n=329)	Retrospective (n=162)
Research university	21.6%	17.0%
University	32.7	37.1
Four-year college	37.7	38.6
Two-year college	6.8	6.7
Other (please specify)	1.2	0.6

Note: [a]"The current institution at which you work would be best described as a:"

The basic conclusion to be drawn from the above analysis is that the retrospective sample from the group of all attendees at the TIP workshops appears to mirror many of the same characteristics as the workshop attendees. The retrospective sample, therefore, appears to be representative of the full group and is not self-selected in an obvious way. With that commonality established, the focus can turn to the findings from the retrospective survey to provide more insight about the assessment of TIP and other outcomes.

III. OVERALL AND WORKSHOP ASSESSMENTS

Perhaps the most important question on the survey was one that asked about the participants' overall assessment of TIP. These survey responses reveal what participants thought about the entire program and not one component. The use of this type of evaluative item, however, means that each participant supplies this overall evaluation based on an unknown framework for the assessment, perhaps based on the workshop experience, module instruction, or scholarly activity, or some weighted combination. In spite of this ambiguity about the basis for the assessment, the self-reported data are still meaningful as a general indicator of the program's value for the participants.

Table 11.3 reveals that the overall assessment is very positive. Over seven in ten (71%) would give the program an excellent rating and well over two in ten (23.4%) would give it a very good rating. The combination of these two response categories shows that nearly all the participants have a very high regard for the program. The positive results shown in the numerical data are strongly reinforced by written statements supplied by 35 of the 162 respondents (21.6%). These TIP participants almost unanimously described beneficial effects from TIP. A full list of comments is found in Appendix 11A, but here is a sample of five: (1) "The program is outstanding. I have implemented many of the strategies this semester and have seen a major improvement in students' participation in class and retention of material"; (2)

"This sort of training and discussion of pedagogy is sorely lacking in our discipline"; (3) "Great flexibility, many modules, online rapid response and consultation from module leaders was a fabulous and distinguishing aspect of this program"; (4) "I have made many changes in how I teach since participating in TIP. I feel more confident that students are really learning in my classes now"; and, (5) "Great plan for follow up to what is learned at the conference with the online modules and presentation opportunities."

Table 11.3: Overall Assessment of TIP[a] (n = 162)

Responses	
It is an excellent program for economics instructors	71.0%
It is a very good program for economics instructors	23.5
It is a good program for economics instructors	4.3
It is an adequate program for economic instructors	1.2
It is a poor program for economics instructors	0.0

Note: [a]"From an overall perspective, what is your assessment of the Teaching Innovations Program (TIP)?"

Workshop Evaluations

The workshop assessments provide more support for the overall findings. An evaluative question was asked of participants at the time they completed the workshop and also was asked in the retrospective survey. The survey responses that came months or years after completing a workshop are quite similar to the responses given at the time of the workshop, suggesting that the workshops created a lasting impression in the minds of the TIP participants. The workshop assessments are overwhelmingly positive (Table 11.4).

Timing may affect the results, so it was given further study. The workshop rating responses from the retrospective survey were re-analyzed after eliminating the two most recent workshop groups, whose responses to the survey came only about four months after completing the 2009 workshops. The results from this subsample show that the responses from those workshop attendees who were at least a year or more beyond the program (n = 128) were essentially the same (78.1% better; 15.6% good; 6.3% some) as the retrospective assessment from all workshop attendees as reported in Table 11.4. Moving the cutoff back another year to study the responses from the subsample of respondents (n = 87) who participated in the first six workshops (during 2005 through 2007), and who were more than two years away from workshop attendance, produced a pattern similar to that found for the total group (75.9% better; 16.1% good; 8.0% same). These results indicate that there is good stability in the responses over time.

Table 11.4: Evaluation of TIP Workshop Attended

Responses	Workshop[a] (n=329)	Retro[b] (n=160)
A better use of my time than my next best alternative	78.4%	76.9%
As good a use of my time as my best alternative	19.4	17.5
Of some value, but I could have put my time to better use	2.1	5.6
Almost a complete waste of my time	0.0	0.0

Notes: [a]"What is the overall value of the workshop compared to the opportunity costs of your time?" [b]"In retrospect, how would you evaluate the TIP workshop you attended?"

What also is interesting about this evaluation item is its wording. The question was stated in the economist's terminology of opportunity cost and asked for a relative rather than an absolute assessment. Travelling to and attending a three-day workshop has a substantial opportunity cost in the form of other activities or work projects not done to make time for the workshop. The opportunity cost of a workshop can be substantial. One participant took his or her time into account and gave the workshop only a good rating because "I'm on a really tight timeline for a consulting project so the value of my time is unusually high right now." Another participant stated in the evaluation comments that "It was my birthday that weekend so I may have had a better alternative, but it was still an excellent use of my time," and rated the program accordingly. The fact that almost eight in ten economists, who often have busy personal and work schedules, said it was a better use of their time indicates that there was strong support for this phase of the program.

IV. ONLINE INSTRUCTION

After participating in one of the ten residential workshops, TIP participants were invited to enroll in one of the online teaching modules developed for the program. Through the module instruction, TIP participants learned more about an instructional strategy (e.g., interpretive discussion, classroom experiments, context-rich problems, cooperative learning, case studies, assessment, and interactive learning in large classes) by reading and receiving feedback on their teaching ideas or plans related to that strategy. They would then develop a teaching innovation for one of their economics courses that used one of the module strategies and try it with students in their classes. All of this module work would be conducted under the guidance and mentoring of the module developer, who was an economist with teaching expertise in using this instructional strategy. A main purpose of the module work was to get the TIP participants to take what they had learned about a teaching strategy in the workshops, adapt it for their economics courses, and then implement the adapted strategy in their economics teaching.

First Module Assessment

Enrollment in the instructional modules was strictly voluntary for each TIP participant. Near the end of the TIP workshops a session was held to describe the follow-on instructional modules and their importance for learning more about and using the teaching strategies in the classroom. The workshop exit survey asked about the likelihood of participating in follow-on instruction through an online module. The responses showed overwhelming interest among the workshop attendees in further education: 90.2 percent stated they were highly likely to participate in the module phase and another 8.8 percent said they were fairly likely to participate in the online phase of the program. Of course, there is often a difference between what people say they are highly likely to do and what they actually do. This observation turned out to be the case for many of the workshop attendees. Based on module records, seven in ten (70.4% or 236) of the 335 workshop attendees enrolled in at least one online module.

The most likely reason for the difference in intentions and follow-through is time constraints. When the TIP economics instructors returned to their colleges and universities, their other professional or personal responsibilities became more important and crowded out the time to be allocated for follow-on instruction. The support for this explanation comes from the retrospective survey. When survey respondents who did not enroll in a module were given a list of reasons for why they did not, the predominant response selected was: "I did not have time to complete an instructional module" (64.7%). The remaining explanations drew much smaller percentages: (1) had other reasons (15.7%) (e.g., was not teaching); (2) did not see sufficient value in completing an instructional module (13.7%); and, (3) did not like the instructional modules offered (5.9%).

Enrolling in a module is only the first step in the second phase of TIP. Completing the module requires that the participant learn more about the teaching strategy and implement it in the classroom. Not everyone who enrolled in a module completed it. Module records indicate that over half (55.1%) of module enrollees completed a module (130 of 236).[4] The module completion data also can be viewed over a longer time period. Of the 335 participants who started TIP and completed a workshop, almost four in ten (38.8% or 130) went on to complete at least one module.

The question that arises is how the module completion percentage, based either on module enrollees (55.1%) or workshop completers (38.8%), should be interpreted. At first glance, the percentages appear low and suggest that TIP was not effective in getting *all* participants to make a lasting commitment to improve their economics teaching. That interpretation is too harsh and does not account for other factors. The first and most obvious reason is that some of the more recent module enrollees (from 2009) may not have had sufficient time to work on and complete a module because they only had a year to work on modules. This explanation, however, is only part of the story because it applies only to the 67 TIP participants from 2009.

A second and more important reason is that there usually will be some inertia with follow-through associated with participation in most educational activities even if the initial experience was a good one. People attend self-improvement courses and programs in education and health care all the time, but only a small percentage may act on the information or do the follow-up that is requested to take full advantage of the experience, even if it is considered to be very beneficial to do so. Time pressures can shift attention to other responsibilities and personal behavior may limit the continuing commitment to a worthy endeavor. In fact, when a subsample of TIP participants was surveyed retrospectively for the reasons why they had not completed a module, almost all of them who were not still working on a module gave the response "I found I did not have time to complete it."

The third reason is that relative comparisons or perspectives matter when interpreting outcomes. A 55 percent or 38 percent rate of profit as a return on investment would be considered to be very profitable from a business perspective whereas a 100 percent return would be highly unlikely and might raise questions about fraud ("It is just too good to be true."). A similar perspective seems reasonable to apply to most educational ventures that depend on voluntary participation, have limited incentives for participation and completion, and whose success is often affected by many uncontrollable factors. From this perspective, it is no small accomplishment to get a third of economic instructors who have already invested substantial time and effort in attending a TIP workshop to make an additional and substantial commitment to spend more time on their economic education, adapt or change their teaching practices, and take the risk of trying out what they have learned and developed with undergraduate students in their economics courses and classrooms. In this case, a 100 percent or some other very high rate of participation and completion is just not very likely and would be suspect.

One other factor needs to be considered when assessing module completion rates: it is an all-or-nothing counting. Some TIP participants signed up for a module, did the readings and assignments, and received some expert instruction, but for one reason or another they did not finish it. To paraphrase what one TIP participant stated during a presentation on TIP findings: "just because we did not complete a TIP module, does not mean that they did not benefit from the module instruction." Although no data are available for assessing how many of the 106 TIP participants who did not complete a module fell into this partial completion category, anecdotal feedback received from TIP participants suggest that it was not a trivial percentage and that perhaps it was a substantial percentage.

Once TIP participants completed a follow-on module, it was worthwhile to investigate their assessments of the effects of the module on their teaching. Two questions from the retrospective survey supply this data, although each question offers a different perspective on the matter. The first question asked for an absolute rating based on a positive or negative evaluation of the module effects. The second question asked for a relative rating, one based on comparing the module benefits with the module costs. The responses from the two questions are shown in Table 11.5.

Table 11.5: Assessment of First Module on Teaching (n = 63)

Q1: Responses[a]	
It was very positive	54.0%
It was positive	41.3
It had no effect	3.2
It was negative	1.6
It was very negative	0.0
Q2: Responses[b]	
The benefits were much greater than the costs	52.4%
The benefits were somewhat greater than the costs	36.5
The benefits were about the same as the costs	4.8
The costs were somewhat greater than the benefits	4.8
The costs were much greater than the benefits	1.6

Note: [a]"How would you assess the effect of the first module on your teaching?" [b]"How would you assess the benefits of completing the first module relative to the costs?"

The results from both questions reinforce each other and provide multiple sources of evidence that, for most module completers, the follow-on and web-based instruction made a valuable contribution to their teaching (94% stating it was positive or very positive and 90% stating the benefits were greater than the costs).[5] The responses to these questions are, of course, only perceptions, and questions can be raised about whether these perceptions reflect actual outcomes. Nevertheless, the responses come from economics instructors who completed TIP modules and who are the best judges of whether they thought that participation was beneficial.

Second Module Assessment

Another indicator of the value of the TIP module instruction is whether a TIP participant who completed one module also enrolled in and completed another module because if economics instructors did not find the first experience to be worthwhile, it is highly unlikely that they would continue their module participation and education. In the case of TIP, it should be noted that there was an additional incentive included in the program for those economics instructors who completed a second module. They would be eligible to receive a Certificate of Achievement awarded by the Committee on Economic Education of the American Economic Association. This teaching certificate might hold value for some TIP participants for reasons related to improving annual job evaluations or to contribute to a dossier for tenure and promotion. Other TIP participants may have decided to enroll in a second module for intrinsic reasons, and without regard for receiving external recognition, perhaps because they enjoyed learning more about a new teaching strategy. Which motivator, internal or external, was more important for continuance to a second module is unknown.

What is known from TIP records is the number who did continue their TIP education and training with a second module. Of the 130 TIP participants who completed their first module, well over eight in ten (112 or 86.2%) enrolled in a second module. Changes in costs and benefits were likely at work that account for this high percentage. From an economic perspective, the marginal cost of completing a second module was probably lower than for the first module because learning-by-doing from the first module would reduce the time or hassles associated with completing the second module. If the marginal benefit of completing the second module was the same as the first, or increased because of greater satisfaction with teaching or interest in obtaining a certificate, then given the lower marginal cost, the net benefit of doing a second module would be greater and more TIP participants who had completed one module would enroll in another module.

The percentage enrolling in a second module is one type of indicator, but a more valuable one is the percentage of enrollees who complete it. Among the 112 TIP participants who enrolled in a second module after completing the first, eight in ten (90 or 80.4%) completed it. This percentage is substantially higher than the completion rate for the first module (55.1%). The reasons for this difference in first and second completion rates is most likely because of the learning-by-doing factor previously described and that the subsample for the second module is likely to be more persistent and achievement-oriented.

There is value from an assessment perspective in studying the perceived effects of the second module on the teaching of TIP participants. The two questions used to assess these effects with the first module (Table 11.5) were adapted and used to assess the effects from the second module (Table 11.6). One question asked for an absolute assessment, positive or negative, and the other question asked for a relative assessment, benefits compared with costs.

Table 11.6: Assessment of Second Module on Teaching (n = 30)

Q1: Responses[a]	
It was very positive	66.7%
It was positive	20.0
It had no effect	13.3
It was negative	0.0
It was very negative	0.0
Q2: Responses[b]	
The benefits were much greater than the costs	63.3%
The benefits were somewhat greater than the costs	20.0
The benefits were about the same as the costs	10.0
The costs were somewhat greater than the benefits	6.7
The costs were much greater than the benefits	0.0

Note: [a]"How would you assess the effect of the second module on your teaching?" [b]"How would you assess the benefits of completing the second module relative to the costs?"

The value or net benefits from completing the second module are viewed favorably by the small group of TIP participants who submitted an online survey. The ratings are higher than for the first module (see Table 11.5) if the most positive or most benefit categories are considered, but that comparison is speculative because of the limited sample and data. What this survey item shows is that a great majority of TIP participants who completed a second module recognize its contribution to their teaching.

Certificate of Achievement

The final step in the assessment of the online phase of TIP is to consider the value of the Certificate of Achievement. Of the 335 TIP participants who attended a workshop, over a quarter (90 or 26.9%) earned one. Of course not all workshop attendees were interested in module instruction and participation in the module phase of TIP was strictly voluntary. A better perspective for assessing this outcome would be to compare the number completing a certificate with the number who originally showed an interest in online instruction by enrolling in a module. Of the 236 TIP participants who enrolled in a module, almost four in ten (38.2%) went on to earn a certificate.

How the completion percentages should be interpreted depends on the frame of reference. If a 100 percentage completion rate is adopted as the standard for comparison, then the TIP completion percentages would be considered low. This 100 percent standard, however, is not realistic. The TIP certificate completion rates (27% or 38%) should not be viewed as low or given a negative interpretation for the same reasons previously discussed about the percentage of TIP participants who completed their first module. There are many work problems, time constraints, and motivational factors to consider that affected an individual's capacity to complete a second module and earn a certificate. In addition, from an economic perspective, a 27-percent rate of return for all TIP workshop participants or a 38-percent rate of return rate of return for all module enrollees from an investment in human capital through TIP is sizable.

Other evidence related to the certificate comes from one question on the retrospective survey. It asked: "How valuable was it for you to receive a Certificate of Achievement from the Committee on Economic Education of the American Economic Association?" This item was completed by slightly less than half (48.5%) of TIP participants. As expected based this subsample, survey respondents for the certificate item should represent slightly less than half of certificate holders. This relationship holds because the respondents are slightly less than half (47.8%) of all those TIP participants who had received certificates by the time the survey was administered (22 of 46).

After doing all the work required to complete two modules to earn a certificate, it would be expected that receiving a certificate would be highly valued, especially given the very positive ratings for completing modules (see Tables 11.5 and 11.6). Although the responses for this item were fairly positive, because over two in ten (22.7%) considered receiving the certificate to be very valuable and another over three in ten (31.8%) stated that it was valuable, the responses were not overwhelmingly positive. In fact, over three in ten (31.8%) replied that they were uncertain about the value of a certificate and the other respondents (13.6%) did not think that earning a certificate was valuable for them.

The certificate responses need to be placed in context. What is most important about completing a module is its positive effect on teaching, which was highly valued by those who completed a module based on the survey data. Whether being awarded a certificate is valuable apparently depends more on personal circumstances and the criteria for the valuation. If some TIP participants are internally motivated to achieve and not externally motivated by an award, they might be uncertain or even negative about the value of receiving a certificate because it is not considered important by them. Other TIP participants who qualify for a certificate also may not rate it as valuable if it does not count for job evaluations or personnel decisions.

V. SCHOLARSHIP OF TEACHING AND LEARNING

The third phase of TIP encouraged TIP module completers to participate in what is generally referred to in higher education circles as the scholarship of teaching and learning (SoTL), and which in more recent years has been applied to economics (e.g., Johnston, McDonald, and Williams 2001). This broad concept describes a wide array of professional and scholarly activities within a discipline such as developing new instructional materials, making a teaching presentation, being a discussant at a teaching session at a profession meeting, writing a descriptive or research-oriented paper about teaching, and submitting a scholarly paper about teaching to a referred academic journal.

Some limited evidence of TIP participation in SoTL is provided by one survey item: "Did you participate in any activity related to the scholarship of teaching and learning economics based on or because of your TIP experiences?" About a third (34.2%) said yes and less than two-thirds (65.8%) said no.[6] Although this percentage appears to be low, the path to SoTL needs to be considered. TIP participants were encouraged to engage in SoTL only after they had completed one TIP module. Table 11.7 reports the SoTL activity for TIP participants who responded to this survey item.

Table 11.7: Scholarship Activity[a] (n = 60)

Responses	
Developed instructional materials	66.7%
Made a presentation	46.7
Served as a discussant	21.7
Participated in a program	16.7
Wrote a paper related to teaching or learning	46.7
Submitted a paper related to teaching or learning for publication	16.7
Other	21.7

Note: [a]"What did you do related to the scholarship of teaching and learning? (check all that apply)"

The evaluative question to be asked was whether it was worthwhile to be involved in SoTL activities. The replies to one item on the retrospective survey indicate that it was. Over half (52.6%) of the TIP participants who were engaged in SoTL activities stated that it was very valuable and another third (33.3%) stated that it was valuable, which means that well over eight in ten (85.9%) respondents thought SoTL in economics was worthwhile. Although there was some uncertainty among a few TIP participants (14.0%), no survey respondent gave a negative assessment of participating in SoTL.[7]

VI. CONCLUSION

The Teaching Innovations Program (TIP) was a multi-dimensional project designed to improve the teaching of economics faculty. TIP provided residential workshop training for economics instructors to learn about interactive teaching strategies that can be used in the economics classroom to motivate and engage students in the learning process. One of the most unique and inventive features of the program was the opportunity for workshop participants to return to their colleges and universities and continue to receive follow-on instruction. This additional education was offered through a set of online modules and mentoring by economists who also were teaching experts with a particular interactive strategy or method. In this stage of the project the economics instructors developed classroom activities and innovations to try out in the classroom and receive feedback from their module mentor. After completing a workshop and the follow-on instruction, the TIP participants were encouraged to be involved in the scholarship of teaching and learning in economics so they could share their teaching innovations with other economists through presentations, papers, and other scholarly works.

An assessment plan was designed and executed for each phase of TIP. The assessment conducted formative evaluations to provide feedback to project staff as the program developed over its years of operation, and which was used to make yearly improvements. There also was summative reporting to NSF on the annual outcomes from the project. In addition, a longitudinal survey was administered to obtain a retrospective assessment of the program and its different components. What emerges from the analysis of participant surveys given at each phase of program activity, and reconfirmed with the longitudinal survey months or years after attending a TIP workshop, is a very positive perception of TIP among the participants. The survey responses showed that the TIP participants valued very highly the workshop experience, felt that the follow-on instruction improved their teaching, and thought they benefited from engaging in activities related to the scholarship of teaching.

NOTES

1. The survey was prepared by the author of this paper with valuable comments and suggestions on several survey drafts from Michael Salemi and KimMarie McGoldrick.
2. The number of workshop respondents was 311 because not all workshop participants supplied a response to this question.
3. It also is interesting to note that the 162 economics instructors who completed the retrospective survey reported teaching an average of 260 students a year, which represents an aggregate of 42,130 students taught per year. No comparable data

was obtained on the average number of students taught by the workshop attendees, so a comparison between the two groups could not be made on the average number of students taught.

4. This calculation is based on data collected through June 30, 2010. The responses from the retrospective survey showed a similar percentage (58.8%) for module completion, indicating that it provided fairly accurate data on this outcome.
5. An anonymous survey also was answered by all TIP participants who completed a module through the Blackboard system in which participants were enrolled at the University of Nebraska–Lincoln. The question asked and the responses associated with each category was: "The time I spent completing follow-on instruction using this module has been: (a) a better use of my time than the next best alternative (59%); (b) as good a use of my time as the next best alternative (37%); of some value, but I could have put my time to better use (3%); and almost a complete waste of time (0%)." These results provide additional evidence from another source to show the perceived value of the module instruction in the opinion of the module completers.
6. A total of 152 of the 162 TIP participants who returned a survey answered this question.
7. Data collection for SoTL from TIP will continue even though TIP officially ended in January, 2010. Many TIP participants only started a SoTL activity after they completed a workshop and also completed a module. This assessment of SoTL and TIP will be given further study once there is a more comprehensive dataset of activity from all TIP participants, especially from the more recent cohorts of workshop participants.

REFERENCES

Fitzpatrick, J.L., J.R. Sanders, and B.R. Worthen (2004), *Program Evaluation: Alternative Approaches and Practical Guidelines* (3rd ed.), Boston: Pearson Education.

Johnston, C., I. McDonald, and R. Williams (2001), "The scholarship of teaching economics," *Journal of Economic Education*, **32** (3), 195–201.

Salemi, M.K., P. Saunders, and W.B. Walstad (1996), "Teacher training programs in economics: Past, present, and future," *American Economic Review: Papers and Proceedings*, **86** (2), 460–64.

Salemi, M.K., J.J. Siegfried, K. Sosin, W.B. Walstad, and M. Watts (2001), "Research in economic education: Five new initiatives," *American Economic Review*, **91** (2), 440–45.

Walstad, W.B., and P. Saunders (1998), *Teaching Undergraduate Economics: A Handbook for Instructors*, New York: McGraw-Hill.

APPENDIX 11A
Written Responses to Overall TIP Assessment

"From an overall perspective, what is your assessment of the Teaching Innovations Program (TIP)?"

1. I learned so much that I am currently using in my classes. The best thing about it was they helped with big classes as well as small. I teach 2 small classes and one very large lecture class so was pleasantly surprised that I took away things that would help in both.
2. The program is outstanding. I have implemented many of the strategies this semester and have seen a major improvement in students' participation in class and retention of the material.
3. Phase I presents very useful teaching strategies. My only regret was that it was not longer (1–2 extra days) and did not cover additional strategies. Phase II helps to implement strategies, an important follow-up to what you learn in Phase I.
4. I have learned a lot about teaching innovation.
5. TIP deserves a higher rank than excellent – at least outstanding. I have done a number of teaching workshops run by general educators. The TIP program was head and shoulders above any of those both because of how well organized the residential workshop was and because of the Phase Two follow-up online.
6. Very worthwhile. I received substantial, tangible strategies to better engage and teach students.
7. Provided me with ideas for alternative teaching methods through interaction with other Econ faculty as well as resources for Economics teaching.
8. They talk about things no one else in the profession talks about.
9. Truly beneficial – one of the more relevant workshop ever attended
10. I wish that I had such an experience much earlier in my career. It has made a difference in my teaching even this many years into my career.
11. My university attempts to run a program to help instructors with large classes. Since disciplines vary greatly, that seminar is neither fish nor fowl. Concentrating on just economics is highly productive.
12. This sort of training and discussion of pedagogy is sorely lacking in our discipline.
13. I would have welcomed the opportunity to do one or two additional modules.
14. I found it very useful. I especially liked the mix of experience amongst the participating candidates. This provides a very rich exchange of ideas and opinions
15. I believe it is an excellent program even though I have not yet engaged in Phase Three. But I intend to do so very soon.

16. But much more demanding than I expected
17. It is good at what it does, which is to help teachers devise more active learning techniques, to better evaluate their students, etc. ... but in terms of addressing the ailments of undergraduate teaching of economics, the program falls flat.
18. This program helped me improve learning and student evaluations in all my classes.
19. This provided the teaching support within the context of economics rather than a generic presentation.
20. I wish I had more time available to complete more modules.
21. As an adjunct, I do not get a chance to interact with other economists. I was wonderful interacting with my workshop peers
22. Great plan for follow up to what is learned at the conference with the online modules and presentation opportunities thereafter.
23. I found many of the ideas useful. Some I already used before the workshop. One thing I would like to see is more emphasis on how to apply the ideas to larger courses.
24. The opportunity for hands-on, guided use of innovative pedagogies after the on-side workshop is one of the best qualities of the program. This helps to produce enduring effects in the classroom.
25. I have learned so much from the program.
26. I recommended it to several colleagues
27. Great flexibility, many modules, on-line rapid response and consultation from module leaders was a fabulous and distinguishing aspect of this program
28. I have made many changes in how I teach since participating in TIP. I feel more confident that students are really learning in my classes now.
29. It has positive externalities, not only do the instructors benefit, but also students benefit.
30. It is most appropriate for instructors at non-research universities.
31. Every economics teacher should participate in this program. Great ideas and excellent networking.
32. The process of getting the modules approved is too long and cumbersome. It just wore me out.
33. The think–pair–share idea that was communicated has made my courses much stronger.
34. I am really impressed with different possible ways to teach economics. I am still in Phase two.
35. I wish there'd been a module addressing the case of those of us for whom, with no apparent reason, teaching has become a struggle. Perhaps one obstacle to teaching improvement may be something to do with classroom dynamics, and that was largely left unexplored. But, in what it did address, the program was undoubtedly very good.

INDEX